Wolfe & Montcalm

Wolfe & Montcalm

THEIR LIVES, THEIR TIMES, AND THE FATE OF A CONTINENT

JOY CARROLL

FIREFLY BOOKS

A FIREFLY BOOK

Published by Firefly Books Ltd. 2004

First printing

Publisher Cataloging-in-Publication Data (U.S.)

Carroll, Joy

     Wolfe and Montcalm : their lives, their times and the fate of a continent / Joy Carroll. —1st ed.

[302] p. : maps ; cm.
Includes bibliographical references and index.

Summary: A historical account of the lives and times of the two generals and the events surrounding the battle between the British and the French on the Plains of Abraham, Canada, 1759.

ISBN 1-55297-905-9 (pbk.)

1. Wolfe, James, 1727-1759. 2. Montcalm de Saint-Véran, Louis-Joseph, marquis de, 1712-1759. 3. Plains of Abraham, Battle of the, Québec, 1759. 4. Canada — History — To 1763 (New France). 5. United States — Colonial history, 1607-1775 — By period —1689-1775 — French and Indian War, 1755-1763. I. Title.

973.26/ 0922 dc22   E199.C377 2004

National Library of Canada Cataloguing in Publication

Carroll, Joy

     Wolfe and Montcalm : their lives, their times and the fate of a continent / Joy Carroll.

Includes bibliographical references and index.

ISBN 1-55297-905-9

1. Wolfe, James, 1727-1759. 2. Montcalm, Louis-Joseph, marquis de, 1712-1759. 3. Plains of Abraham, Battle of the, Québec, Québec, 1759. 4. Canada — History — Seven Years' War, 1755-1763. 5. United States — History — French and Indian War, 1755-1763. I. Title.

FC384.C318 2004   971.01'88   C2004-902480-9

Published in the United States in 2004 by
Firefly Books (U.S.) Inc.
P.O. Box 1338, Ellicott Station
Buffalo, New York 14205

Published in Canada in 2004 by
Firefly Books Ltd.
66 Leek Crescent
Richmond Hill
Ontario L4B 1H1

Cover portraits © 2004 David Jean
Cover and text design: Sari Naworynski
Printed in Canada by Friesens, Altona, Manitoba

The Publisher acknowledges the financial support of the Government of Canada through the Book Publishing Industry Development Program for its publishing activities.

Preface

Six years ago I had the urge to write about Quebec society in the eight-eenth century, using the Battle of the Plains of Abraham as a focal point. After a year of research, a mysterious hole opened up in my collection of stories and facts. Who, exactly, were James Wolfe and Louis-Joseph Montcalm? Clearly, they were the "stars" in this battle for a continent, but little had been passed on about their private lives. In textbooks they sound remarkably stuffy, but no picture of either man emerges. After reading their letters and journals, however, it became obvious that the generals were real men with real problems and moments of consuming passion. Both were brave, ambitious and colourful, but they had not been portrayed this way.

The following account of their lives is meant to be intimate and entertaining, and at the same time as accurate as possible. It should be noted, though, that historians do not always agree on certain points, not even on the spelling of names and places important to the story. I have used material from what I felt were the most reliable sources.

Montcalm was considerably older than Wolfe – he was forty-seven at the time of the famous battle and considered Wolfe (who was thirty-one) a bit of an upstart. Yet there were curious similarities in their careers. Both complained about the lack of support they received from their own officials and, in the hot August days of 1759, both men were sick and depressed (for very different reasons, of course), which generated fears among their troops that they might be too ill to lead in the final confrontation. Wolfe and Montcalm both recovered from bad health. Wolfe was given doses of laudanum by his doctor; Montcalm's treatment is not recorded. Furthermore the two generals died from fatal wounds they suffered on that September morning in 1759.

Each had a ferocious temper that often caused trouble with superior officers. Each enjoyed flirting with women, although Montcalm was happily married and Wolfe was engaged to be married. The two generals had campaigned successfully in Europe, though not at the same time. Montcalm suffered five wounds to the head in one conflict and a single wound in another. Wolfe seems to have escaped this unpleasant side of war, but he was often ill from a variety of complaints like arthritis, rheumatism and kidney stones. Some conditions were undoubtedly real, and his violent seasickness was obvious. He himself suspected he had scurvy and possibly tuberculosis, but these ailments were never confirmed by his doctors.

The generals were aware of each other when they read reports in newspapers and heard military gossip in clubs and coffee houses. As enemies, they were mutually fascinated with each other, but they never actually met. Wolfe was shocked at Montcalm's use of Indians in warfare because he blamed the tribesmen for torturing prisoners. Montcalm was never happy about using them as allies but was ordered to do so by Governor-General Pierre Vaudreuil, who insisted Indians made effective spies when they visited English camps. French soldiers, Vaudreuil said, would be lost without the natives to act as guides in the wilderness. Wolfe, on the other hand, occasionally had Indians as guides, but he was never as friendly with them as were the

French. Wolfe was accused of burning homes along the St. Lawrence River and seizing domestic animals to feed his troops.

After reading dozens of textbooks and official papers in my search, I still knew little about Wolfe or Montcalm. I turned to letters the generals had written to their families, friends and fellow officers. A good example is Wolfe's letter to General Jeffery Amherst blaming him for giving orders to set fire to fishermen's huts and fishing equipment on the Gaspé Peninsula and for *not* buying huge amounts of fish – when it was cheap – to feed his army. The letter shows Wolfe was confident enough to criticize his superior officer and had business sense, as well.

Historians have covered the battle inch by inch, regiment by regiment and cannon by cannon, but Wolfe and Montcalm end up being little more than names. Who were these men and how did they come to be in or near Quebec in the first place? Wolfe seemed to spring up out of the ground like a cardboard cutout in a scarlet coat, more like an actor on a stage than a real man with real fears, failures and frustrations. Montcalm was easier to explain – obviously King Louis XV had sent him to defend French colonies in "Canada," as New France was called by that time. But why had Montcalm been chosen? Nobody who wrote about him seemed to care. Actually, it is said that Montcalm didn't want to be major-general in command of the war against Canada, but the king had no other officer experienced enough for the job and willing to accept the position. Frenchmen tended to see Canada as a snowy wasteland for six months of the year and a vast mosquito-ridden swamp for the remainder.

As for Wolfe, he had had a stormy time in the army until he gave a bravado performance at the taking of Louisbourg. He was chosen by Prime Minister William Pitt to win Canada for Britain at any cost. And there he was on the appointed day, striding up and down in front of four thousand redcoats, waving his cane to urge them on, flashing like a dragonfly in his bright red coat. (It had been fashioned by a London tailor just for this occasion, and Wolfe had never before worn it. He was always a snappy dresser.) And there was Montcalm on his big black charger, riding down the slope, cutting the air with his sabre and wearing a green or perhaps blue coat. After it was all over, the colour of his coat would be much debated.

Why was Wolfe on foot and Montcalm on a horse? That is part of the story, too. One historian describes Wolfe wearing "gaiters," which were cloth leggings buttoned down one side and worn by the ranks along with a uniform and shoes. Officers bought their own clothes and, since most of the men came from rich or well-to-do families, they wore handmade leather boots and tailored coats. Officers also provided their own food and a chef to cook it, as well as horses and grooms to care for them. Officers employed personal servants and might have two or even more. They were called "valets," and Wolfe employed two. As an extremely clothes-conscious man, Wolfe achieved all this by borrowing money from his father and mother. He wouldn't be caught dead in gaiters.

The battle had lasted only a few minutes when Wolfe was fatally wounded on the battlefield by an unknown sniper hidden in a tree or behind a rock. It's highly unlikely that Wolfe was hit by a spent bullet as some writers have suggested. A spent bullet has little energy left, probably not enough to penetrate a heavy woollen coat or vest. Montcalm, too, was wounded by a concealed gunman, who might have been a traitor or even a redcoat. He died the next day inside the fortress of Quebec. Montcalm was given a modest funeral in the chapel of the Ursuline convent. Wolfe's body was carried back to England and buried with some pomp in the family crypt. Later, Wolfe's enemies tried to defame him, but he had had his moment of glory just as he had hoped.

Wolfe was a romantic – he fell in love three times, dressed like a duke and swaggered like a dandy. Being practical, he was always a student, studying something new whether it was polishing his French or learning how to play the flute. But above all, he was a soldier, tender with his friends and family and fearless in battle. Montcalm was loyal, brave and dutiful. Montcalm's ideas for the defence of Quebec would have been more effective than those of the officials, but they refused to listen to his suggestions.

This book is dedicated to Major-General James Wolfe and Lieutenant-General Louis-Joseph, Marquis de Montcalm de Saint-Véran.

Acknowledgments

Thanks to my researcher, Freda Gough, who found many treasures in the University of Toronto libraries; to my editor, Dan Liebman, for his patient handling of the manuscript; to Stephen Chellew, for his great knowledge of weaponry; to David Jean, for the cover portraits; and to Matie and Julius Molinaro, whose encouragement makes them so much more than agents, but good friends as well.

I dedicate this book to General James Wolfe and General Louis-Joseph Montcalm. They were admirable men, and not just names on a page of Canadian history.

Contents

Prologue

THE BATTLE THAT GAVE ENGLAND HALF A CONTINENT

*"The officers and men will remember what a determined body
of soldiers inured to war is capable of doing against five weak
French battalions mingled with a disorderly peasantry."*
— MAJOR-GENERAL JAMES WOLFE, on the eve of the battle

One morning in the fall of 1759, ten thousand men gathered on an empty tract of land just west of Quebec. In those days, soldiers dressed to kill. British privates fought in scarlet jackets faced with yellow and tall caps embroidered with the letters GR for *George Rex*. French regulars wore big black tricorns and long greyish-white coats with brass buttons that glinted in the sun. Each array of troops flew a national flag: the sleek gold lilies of France on white silk, and England's flame-red cross of St. George over St. Andrew's white cross on a sea of blue. They were about to fight a battle that would determine the future of North America.

And yet the presence of Major-General James Wolfe and his little army on the Plains of Abraham was, in itself, impossible. The field was a small square of grass and corn stalks perched two hundred feet above the mighty St. Lawrence. A few miles upriver from the fortress of Quebec, one faint trail led up the sheer bank and a second was clogged with fallen trees. General Louis-Joseph Montcalm had scoffed at his cohorts' fears that Wolfe might land on the beach, climb to the plateau and threaten the town. "We need not suppose that the enemy has wings," he told Canada's ruling council. But he was wrong, and his next pronouncement on the subject was less fanciful: "There they are where they should not be!"

At dawn on September 13 the sky over Quebec was leaden. Both generals dreaded thunderstorms because pouring rain stopped musket fire and violent winds ruined even the cleverest plan. This morning, troops on both sides were revved up for a final confrontation – and it had to take place before the men lost their edge. The lateness of the season was a factor, too. Winter was approaching and a death-struggle in the snow was out of the question. Who was going to control Canada? The issue needed to be settled.

The siege of Quebec, occurring at "half-time" in the Seven Years' War, was the most decisive battle in the eighteenth century. This conflict, which for many years had been called the French and Indian War, was based mostly upon squabbles between France and England over colonies. England turned these endless skirmishes into a larger conflict by declaring war on France on May 18, 1756. France responded in June. The two countries had been warring for centuries for one reason or another, so the latest outbreak came as no surprise. Three years later, the battle on the Plains of Abraham was part of this ongoing struggle. The generals who fought it were players in a drama that had consequences they could never have imagined.

The two armies faced each other. The rain stopped. Tension mounted as officers on both sides tried to make themselves heard above the clamour of rattling gun-carriages, cursing soldiers and keening bagpipes. The rules of combat on an open field were rigid: all rows of costumed puppets must be in place, the lines perfectly straight; and they must be ready to wheel like clockwork. An hour passed before both generals were satisfied, and by then the sun had come out from behind the clouds. When at last the French advanced, it was a pretty sight: pale waves of white and blue rushing toward a frail scarlet ribbon sparked with gold. Uniforms were brighter than the autumn leaves, for this was a time when kings dressed their troops in the fancy outfits of the toy soldiers they had loved as children. But there was a practical side to the dazzle, too. In hand-to-hand fighting, a man could identify his enemy by the colour of his coat.

The idea of camouflaging armies was still far in the future, unless you counted the North American natives who slipped through primeval forests, silent and unseen. In Canada, an amorphous territory once known as New France, some of the wilder white bushrangers liked to imitate those Indian skills and went to war wearing paint, feathers and very little else. To the south, in the Thirteen Colonies, Major Robert Rogers trained a body of volunteers to fight Indian-style, creating the legendary Rogers' Rangers. But on that day on the Plains of Abraham, such tricks played only a minor role.

"The people long eagerly for two things – bread and circuses," Juvenal wrote in the first century. It seemed to King George II of England that the Roman poet had got it right. In England, people loved a parade, especially a glittering army led by a marching band. King Louis XV of France noticed much the same thing in his country: soldiers who were brightly and tightly garbed became romantic figures, flirting their way through country fairs and Parisian masques, strutting into bloody frays. It suited men in high places to adorn the ranks with lace cuffs and greased pigtails, to doll up their officers in shiny braid and singular hats.

In the eighteenth century, privates and non-commissioned officers were always in the forefront, directly under fire from muskets and cannon, and senior officers and generals took their chances alongside them. How could it be otherwise? The huge underclass back home was hungry for heroes, men who inspired admiration and even awe. Such gods must be created, and a battlefield was the place for it. Glory for its own sake was still a strong driving force.

Under certain conditions, war was a spectator sport. A scrap between two armies was often confined to a specific area (a valley, town or bridge), and civilians who loitered around the edge were relatively safe. A great many accounts of battles were provided by curious onlookers, tourists or friends of those involved in the action. It was a form of entertainment for townspeople, much more thrilling than watching a simple hanging. Here was an opportunity to see men die, to shiver at the cries of mangled horses, to recoil from explosions and to vomit at the sight of spilled guts. During the siege of Quebec, the field was fringed with bushes and evergreens sheltering watchers along the cliff as well as roads to the west. The town's fortified wall overlooked the Buttes-à-Neveu, a ridge where military forces often mustered. On that September day, people peered over the parapets. Some held spyglasses, as if they had a balcony seat in a theatre.

Crowds came to cheer on their friends and relatives and to pray for a French victory. Most Canadians kept an eye on the veteran campaigner Lieutenant-General Louis-Joseph Montcalm as he plunged along the lines on his big black charger, firing up his men with cries and gestures. Others were fascinated by a spindly, scarlet-coated Major-General James Wolfe as he inspected his battalions on foot and directed the action with a walking stick. Aficionados might have noticed that Montcalm and Wolfe had one thing in common: they led by example, always out front, always an easy target.

Part One

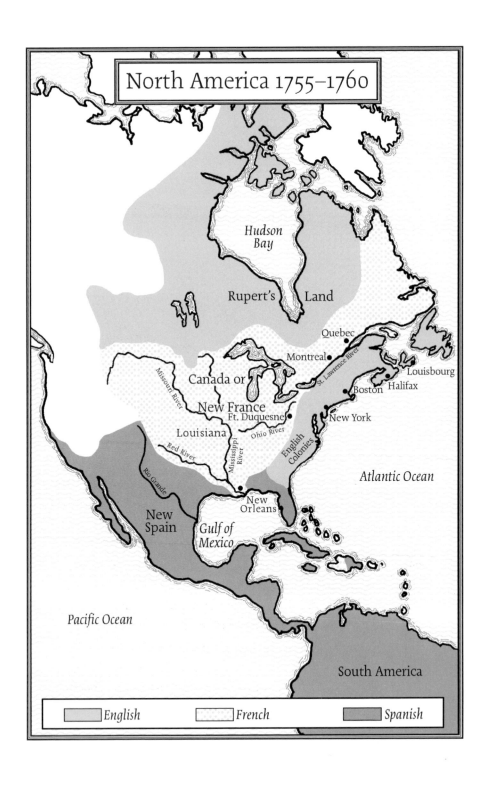

North America 1755–1760

Hudson
Bay

Rupert's   Land

Quebec

Montreal

St. Lawrence River

Louisbourg

Canada or

Missouri River

New France

Halifax

Boston

Ft. Duquesne

New York

Louisiana

Ohio River

Red River

English
Colonies

Mississippi River

Rio Grande

Atlantic Ocean

New
Spain

New
Orleans

Gulf of
Mexico

Pacific Ocean

South America

English   French   Spanish

1

Wolfe's Military Heritage

"I will not go back defeated to be exposed to the censure and reproach of an ignorant populace."

— JAMES WOLFE, 1759

General Wolfe's connections with the military went back a long way. In the sixteenth century a family named Woulfe emigrated from Wales to Ireland in the hope of a better life. At the time they settled in Limerick the Woulfes were Roman Catholics; it's possible they accepted the faith to better fit into society. By the year 1613, James Woulfe was a bailiff and George Woulfe, a sheriff. Unfortunately, both men were deposed for refusing to take an oath of allegiance to England. Forty years later, Henry Ireton (acting for Oliver Cromwell) attempted to install British citizens on Irish farmland. Ireton, then Lord Deputy of Ireland, was thwarted by George Woulfe, an army captain, and his brother Francis, a Grey Friar. Both Woulfes were proscribed and, despite his position in a religious order, Francis was executed. George fled to Yorkshire where he turned Protestant, dropped the letter 'u' from his name and married a local girl. Captain George Wolfe was the great-grandfather of General James Wolfe.

James Wolfe's father, Edward, was born in 1685 and entered the service of Queen Anne as a second lieutenant of marines when he was barely seventeen. By the year 1717, Edward had risen to lieutenant-colonel. Since he had neither wealth nor family influence, it seems fair to say he was promoted for excellence. A few years later, during a pause in the incessant wars between England and France, the colonel realized there was limited scope for doing glorious deeds – so he decided to marry and settle down. His bride, Henrietta, was a beauty of strong character, the daughter of Edward Thompson, Esq., of Marsden, Yorkshire. Colonel Wolfe was thirty-eight and Henrietta was nineteen, but the age difference didn't seem to matter. The Wolfes were apparently well-suited.

Their first son, James, was born in the village of Westerham, Kent, in 1727, and one year later his brother, Edward – always called Ned by the family – arrived to complete the family. The Wolfes rented Spiers, a Tudor mansion they occupied for the next ten years. A strange setting for a budding military prodigy, its dusty attics were filled with trunks and treasures and its unlit upper passageways hinted at secret rooms, inspiring many an imaginative game for two little boys who spent their winters indoors.

Henrietta Wolfe, a hands-on mother in a day when nannies ruled the nursery, took up herbal medicine so she could prescribe for James and Ned instead of calling on doctors. Her methods probably did less harm than those of professional medical men, who made a habit of drawing blood for almost every ailment. The use of leeches may sound creepy but the insects were no more contaminated than doctors' instruments. At the time, the germ theory hadn't been discovered and the role of unwashed hands in spreading infectious diseases remained a mystery.

After James Wolfe became famous, he often was described as a life-long hypochondriac. But logic suggests that a bright boy like James would know better than to fake illness once he'd tasted the ferocious tonics his mother called cures. Henrietta's notion of a potion was a combination of minced green garden snails washed in beer and mixed with angelica, bilberry, turmeric and rue. To this, she added a quart of chopped garden worms, soaked the whole mess overnight in milk and boiled it in the morning. Once the brew cooled, the patient was forced to swallow at least two spoonfuls. Surely it would have been easier to hit the schoolbooks than down such a horrid-sounding pick-me-up.

During the early years, Colonel Wolfe was away with his regiment a large part of the time. But when he *was* home, talk centred on military matters. Young James was a good listener. The flavour of army life seeped into his bones and led him to read every book he could find on military tactics. He fought historic battles over and over in his mind, analyzed mistakes, memorized brilliant moves and, when he was abroad, took the time to visit ancient sites.

Until James was ten and Ned was nine, they attended day school in Westerham, unlike their friends who were sent away to boarding school. In his developing years, James spent many hours with his mother and the two became close. The first time his father took James hunting the boy fell in love with the sport, and from then on he kept dogs and horses. His mother later made this possible by looking after his animals when James was off campaigning. Young Wolfe's lack of experience in the field of animal care didn't prevent him from giving his mother instructions. "Please feed them yourself," he suggested. "The servants give the dogs too much meat."

In the summer of 1740, Edward Wolfe was appointed colonel and, although James was barely fourteen, his father enlisted him in his own regiment of marines. England was at war with Spain then and the regiment joined an expedition to Cartagena, a Spanish possession on the coast of Colombia. James begged to go along. Henrietta vetoed the idea but Colonel Wolfe sided with James and, in August, father and son were aboard ship off the Isle of Wight, waiting to sail for the Caribbean. Two brief excerpts from the boy's first letter to his mother, dated August 6, reflect his feelings: "I will certainly write to you by every ship I meet because I know it is my duty. Besides, if it is not, I would do it out of love." He further promised, "I will, as sure as I live, let you know everything that has happened, therefore pray dearest Mamma, don't doubt about it. I am in a very good state of health and am likely to continue so."

When it came to his own constitution, James was a poor prophet. Shortly after sending the letter, he fell seriously ill and was taken home to recuperate. James may have viewed the lost voyage as a tragedy, but it was a blessing for his health. The fleet was in trouble from the outset, nearly wrecked by a violent storm while in the English Channel. Since James was seasick even on calm water, such wild pitching and tossing would have been agony for him. By the time they reached the waters off the port of Cartagena, pestilence on poorly run hospital ships had managed to kill more British soldiers than bullets fired by the enemy. Lord Cathcart, the original commander, died suddenly; and since no officer was available to replace him, the enterprise fell into confusion. Bad blood had long existed between the army and navy. Now it turned from jealousy to hatred.

The combination of setbacks caused the British to lose the forts they had taken earlier. The expedition – what remained of it – headed for Jamaica to prepare for the long voyage home. Colonel Wolfe was embroiled in the failed Cartagena venture for two years and, before it was over, he realized James might have died had he been part of it. The boy wasn't cut out for the navy. By letter, the colonel arranged to transfer his son to the 20th Foot, an infantry corps.

The Wolfe family had moved to Greenwich in 1737, where the brothers attended Samuel Swindon's day school. James was a good student and Mr. Swindon became a family friend, but no one considered the boy brilliant. His schoolmates thought him a stuffed shirt because he refused to gamble and drink, preferring to bury himself in his books. All this brainwork didn't squelch Wolfe's romantic feelings, however, and he developed a painful crush on the sister of his best friend, George Warde. The Wardes, a prominent family in Westerham, still lived in Squerryes Court, up the hill from Wolfe's former home. Miss Warde, thinking James too young to be taken seriously, rejected him. He was devastated. Nine years later, when his mother told him the young woman was engaged to be married, James retorted bitterly, "Is she pleased with her coxcomb companion? She'll repent her bargain!"

One wintry day Wolfe was visiting Squerryes Court when a message arrived stamped "On His Majesty's Service." Dated November 3, 1741, and signed by George II, it was an order for James to join his regiment. The following spring, Wolfe was posted to Ghent in Belgium. Before the expedition sailed, King George reviewed the troops at Blackheath. James was selected to carry his regiment's colours.

Even in his teens, Wolfe was a head taller than most people around him. At twenty, he was six-foot-three. His family said he "grew too fast." Rail thin, which accentuated his height, Wolfe was a dashing figure in the red, white and gold of the British officer's uniform. His profile was no prize – he had a weak chin – but when his face was seen from the front, his flashing blue eyes signalled a sharp mind. A lively talker, he could hold forth on topics from the practical uses of Latin in European society to playing the flute or leading a charge. At times he was moody and short-tempered, but when he was engaged in a project that interested him, he focused on it with childlike eagerness.

Wolfe's red hair was thin and, according to the fashion of the day, he pulled it back in a queue and tied it with a ribbon. Once in the army, he took to wearing wigs and wore one the day he carried the colours at Blackheath. During his years of service in Scotland, his mother acted as agent between Wolfe and his wigmaker, passing on strict instructions from her son and arranging for delivery of the finished product.

Usually, Wolfe's skin was pale like that of most redheads, and he blushed easily; but on at least one occasion he sported a dark tan. After marching with his regiment from the Scottish border to

Reading in the south of England he wrote, in a letter to his mother, "We have more the look of troops from Spain or Africa than from the north. We are really a good deal browner and more tanned than the battalion from Minorca that relieve[s] us." Always a stickler for detail, he added that the uniforms his men wore on this occasion were threadbare. "I do believe we shall be the most dirty, ragged regiment that the Duke has seen for some years." Wolfe was referring to the Duke of Cumberland, the king's third son.

When Wolfe first became a soldier, England had enjoyed thirty years of peace and, as a result, her forces were dangerously weak. It was the custom of shortsighted parliamentarians to recruit soldiers with vigour in wartime and turn them loose without jobs or pensions once peace was restored, a cruel and risky policy. England's army in 1742 consisted of fifteen cavalry regiments (the Horse Guards), fifty infantry regiments (the Foot Guards) and four companies of Royal Artillery.

Sixteen thousand men had been set apart for Continental service the year Wolfe joined his regiment. Uniforms were picturesque, uncomfortable and, in some ways, inadequate. In the Light Infantry, for example, men wore cumbersome scarlet coats closed by two or three buttons above the waist and folded back in broad lapels to expose the front of the shirt. Coat-skirts reached the knees and hampered swift movements in battle. Turning up the front corners to get them out of the way was originally a practical matter, but it had the advantage of revealing white or yellow lining – adding a contrast to the red jacket. Leg coverings consisted of red breeches and white gaiters.

The jackets were dazzling from a distance, but a keen observer standing up close might notice that some were stretched to the splitting point and others were faded. Once Wolfe was in charge of a regiment, as happened in Scotland, he made some improvements, abandoning the lace cuffs and adding straps under the chin to keep small velvet caps from blowing off in a high wind. The men blessed him for it. But plenty of silly details remained: men still greased their hair, wasted time whitening their shoulder belts with pipe-clay and wore a tight wooden or leather collar to "deflect bayonet points." This device kept every soldier's head stiffly erect, but gave a choking feeling. It also stopped a soldier from turning his head, and in hand-to-hand combat he had no peripheral vision and couldn't look behind him.

Regulation footwear was often a bad fit and wore out quickly. Wolfe soon discovered that much-needed shoes for the lower ranks weren't always available – requests for more shoes often appeared in his dispatches. Military hats came in many styles: tall mitres worn by the Grenadiers were apt to blow off. In other regiments, small velvet caps without winter flaps encouraged frostbite, and floppy brims impaired a man's vision. Soldiers took to turning up the brims of their hats and fastening them to the crown with a jaunty ribbon that came to be known as a "cockade."

Ensign Wolfe landed at Ostend, Belgium, one hot June day. Two regiments, Howard's and Duroure's (his own), set out at once for Ghent, a town located in the province of Flanders. Wolfe said it felt more like running the gauntlet than a march because curious peasants with sour faces lined the roads to stare. Hostility to the British stemmed from the fact that the population in this part of Belgium was a mixture of French and Dutch, but the territory was under the control of Austria. It was Queen Maria Theresa whom British troops had come to support. As a conquered people, the Dutch were not sympathetic to her cause.

A shipload of wives and sweethearts attached to Duroure's arrived at Ostend a few days before the regiment, but no arrangements had been made to feed or house them. After considerable fuss, the women were, at last, forwarded to Ghent to wait for their men. This was only the first of many set-tos between Dutch officials and occupying troops.

In fact, while the British were on Dutch soil, they constantly engaged in nasty scuffles with local burghers. Two weeks after the British encamped in Ghent's marketplace, a savage fight broke out.

With the influx of newcomers the price of beef had risen dramatically and so had the public temper. A British officer, who claimed he was only smelling the meat to see if it was fresh, was accused of stealing. Hot words followed and the butcher slashed the officer across the face with his knife. This prompted the officer's companion to run his sword through the butcher, and in minutes shopkeepers with cleavers and soldiers with sabres got into a bloody mixup. Several men were killed and the cavalry was summoned to restore peace. Officers involved in the affair were thrown in jail for the rest of the day, and Dutch magistrates announced publicly that if any local citizen assaulted a subject of Great Britain in future, he would be "whipped, burned in the back and turned out of town." The threat cooled tempers for a while, but the feeling of hostility dragged on.

Wolfe, with his usual zeal, soon found good lodgings. Ghent was an ancient city with narrow streets, historic canals and old fortifications to explore. He discovered that people here were poorer than folk around Westerham, where he had lived as a boy. The Dutch dressed in ragged, dirty cloaks (James suspected they wore nothing underneath) and rough wooden shoes. Even so, he managed to find a few compatible souls with whom he could share a meal and polish up his French. Henrietta wrote to say that his father had returned home and had been promoted to an inspector of marines. Wolfe replied with a description of life in Ghent: he had met his old friend George Warde (now a cavalryman); he swore that he *had* written to his brother, Ned; and he reported that his shirts were all in order. "[They] will last me a great while," he wrote to Henrietta, "but I fancy not so long as we are in Flanders." Exaggeration was not beyond him when he wanted to lighten a tale.

James, now an adjutant-in-training, spent the winter in Ghent and moaned about the high cost of living since the town was flooded with British soldiers and their hangers-on. It didn't seem to occur to him that he and his companions were part of the problem. The old houses, "overtopped by fantastic gables," were charming on the outside but uncomfortable on the inside, and he practised the flute in a chilly, poorly lit room.

Wolfe attempted to cheer up his mother by omitting criticisms he often included in letters to his friends. To her, James said he was "eating well," but slipped when he mentioned the prevalence of sour bread. On the other hand, rum and brandy were cheap, so he "took a little sneaker at night to keep warm." For recreation, Wolfe attended a play at least once or twice a week and always spoke French to any ladies he met there. Such trifles were meant to soothe Henrietta's nerves, but at the same time they shed light on the life of a campaigner in a country that was an ally of England.

2

Horrors and Heroics

"The Duke of Cumberland was as brave as a man could be.
I had several times the honour of speaking to him and was often afraid
he would be dashed to pieces by the cannon balls."
— JAMES WOLFE, after the battle of Dettingen

The day Ned Wolfe was fifteen, he joined Duroure's so he could be with his brother. In February 1743 Ned reached Ghent just as his regiment was setting out for the Rhine, where the commander, Lord Stair, hoped to confront the French army. Luckily, Ned spotted James in time and the brothers marched together for several weeks. For the first five days it rained heavily, and eventually it snowed. Walking dozens of miles a day in bitter weather was to be expected, of course, but food supplies were so badly organized the troops were travelling on half-empty stomachs. The Wolfe brothers, as junior officers, had planned to buy their own food along the way but, like their comrades, they had no inkling of how deeply the peasantry despised them – most farmers refused to sell provisions to the British. By the time the army reached St. Tron, near Liège, officers and men alike were always hungry.

In a breezy letter home, however, Wolfe made the mistake of turning gloomy. "I never come into quarters without aching hips and knees," he wrote. Ned, less resilient than his brother, was in worse shape. The Wolfe brothers were too delicate for army life, but their family in England seemed oblivious to their plight. At this low point in James' affairs, he bought a horse so he and Ned could each ride it on alternate days.

The march to the Rhine was painful for everyone. Wolfe stopped trying to conceal the terrible conditions under which he and Ned were living, admitting to Henrietta that, on one occasion, he was "glad to take a little water out of a soldier's flask and eat some ammunition bread" because his own food pouch was empty. Not only were they finding it difficult to buy provisions, but a breakdown in the army supply system left no efficient canteen to rescue them.

In April, Duroure's regiment was still thirty miles from the banks of the Rhine. For a short time, the brothers' duties took them in different directions. James, at sixteen, was being groomed as an adjutant, assisting his superior with administrative work. The whole army was scrabbling for food and Ned was sent to Bonn to buy any provisions he could lay his hands on. At fifteen, Ned, who was now miserable and physically ill, wrote a touching letter in which he addressed his father as "Dearest Sir." Ned probably ate well enough on the Bonn food-finding mission, but he had been ill-fed and cold for some time and, with his delicate constitution, was a prime target for any disease spreading through the ranks. Winter weather still prevailed and, despite owning half a horse, Ned often found himself walking knee-deep in snow.

A month later, the British were camped near Aschaffenburg (southeast of Frankfurt) and James took up the story where Ned left off. King George and his son the Duke of Cumberland had arrived unexpectedly, Wolfe wrote to his parents, and with their entourage, the two royals were staying in a small castle nearby. The king's presence definitely bucked up morale, but it failed to produce better rations. "We have left a very fine country to come to the worst I have ever seen," James went on. "It has been ruined by Hanoverians. They and our men now live by marauding … I don't know how it will be possible to get provisions … [T]he French are burning all the villages on the other side of the Main and we are ravaging the country on this side."

After months of marching, the two armies faced each other across the Main River; the Earl of Stair commanded forty thousand men and the Duc de Noailles, sixty thousand. Unfortunately for the British, Lord Stair was incompetent and had blundered his way into an extremely dangerous position in a narrow valley surrounded by rocky hills. The only way to bring in relief troops, or to escape, was through a narrow mountain pass. Noailles, camped near the village of Dettingen, had only to march across a bridge, form his army at the mouth of the gorge and bottle up his enemy. Lord Stair was at a loss. Should he surrender without a fight or try to sneak his army out through the dangerously narrow pass?

While Lord Stair hesitated, King George II, a rotund, greying little man with a red face, suddenly took command of the British forces. Plunging up and down the front line, he roared, swore and urged his troops forward. Officers close to him noticed that the king appeared to be enjoying himself, and his men were thrilled at his courage. But the king's horse had other ideas and bolted, carrying the struggling monarch to the rear. George dismounted and, on foot, pushed his way through the ranks to the front. "I can be sure of my legs," he said to the nearest officer, dismissing the horse. "*They* will not run away with me." It was the last time a British monarch would lead his troops in battle: a historic occasion, although no one realized it at the time.

Meanwhile, the Duc de Noailles sent his nephew, the Duc de Grammont, with a detachment of thirty thousand men to cut his enemy off at the pass. If Grammont waited at the mouth of the gorge, he could pick off the British as they tried to squeeze through. King George drew up his army under heavy fire from French guns across the river. His troops, recognizing their dangerous position, felt certain they were about to be destroyed. But Grammont was too impatient to follow his uncle's orders and advanced into the gorge until the two armies met on even ground. The quality of the British soldier, the fact that the king himself was leading them, and, above all, the fatal mistake made by Grammont, produced a victory for the British. This action, pitting Grammont's impetuosity against the bravery of the redcoats, would become known as the battle of Dettingen.

The horrors and heroics young Wolfe saw that day remained the high point in his life for many years. He had found his niche at last. During the action, he learned that war was down-and-dirty, but it lifted his spirits like nothing else. Even in the cut and thrust of hand-to-hand fighting, Wolfe was cool enough to observe the way men behaved in the face of death. For example, the Duke of Cumberland was as brave as a man could be, slashing and thrashing in the midst of his enemies although the royal leg had been pierced by a musket ball. "I had several times the honour of speaking to him and was often afraid he would be dashed to pieces by the cannonballs," Wolfe reported.

James Wolfe learned two important lessons in his first battle: being noticed by a VIP was very useful (two weeks afterward, the Duke of Cumberland had him promoted to lieutenant); and a victorious army must pursue a beaten one at all costs. He couldn't help noticing that the king and the duke loitered on the field to receive compliments from their fawning courtiers while the whole French army escaped.

By October 1744 young Ned Wolfe, still in the Netherlands, was dying of tuberculosis in a camp several miles from his brother. No one bothered to send word to James about the seriousness of his brother's illness, and James was shocked and furious to learn the boy was dead. He confessed in a letter to his mother, "It gives me many uneasy hours when I reflect on the possibility there was of my being with him before he died." James disposed of Ned's effects and provided his mother with details. "I have his watch, sash, gorget [a metal crescent worn around the neck that denoted rank in the army], books and maps, which I will preserve to his memory." Ned was sixteen when he died. He was surrounded by his army friends and a servant, but James felt guilty. After all, Ned had joined the army to be near him. "There is no part of his life that makes him dearer to me than what you have often mentioned – *he pined after me*," he assured his mother.

From a very young age, romantic attachments disturbed Wolfe's studies. At the age of twenty, when he was in camp near Brussels, he became friendly with the daughter of General Lacey, then in the Austrian service. Wolfe's letters to Miss Lacey were sprinkled with inside jokes, bits of banter and intimate references to the young lady's supervision of a scarlet officer's frock coat he was having made by a tailor in Liège. But Miss Lacey was merely a diversion. James still harboured his youthful passion for Miss Warde. His feelings were about to change, however, because that same year, 1747, he fell in love with another pretty girl and wooed her passionately.

Elizabeth Lawson's father was Sir Wilfrid Lawson and at the time Wolfe met her, she was maid of honour to the Princess of Wales. For the romantic Wolfe, it was love at first sight. Not long after their first encounter, he was sent to Scotland and confided to his close friend Captain William Rickson, "She won all my affections. I, who am her lover don't think her a beauty. She is tall, thin, about my own age." Was James being truthful or merely modest? Since Miss Lawson had many other suitors, she was probably more attractive than his description suggests. Wolfe was often playful in his letters to Rickson.

Miss Lawson had a dowry of £12,000, a considerable amount in those days. Wolfe's mother didn't approve of Elizabeth partly because she had her own candidate, Miss Hoskins, with a dowry of £30,000, and partly because the girl's mother had a dubious reputation. Wolfe was mad about Elizabeth and quarrelled violently with his mother, not only over the merits of the girl, but over Henrietta's nasty remarks about Lady Lawson. Wolfe's father took his wife's side in the argument. Wolfe's break with his parents over Elizabeth Lawson drove him into a two-week spree, a thing he'd never done in his life.

According to Wolfe himself, he plunged into all the vices London had to offer – women, drinking and gambling – and made himself so ill he wasn't fit to return to his duties in Scotland for several weeks. After a time, his relations with his parents warmed and eventually returned to normal.

Wrangling over dowries may sound unsavoury, but General and Mrs. Wolfe were far from wealthy and they had been pouring money into their son's career for several years. Perhaps they were looking for financial relief by trying to marry him off to a rich woman. Having patched up his quarrel with his parents, James sulkily agreed to court Miss Hoskins. But it was too late; she had been snapped up by a more persistent suitor and was now engaged. Wolfe hinted to his closest friends that he still longed for Elizabeth but, giving no reason, he seemed to stop pursuing her.

Wolfe was judged a fine regimental officer not only because of his bold strikes in action, but also because he was a stickler for detail. He tackled every sort of problem, from caring for teeth, wigs and dogs to dressing elegantly on very little money. Being penniless didn't appear to make much of a dent in his self-confidence. Wolfe was eager to offer financial advice to his mother and didn't hesitate to suggest treatments for her gout and rheumatism. At one point, he even suggested she might wish to be fitted for false teeth.

"Teeth are valuable from their great use," Wolfe told his mother pompously. "[T]he other day I broke a fine large one all to pieces." Wolfe went on to say someone had told him that in Paris they put in artificial teeth "as serviceable as natural ones," and that "perhaps they do the same in London. I see no harm in repairing any loss of this kind as we really can't eat or speak properly without them." Later, when in Paris, Wolfe noted dozens of interesting details about life in that city, including the French fondness for umbrellas. The English might eventually take to this custom, he speculated, in view of the island's rainy weather.

Wolfe was a networker, a custom referred to in those days as "knowing the right people." His father, who ended his military career with the rank of lieutenant-general, had helped James transfer from the marines to the infantry when the lad was barely fifteen. After observing Wolfe's courage under fire at Dettingen, the Duke of Cumberland promoted him to lieutenant and later to brigade-major. Wolfe paid his military dues in Scotland – his experience there began when he was posted to Stirling and found himself in command of the 20th Foot. The responsibility was foisted on him because the colonel, Edward Cornwallis, was absent. This was a common enough state of affairs when a regiment was serving in some "uncivilized" part of the world. It happened that the lieutenant-colonel who ought to have taken over had just sailed for Nova Scotia to become governor. This left Wolfe heading a regiment in which many officers were older and more experienced than he. Such a situation was bound to produce keen resentment and make his job more difficult.

In 1745, after their failed rebellion, Highland clans still seethed against the English. In the hills where they could hide, they were particularly restless. It was Wolfe's unpleasant task to enforce tough new regulations that would keep the lid on a possible revolt. The northern climate was bad for his health (most climates were bad for his health), and he despised the town of Stirling because it was "dirty and drunken." But none of this dampened Wolfe's military ardour. Day after day he picked away at what he considered essential details: improving drills and demanding neat uniforms, proper church parade and clean latrines. Nothing escaped his sharp eye. There was to be no "letting down the side" just because the regiment was stationed in a place Wolfe considered the back of beyond.

A typical order dated February 1746 and intended for all Wolfe's fresh-faced junior officers to read, ran, "They must occasionally go round the quarters between nine and eleven at night – not always trusting to the reports of sergeants. If any [of the men] are thinner or paler than usual, the reasons may be inquired into and proper means used to restore them."

Wolfe and his regiment were sent to Glasgow, a city that boasted a university and where he seized the opportunity to improve his mathematics and Latin. As usual, he was sadly short of cash and asked his mother for a loan. The request was accompanied by intimate details of life in that city.

"My horses will be here in a day or two, they have cost me 45 guineas," he wrote. "I am half-undone with these expenses. Be so good as to pay Mr. Fourmantel for the wig: it was 30 shillings." He assured Henrietta that a trustworthy sergeant would stop by her house to pick up the wig and bring it to him in Glasgow, after which he went on to report his budget for a week: "Horses, servants, washing, lodging and diet is no less than 3 pounds 10 shillings. I reckon I have a shilling a day for what they call pocket money."

In April 1746 Wolfe was involved in the battle of Culloden, infamous for its ferocity. The Highland rebels under Bonnie Prince Charlie (who had returned from France to regain his Scottish throne) were outnumbered by the English under the Duke of Cumberland. Wolfe was aide to General "Hangman" Hawley, notorious for his cruelty toward his own men and the enemy. (The nickname was supposedly based on the belief that Hawley imported at least two professional killers to shoot or hang soldiers found guilty of serious offences and slated to die. In any event, his men hated Hawley.)

Although Wolfe was present at the battle of Culloden, he apparently did not fight, nor did he perform any spectacular military moves. Later he described the battle to his uncle William Sotheron: "About one in the afternoon the Duke [of Cumberland] engaged with the rebel army and in about an hour drove them from the field of battle where they left nearly 1,500 dead, the rest except prisoners, escaped by the neighbourhood of hills."

By 1751 James was still stationed in Scotland, and that season the winter was severe even for Inverness. Surprisingly, he claimed his body was in good shape, but his mind was not. "It is in the dead of night when men think of what they really are," he told his mother. His fellow officers were boors and he feared becoming a ruffian himself, feared giving way to the temptations of power. "I hear things said every day that would shock your ears," he wrote, "and often say things myself that are not fit to be repeated."

What was the solution? James had two suggestions: he desperately needed to associate with elegant women, and he had to see Paris at once. To get his own way, he resorted to threats. If he didn't get time off to go abroad he would leave the army altogether – a cry from the heart his parents were to hear more than once in the next few years. Paris at that time was a magnet for any Englishman who aspired to gallantry and sophistication, a city far ahead of London. Since France and England were between wars, a visit in the French capital was not out of the question.

Wolfe made a number of attempts to get permission to go abroad, but it was a year before it came through. His father put up the money and Colonel Lord Bury (who felt he could rely on Wolfe to look after the regiment in the long haul) finally supported his request. In the fall of 1752 James Wolfe set out for Paris carrying several letters of introduction. The most valuable was a note from Colonel Bury to his father, Lord William Albemarle, then British ambassador to the Court of Versailles.

Lord Albemarle changed Wolfe's view of life when he introduced him to some of the most powerful people in Europe. By taking the young soldier into his circle, Albemarle was able to present him to Louis XV, the entire royal family and even the king's mistress, Madame de Pompadour. Wolfe's fluent French made the exercise easier. Eventually, when Wolfe was back in England, he described his visit with Pompadour: "Madame la Marquise entertained us at her toilette. We found her curling her hair. She is extremely handsome and, by her conversation with the Ambassador and others that were present, I judge she must have a great deal of wit and understanding."

Through Albemarle, Wolfe met a very young William Hamilton who, as Sir William Hamilton, would marry beautiful Emma – the ex–artist's model, later to become Lord Nelson's mistress. The Wolfe family knew how to use contacts in high places not only for themselves, but also to help their friends and relatives find jobs or get into the army. Such items often appeared in correspondence between James and his mother.

While he was in Paris, he polished up his French, learned ballroom dancing and improved his skill with the sword. And he accomplished all this in spite of various ailments. Hearing how often Wolfe was sick – with fevers, scurvy, rheumatism, kidney stones and possibly tuberculosis – strikes an odd note today, when the army rejects a man for flat feet or weak eyes. In the eighteenth century, the same rules did not apply. Officers with the right stuff, or the right connections, were accepted without a lot of nosy questions about their health. Battles were spaced weeks or months apart and were usually short and brutal. Having a chronic illness was unlikely to affect a soldier's performance.

Wolfe predicted a short life for himself and often remarked that he might be called upon to die for his country. In the last years of his life, he believed he had tuberculosis and made it clear to his friends that if given a choice he would prefer to die for a great cause than waste away in obscurity. This attitude probably wiped out his fear of dying on a foreign battlefield; better a dead hero than a sick nobody. Horace Walpole, the popular London author and a member of Parliament, put the case this way: "Wolfe looked upon danger as the favourable moment that would call forth all his talents." Colleagues who fought beside him noticed Wolfe seemed to get a thrill out of hurling himself into the line of fire. In moments of great danger, his face expressed intense pleasure – as if he were experiencing the ultimate orgasmic high.

Returning to Scotland was a shock to Wolfe's system after the civilities of Paris, and he was forced to endure a few more months of harsh weather before returning to see England again. When at last he travelled south again, a bystander in Reading caught a glimpse of Wolfe with his regiment, describing him as "a tall thin officer astride a bay horse, his face lit up by a smile." People often remarked on Wolfe's brilliant smile because good white teeth were rare then. Dentistry was still practised by barbers and consisted mostly of pulling teeth, not preserving them.

Wolfe accompanied his regiment to Dover Castle in November 1753. "Here our labour ends," he wrote to his father. "I can't say comfortably or warmly, but in a soldier-like starving condition." His lodging was on the ground floor of a Roman-built tower, drafty, unheated and offering a bleak view of the English Channel. The castle was in such a bad state of repair that the roofless chapel, damaged by years of rain and frost, was used to store coal.

When the weather was foul, there was no entertainment in Dover and Wolfe fell back on his books. During this miserable period, he came up with a brand new fear. "Let me alone six or seven days in my room and I lose all sort of sensation, either pain or pleasure, and I am, in species, little better than an oyster." It wasn't just cold and boredom that bothered him; it was being denied the kind of soldiering that fuelled his inner fires. Sinking lower as the temperature around him plummeted, his imagination took another bizarre turn. "The castle is haunted," he wrote. "Weak conscience or strong imagination, people say they see ghosts."

Christmas was almost upon them and Wolfe longed for the delicious holiday fare of his youth, but there were no mince pies to be had in Dover at any price. It was a village without pubs, newspapers, pretty girls or green tea. He tried to content himself with card games and, when it wasn't raining, horseback riding. At the age of twenty-seven, Lieutenant-Colonel Wolfe remembered the delights of Paris and wondered how he could have landed in this cultural desert. His only comfort was the companionship of a hunting dog his cousin Oliver Goldsmith (who in 1766 would write the classic novel *The Vicar of Wakefield*) had given him. "That [my dog] is my very existence here."

A plague struck the Dover area in February 1755. Citizens and soldiers hoped the frost would kill the disease, but the cold seemed to have no effect upon its spread. Spring arrived at last and Wolfe was given a three-month leave of absence. He hurried to his parents and his six dogs at the family residence in Blackheath, visited his old friends the Wardes at Squerryes Court in Westerham, and spent time with a new friend, Sir John Mordaunt, who had a seat in Hampshire. His greatest love, Elizabeth Lawson (Mordaunt's niece), had rejected Wolfe and he was still fighting his personal demons. When he dined with Sir John, he couldn't look at Elizabeth's portrait without feeling ill.

After his long holiday, Wolfe's regiment moved to Rougemount Castle in Exeter, a posting that turned out to be far more pleasant than Dover. Wolfe, who kept abreast of world events, knew war with France was creeping closer. He might suddenly be ordered to take the field. Since he was a man who liked to be prepared, he took stock of his wardrobe. Among other things, he needed "a quantity of coarse shirts"; but he had no money for such luxuries. This sad fact led him to take a long, hard look at his life. "I am twenty-eight years of age – a Lieutenant-Colonel of Foot and I cannot say I am master of £50," he informed his mother. She discussed the situation with "the old general," as Wolfe now called his father, and James soon received money enough to cover all his needs. But his career was definitely in the doldrums. He had expected to be made colonel of the regiment and, when the promotion had been denied him, Wolfe told his father he would have resigned his commission on the spot, but war with France was about to break out and he had to be part of it.

Still smarting over the loss of the coveted promotion, Wolfe diagnosed himself with scurvy and went to Bath to take the cure. Duty prevented him staying long enough to experience a full course of treatments; his mother was ill again, and he needed to see her. "My utmost desire and ambition is to look steadily upon danger, and the greatest happiness that I wish for here is to see you happy," he wrote in a comforting letter to Henrietta.

This was the summer Wolfe abandoned his white military wig. Legions of men were doing the same thing that year. Wigs were a nuisance on a campaign, they encouraged lice, and in civilian life they made the head hot. Jokingly, Wolfe gave his mother permission to laugh at his short red hair – he was aware that his thin hair wasn't his best feature. Serious again, he asked her to order "a strong pair of boots" for him and half a dozen pairs of "very strong shoes." James might look frail, but like most men of his day he walked long distances and knew the importance of comfortable footwear.

In May 1756 Wolfe and his regiment marched to Wiltshire, leaving behind the blooming orchards of Kent. Rumours of war grew stronger every day. Citizens began protesting the ruthless press gangs that kidnapped young men and carried them off for sea duty. A fund-raising scheme was afoot to raise money to buy blankets for the soldiers in Wolfe's regiment, and he was pleased, since the government had failed to provide them. He heard that Britain had lost the island of Minorca, an event that spawned a high-profile scandal involving Admiral Byng. Byng was said to have refused to defend the base there. But Wolfe had received no word about taking his regiment to the Continent.

On May 18, England declared war on France. Wolfe was delighted at the prospect, but by June 7 he was still awaiting orders. Interested in anything military, he caught sight of Hessian troops (German mercenaries) and took time to describe them. "A fine appearance, being generally straight, tall and slender," he wrote. "Their uniform is blue, turned up with red and laced with white and hair plaited behind, hangs down to the waist." He was impressed with their discipline.

England was now at war with France, but Wolfe and his regiment were sent to Gloucestershire to quell rioting weavers. He didn't relish this kind of "police work" and sympathized with the weavers whose pay was so low they were reduced to begging in the streets. To add to his frustration, political leaders seemed hesitant to prepare for war. Furious in the face of so much stupidity and laziness, Wolfe wrote a number of insulting letters to men in authority and several times questioned their motives in person. It was a dangerous game if he hoped to rise in the army. Apologizing to his mother for his hot temper, he explained, "It is my misfortune to catch fire on a sudden, to answer letters the moment I receive them."

When the year 1756 came to an end, the war was six months old and England had done nothing to defend herself from the expected invasion by France. James Wolfe was disenchanted with the government and with the army, and once again he considered choosing a different career. The following summer, 1757, Wolfe's friend Sir John Mordaunt came to his rescue by suggesting Wolfe be appointed quartermaster on a raid that Acting Prime Minister William Pitt was planning to carry out on a French port. Wolfe, sizzling with patriotic fervour, accepted immediately. A bloody good fight, at last!

3

Montcalm's Army Career

"*Montcalm has changed the very nature of war and has forced us to a deterring and dreadful vengeance.*"

— JAMES WOLFE, 1758

General Louis-Joseph, Marquis de Montcalm-Gozon de Saint-Véran, was short and fat. A few weeks after his arrival in Canada in 1756, an Indian chief, meeting him for the first time, confessed his disappointment.

"We thought you would be so tall your head would be lost in the clouds. But you are a little man, my father."

Montcalm was olive-skinned and dark-eyed. In a stiff portrait typical of the period, Louis-Joseph is shown wearing a mysterious smile and what appears to be the sphinx's wig. He was a man of wildly swinging moods: a sharp temper one minute, a sunny smile the next. At the time of the Battle of the Plains of Abraham, Montcalm was forty-seven, lively and flirtatious around the ladies but blunt and offensive with his colleagues. He was, rare in those times, in love with his wife.

"What a country!" he once blurted during an argument about Quebec's weak defences. "Here all the knaves grow rich and the honest men are ruined!"

The Montcalms belonged to the most ancient order of French aristocracy, the *noblesse d'épée,* although Louis was brought up on the family estate in Provence, far from the elegant Court of Versailles. Even so, his mother believed in loyalty to royalty and instilled in the boy a sense of duty to the king. When Louis was six years old, his grand-father's illegitimate son, Dumas, became his tutor. From the start Dumas struggled to improve the heir's wretched handwriting, and his concern produced a report to Montcalm's father. "The boy had better be ignorant of Latin and Greek than know them as he does without knowing how to read, write and speak well. What will become of him?"

Montcalm's army career began early. At fifteen he was an ensign, at seventeen his father bought him a captaincy, and from then on, he climbed the ladder steadily. When Louis was twenty-four, the old marquis died, leaving his son the title and Candiac, the family seat. Louis loved his château and his olive groves, but the Montcalms belonged to an impoverished aristocracy: men with hoary titles and long lineage who could barely make a living off the land. In one of those practical strokes so common in French society, a marriage was arranged between Louis-Joseph and a wealthy young woman, Angélique Louise Talon de Boulay. Magically, he fell in love with her, and after twenty years of marriage he was still deluging her with florid letters. "Adieu, my heart, I adore and love you!" was a typical closing line.

As well as rescuing Candiac, Angélique produced ten children, putting extra pressure on an already strained family budget. In his memoirs, Montcalm was apologetic about the couple's fertility. "Perhaps it will be thought that the number is large for so moderate a fortune, especially as four of them are girls: but does God ever abandon his children in their need?"

While campaigning in Italy Colonel the Marquis de Montcalm received five saber cuts (two in the head) and was taken prisoner. Although he recuperated at home for several months – he was paroled within a year – he remained in the army. Promoted to brigadier-general in 1747, he soon was back in the fray. This time he was wounded by musket shot. A year later the Peace of Aix-la-Chapelle gave him time to think things over. What should he do with the rest of his life? If Montcalm had followed his heart, he would have played the role of gentleman farmer. But his army pay helped keep the estate solvent, and he stayed on. He spent the next seven years as a country gentleman.

During a visit to Paris in the autumn of 1755, Brigadier Montcalm called on the minister of war, Comte d'Argenson, to say he planned to remain in Provence for an indefinite period. Never one to dance attendance on the Court of Versailles like some aristocrats or involve himself in politics, Montcalm might not have realized d'Argenson was searching desperately for a general to command French troops in North America. All the qualified candidates had agreed among themselves that fighting battles in Europe was one thing; risking one's life in the wilderness was quite another. So far, they'd all refused to take the job. *Yet someone had to go over there and defend Canada!* D'Argenson regarded Montcalm's surprise appearance in his office as providential, mentioned the appointment to his visitor and promised to get in touch with him. The marquis hurried back to his château and forgot all about it.

Early in January 1756, war with England was casting a shadow over France. By the end of the month, Montcalm received an alarming message: "The King has chosen you to command his troops in North America, and will honour you on your departure with the rank of Major-General." Montcalm's heart sank. God knows, he could use the raise in pay that went with such a promotion, but he was happy at home with his olive oil mills and his pretty wife. He was on the verge of saying no. His tough old mother saw things differently: she pointed out that the Montcalms had supported the monarchy for generations, and Louis-Joseph must accept the honour without delay. Montcalm did as he was told.

Major-General the Marquis de Montcalm made plans to sail from Brest at the end of March. His second-in-command, Chevalier François de Lévis and his third, Chevalier François-Charles de Bourlamaque, were scheduled to sail with him. The king was paying Montcalm twenty-five thousand livres a year with an additional twelve thousand for equipment, but Montcalm doubted the amount would cover his expenses. Instead of augmenting his income, he now feared the promotion was going to cost him money. Even so, Montcalm took great pride in his lavish retinue. Among others, he listed "an assistant cook, two livery-men … I have got a good cook … Estève, my secretary will go on the eighth." The staccato phrasing was an echo of the way he spoke.

During his final days in France, Montcalm commuted from Paris to Versailles with his eldest son in tow "to coach him and get his uniform made. He is thin and delicate as ever but grows prodigiously." The boy had just been given command of a regiment, although the father's description of him suggests he wasn't sufficiently robust to survive army life.

While the two were at Versailles, Montcalm arranged to present his son to the royal family, one of the privileges that came with his new rank. His last scrawl to his wife before departing struck a poignant note. "Perhaps I shall leave debts behind," he wrote to Angélique. "I wait impatiently for the bills. You have my will. I wish you would get it copied and send it to me before I sail."

General Montcalm met his third aide-de-camp, Captain Louis-Antoine, Comte de Bougainville, while he was still in Brest. Bougainville was handsome, charming and ambitious. He had started out as an advocate in the Parlement de Paris (a judiciary body) and switched careers to become a captain of dragoons. He was also a scientific prodigy with a treatise on integral calculus to his credit. Because of that paper, he was elected a Fellow of the Royal Society of England, an unusual honour for a Frenchman. Captain Bougainville was one of those men instantly recognized as brilliant, the kind who move ahead quickly in the world. (After the war ended, Bougainville set out on a two-year voyage around the world at his own expense, stopping at Tahiti and Samoa and rediscovering the Solomon Islands. A strait in the New Hebrides and the tropical vine bougainvillea are named after him.)

When Montcalm left for Canada, two battalions of regulars accompanied him, one from the regiment of La Sarre and the other from the Royal-Roussillon, a total of twelve hundred men. The king's antipathy toward Canada must have been obvious to anyone who compared that figure with the hundred thousand men he had sent to Austria to support the Empress Maria Theresa. But as Montcalm and Bougainville stood on the deck of the *Licorne* watching troops board the *Léopard*, the *Héros* and the *Illustre*, they were elated at the prospect of glory and adventure. "What a nation is ours! Happy he who commands it, and commands it worthily," Bougainville exclaimed.

Shortly after leaving Brest, the *Licorne* was engulfed by high seas. Montcalm and Bougainville were the only two officers who managed to stay on their feet. During a gale that lasted ninety hours, the forecastle and afterdeck were often underwater. A huge iceberg grazed the bowsprit, and only quick action by the deck officer prevented the ship from being crushed. But there were other times when the general enjoyed fishing for cod. "The taste is exquisite," he reported. "The head, tongue and liver are morsels worthy of an epicure."

Montcalm had his darker moments. His scribblings reveal he was homesick long before he reached Quebec. On May 11, the *Licorne* was stuck in ice thirty miles downriver from the capital. "I have taken very little liking for the sea," he wrote to his wife, "and think that when I shall be happy to rejoin you, I shall end my voyage there."

Finally stepping ashore, he learned that the troop transports were safe in the Gulf of St. Lawrence. "Our campaign will soon begin," he told Angélique. "Don't expect details about our operations: generals never speak of movements until they are over. I can only tell you the savages have made great havoc in Pennsylvania and Virginia and have carried off, according to their custom, men, women and children. I beg you will have High Mass at Montpellier or Vauvert to thank God for our safe arrival and ask for good success in the future."

For a brief time Montcalm was naïve enough to think that he and the ruling officials were on the same side in the present war, but he soon discovered this wasn't the case. His colleagues worried more about outmanoeuvring their associates than they did about defeating the enemy. There were two "parties" in the colony – those who cared solely about New France (Canada), and those loyal to Old France. Pierre de Rigaud de Vaudreuil de Cavagnial, Marquis de Vaudreuil, born in Quebec while his father was governor-general, was deeply attached to the country of his birth. After Vaudreuil's eleven-year stint as governor of Louisiana, in 1755 the king appointed him governor-general of Canada. He was fifty-seven. In Vaudreuil's eyes, everyone who came from France was to be mistrusted and every Canadian citizen was his natural ally. By definition, then, Montcalm was an enemy. It took Montcalm a while to grasp this disturbing view. He wanted to believe Vaudreuil was friendly, but he gradually realized this situation was otherwise.

Upon arriving at Quebec, still unaware that he was unwanted, the general wasted little time making his way to Montreal, where Vaudreuil was in residence. Before Montcalm left France, Minister of War d'Argenson had assured him he was to command the battalions of regulars as well as colony troops and militia. This appears to have been a verbal commitment. It was a shock to find Vaudreuil claiming *he* was supreme commander. Weeks later, Montcalm became privy to the fact that the ambitious governor had tried unsuccessfully to discourage King Louis from sending *any* general officer. The governor's dislike of the fiery little general was inevitable.

Montcalm had his flaws. He was haughty and opinionated, but he was also a realist and it didn't take him long to discover he had stepped in a hornet's nest. More frightening than his personal dilemma, he had little confidence in his army. The regulars from France (*troupes de la terre*) numbered three thousand and were, on the whole, disciplined and dependable. But the bulk of his force was made up of colonial troops (*troupes de la marine*) and militia – 15,000 farmers, untrained and unhappy, who fought best from behind a tree.

Governor Vaudreuil begged to differ. He believed bushrangers, Indians and colonial troops were the only men fit to fight in the forest. French regulars with their uppity ways might be brave on an open field, but in the woods they were useless. Montcalm despised the lack of discipline he saw among the colonials and, from what he'd heard of his Indian allies, they were apt to vanish whenever the fancy took them. How could he rely on such troops? Obviously, two powerful men with such diverse opinions were unlikely to agree on a strategy for the defence of Canada.

Montcalm showed the first signs of uneasiness in a dispatch to Minister of War d'Argenson: "Vaudreuil overwhelms me with civilities. I think he is pleased with my conduct towards him … but I am not in his confidence, which he never gives to anybody from France." Montcalm was correct as far as he went, but he still didn't know the real reason for Vaudreuil's rage against him. Vaudreuil wanted to win the war and become a hero by driving Wolfe away.

Three men ruled the colony: Intendant François Bigot, Commissary-General Joseph Cadet and Governor Pierre Vaudreuil. Bigot's fiefdom included the government's financial and judicial affairs; his henchman, Cadet, controlled provisions imported from France and sold in the company store, a warehouse the people secretly called *la friponne*, meaning "the cheat." Governor Vaudreuil, who represented the interests of the king, held a miniature court away from Versailles. It didn't take long for Montcalm to hear gossip about the trio. He made it clear he wasn't going to join the club. Gambling was the chief amusement of the rich, an obsession with Bigot, who lost huge sums month after month. Montcalm couldn't afford to throw away money on bets; he had trouble living in the required style even if he scrimped. There was also the question of women: the Bigot crowd (with the exception of the governor) all kept mistresses or swapped wives for a change of face. Montcalm dabbled in flirtations, but didn't indulge himself in blatant love affairs. Above all, he refused to become a part of Bigot's fraudulent schemes. So the ruling group, who called themselves "the grand society," eyed him with suspicion. How could they trust a man who didn't steal?

Despite their sexual conquests, the rulers of Quebec could not be called clones of Romeo. Bigot is described as having pimply skin, small black eyes and a considerable paunch. He suffered from painful gout, made worse by his relentless consumption of fine wines and rich food, and must have been blessed with a strong constitution, because he never missed a private feast or a public fight. Somehow, he always kept a beautiful mistress; it seems the belles of Quebec had a fondness for luxurious living rather than male beauty. It was Intendant Bigot who gave Joseph Cadet, the butcher's son, a nine-year contract to supply clothing, ammunition and food for the Canadian army: what we would call today a licence to print money. Cadet was a giant of a man with coarse manners and an insatiable greed for gold. But he was bold, brave and obedient, and Bigot found him extremely useful.

The third member of the unholy trinity was Governor Pierre de Rigaud, Marquis de Vaudreuil, by virtue of his office the most influential man in Canada. Even so, everyone with any common sense could see that Bigot really ruled the roost. The fact that Vaudreuil was blind to the corruption all around him only revealed his weakness and hypocrisy.

Vaudreuil began pitching off venomous letters to Versailles before Montcalm had time to unpack his bags and, in the same dispatches that vilified the general, the governor flattered Bigot and his toady Cadet. Time and time again he wrote to the minister of marine to say no task was beyond the abilities of Bigot and Cadet, and that their loyalty was unquestionable. While there was no proof Vaudreuil accepted bribes, he and his wife long enjoyed a vice-regal lifestyle without fear of complaint from his colleagues.

In Paris, the prestigious French publication the *Encyclopédie* dismissed Canada as a place "inhabited by bears, beavers and barbarians"; but the academics making this pronouncement were not entirely correct. Even at the Court of Versailles, Quebec was known (and criticized) for its lavish balls and gargantuan feasts. And Montreal, perched on the very edge of civilization, glowed with candlelight assemblies each time the governor and his entourage dropped in for a visit. "In Quebec they live better than we do," Madame de Pompadour once huffed during a cabinet meeting.

What a shock it must have been for the civilized Marquis de Montcalm to find himself marooned on a flat little island (except for the Mountain backdrop) in the middle of nowhere. Montreal was a trading post surrounded by a low wall built many years earlier to protect settlers from Iroquois bows and arrows. As a barrier against cannon fire, it was useless. The town was a collection of log huts, stone barracks and half a dozen creditable houses where the elite could alight to do business and have a bit of fun. And finally, there was a community of hard-working labourers and merchants exposed constantly to the wild doings of *coureurs de bois* (independent fur trappers) and Indians selling furs and buying brandy.

When Montcalm found he was expected to use Indian allies in the war against the English, his hackles rose. He was aware of tales about native cruelties in the long-standing border war and was shocked to discover Vaudreuil seemed unmoved by them. Vaudreuil explained that the French couldn't find their way through the dense forests or along uncharted rivers without Indian guides. Montcalm, he said, would soon realize that friendly Indians made good spies since they moved constantly between English and French camps and had plenty of opportunities to observe what was going on. Montcalm gave in, convincing himself he would find a way to establish good relations with the natives.

At first, he thought they liked him. "My friends the Indians," he bragged, "who are often unbearable and whom I treat with perfect tranquillity and patience, are fond of me." His aides would have been amused had they read his version of affairs. Friends like Bougainville, Bourlamaque and Lévis were aware of the general's good qualities and even confided in him, but they never denied he was prickly and outspoken. Indian chiefs, unlikely to see Montcalm over a long period, wouldn't be so tolerant of his bursts of temper.

In 1756, June's fine weather brought greenery and wild flowers. It also brought mosquitoes and the fear of invasion. Although Montcalm was still in Montreal, his prime concern was to strengthen Quebec's walls and plant cannon along the banks of the St. Lawrence. The preceding winter Governor Vaudreuil had upgraded border posts between Canada and the Thirteen Colonies, but everyone knew that wouldn't keep the British at bay. By mid-June, Indian spies became specific: ten thousand redcoats were mustering to overwhelm Fort Ticonderoga (formerly Carillon), an important French stronghold situated between Lake Champlain and Lake George.

The governor acted swiftly. At the end of June, he sent Montcalm and Lévis to Ticonderoga with colony troops, militia and a battalion of Royal-Roussillons, three thousand men in all. The fort itself consisted of a large square with four bastions, a ditch blown out of solid rock and a clearing large enough to accommodate soldiers' tents and huts. But despite the governor's ambitious rebuilding program, the outer works at Ticonderoga were still incomplete.

Lévis was in high spirits and spent several days scouting woods and mountains in the area. Montcalm was impressed with his vigour. "I do not think," he commented, "that many high officers in Europe would have occasion to take such tramps as this." Lévis returned the compliment: "I do not know if the Marquis de Montcalm is pleased with me but I am sure that I am very much so with him." Pleasantries at the top made a nice change from complaints in the officers' mess.

Captain Duchat of the Languedoc Regiment was more in touch with life at the bottom, where food was a key concern. For him, the exciting thing was the plentiful and varied game birds: ducks, geese, partridges and pigeons in flocks so thick they darkened the sky. Comparing a soldier's lot in North America with that of his European counterpart, Duchat displayed an unusual flash of insight: "It is a pleasure to make war in Canada. One is troubled neither with horses nor baggage: the king provides everything … but one pays for it in another way, by seeing nothing but pease and bacon on the mess table. Luckily the lakes are full of fish and both officers and soldiers have to turn fishermen."

The British soldier's legendary fighting qualities preceded him, and the inmates of Ticonderoga waited fearfully for the red tide to swallow them up. It was hot. Insects swarmed anyone foolish enough to wander into the bush. Fishing was an option, but only after scouts had reassured the troops there were no redcoats in the neighbourhood. And still the British did not come.

Unknown to the French, there were internal reasons why the British failed to make a move on Ticonderoga. For all their talk, for all their promises, for all the wild tales of how they would demolish the French, the British Army in North America and volunteer regiments from the Thirteen Colonies were in disarray. Senior officers had known for a year that Oswego, that miserable little fort on Lake Ontario, must be improved and reinforced or they would lose it. By the time they were ready to tackle the project, they found themselves involved in a struggle between the British high command and the local governors. The separate colonies were jealous of one another, desperately afraid of paying a larger share of the war chest than the colony next door; desperately afraid of being shut out of meetings where vital decisions were being made. Then, too, a new commander-in-chief, Lord John Campbell Loudon, was due to arrive from London and no one wanted to take responsibility for anything without his approval.

Oswego was dangerously low on supplies, men were dying and the three forts that made up the post were crumbling. That spring, Lieutenant-Colonel John Bradstreet, the only colonial officer willing to help Oswego, on his own initiative arranged to carry provisions to the starving garrison. In May, he hired a thousand boatmen and several hundred flatboats, armed each civilian with a gun and a hatchet and sent them down the Mohawk without an escort – no officer was willing to provide one. Bradstreet managed to deliver much-needed food and ammunition and was returning to Albany with the first one hundred boats and three hundred men when he was ambushed only nine miles from Oswego.

Governor Vaudreuil had sent Chevalier Coulon de Villiers and a party of militia and Indians on a military "dress rehearsal." The aim was to discover how difficult it would be to stage a full-scale attack on Oswego and other British forts between there and Albany. The arrival of reinforcements from Oswego saved most of the boatmen; otherwise, the attack would have turned into a slaughter. Bradstreet and the bulk of his party managed to escape and reach Albany safely. He reported "between sixty and seventy taken prisoners, wounded and dead." Vaudreuil, in his usual self-promoting fashion, declared the raid a French victory. This minor win at Oswego only increased his itch to control it and thus Lake Erie.

In mid-July 1756, Vaudreuil told Montcalm he must prepare for an attack on Oswego. By pressuring his boatmen to row day and night, the general's little army reached Montreal on July 19. Eight days after that, he was in Fort Frontenac (at present-day Kingston, Ontario) on the north shore of Lake Ontario, where his troops were to muster. Rigaud, the governor's brother, had already rounded up three thousand colony troops, Indians and militia in a camp near Sackett's Harbour where the two parties would meet.

Montcalm, with his regulars and heavy artillery, joined Rigaud and his Indians and militia on August 6. Two days later the second division arrived at Sackett's Harbour from Frontenac. By August 10 they were crossing Lake Ontario to a spot near Oswego, Rigaud's troops marching under cover of the forest and Montcalm's force sailing in bateaux close to shore. The entire expedition fetched up at midnight, a mile and a half from its target. The British, who were too weak to post a sufficient number of guards, discovered the French presence the following morning.

The British force numbered four hundred – the rest of the garrison was either bedridden or dying or dead. Like other military bases in the eighteenth century, Oswego sheltered women, children and a handful of wandering traders. The name "Oswego" actually covered three small forts grouped together. Old Oswego sat on the west bank of the Onondaga River with its dilapidated fur-trading post at the centre, and Fort Rascal was perched on a hill about a quarter mile distant. The name "Rascal" was the soldiers' idea of a joke – it was never completed, and there were no loopholes in the flimsy stockade. Fort Ontario, the best of a bad lot, was on the east bank. Vaudreuil's spies had been right when they said Oswego was easy prey.

Long before the French raid on Bradstreet's supply boats revealed the alarming state of Oswego's defences, the British knew they couldn't hold the post without more troops and some serious reconstruction. The previous autumn, Albany had sent British engineer Captain John Vicars with a squad of fifty men to inspect Oswego and bring back a report. Vicars and his company wintered there with the result that forty of his men died and Vicars himself fell ill. Barely recovered by spring, Vicars dragged himself and the ten other survivors back to Albany where he told a heart-wrenching tale: scurvy, dysentery and starvation had killed twelve hundred men in the past year; and on the day he left, everyone was suffering from one disease or another. "We were seldom able to mount more than sixteen or eighteen guards and half of those were obliged to have sticks in their hands to support them."

Throughout the winter, Vicars reported, men had slept on dirt floors in draughty huts, and Fort Ontario's barracks had no beds. When it came to light that troops posted at Oswego were not hardened soldiers but farm boys and labourers who had joined colonial regiments for the initial payment of six dollars and a handful of clothing, it damaged the army's reputation without improving the conditions. Vicars added that during the winter, food had been so short officers considered moving their men out and abandoning the place. About the high death toll, Vicars' words were chilling: "[H]ad the poor fellows lived they must have eaten each other." In the weeks between Vicars' departure and the raid by Chevalier de Villiers and his small force, Oswego had not improved. Oswego was more "Potemkin" than the fake villages described in Russian history.

The siege of Oswego led by Montcalm and Rigaud was short and bitter. On the night of August 10, Montcalm's troops landed on the beach near Fort Ontario and bivouacked beside their boats. Before the British discovered their presence next morning, the French had managed to set up four cannon. On the morning of the eleventh, an engineer called Descombles, reconnoitring Fort Ontario with a party of officers, was mistaken for an Englishman by one of his Indian allies and shot dead. A freak accident like that was bound to dampen French bravura, but Montcalm pressed on with his original plan. Rigaud's Indians hid in the woods and fired happily all day – sniping from dense cover was their favourite style of warfare. Montcalm set up one of his big guns a mere two hundred yards from the wooden ramparts and it became clear the end was near. If Fort Ontario were hit by cannon-shot, the whole structure would splinter.

On Friday the thirteenth, Colonel Mercer, in command of all three forts, ordered everyone in Fort Ontario to move out and take shelter across the river in Old Oswego. Early next morning, Colonel Mercer was directing his gunners when a cannonball cut him in half, right before their eyes. His men were horror-stricken. Women screamed and begged the officers in charge to surrender, men panicked and the British raised the white flag. Vaudreuil, who wasn't there, did not hesitate to describe the scene from reports he received: "Cries, threats and the hideous howlings of our Canadians and Indians made them quickly decide."

The French took a thousand prisoners including women, sailors and labourers. Montcalm's pride in victory soon vanished. A small group of Indians and Canadians split open several rum barrels and got drunk. Frightened prisoners, thinking they saw a chance to escape, tried to run off into the woods. Indians, and Canadians who had painted themselves to look like Indians, began applying the tomahawk to fleeing prisoners. Montcalm, new to this cruel side of surrender, rushed through the mob begging his Indian allies to stop and, in desperation, promised them valuable gifts. Eventually, the troublemakers calmed down, while Montcalm was heard to mutter, "It will cost the king eight or ten thousand livres in presents."

Colonel Bougainville gave the dead at Oswego as fifty English and thirty French. The victors seized one hundred light guns, a quantity of ammunition, any remaining provisions and a thousand prisoners. Within ten days, the French were gone, leaving the ruins to the bears and wolves. A party of travelling Englishmen, who arrived close on the heels of the French army, found Fort Rascal still burning, Fort Ontario in ashes and Old Oswego a smouldering shell. Oswego was Montcalm's first victory in North America.

No attack on Ticonderoga occurred, and Montcalm and Bougainville left at the end of October and headed for Montreal by boat. The French regiments had been assigned their winter quarters according to a system devised by Montcalm: the battalions with the worst quarters the year before and those who had suffered most in the current campaign would have the best winter quarters this time. When his party arrived at Fort St. Jean on the Richelieu River, Montcalm found an order from Vaudreuil cancelling all his prior arrangements. The new plan upset the general and made the troops discontented. "One must be blind not to see it," wrote Colonel Bougainville, siding with the general. The captain made a list of things he thought should be changed at Fort St. Jean. The dried-out stockade was a fire hazard and should be repaired at once, and there was a pressing danger that no one else had addressed. Gunpowder was stored in the cellar "where they go every morning and night to get the wine." In Bougainville's view, a wine supply in danger of blowing up was not to be tolerated.

Despite the recent victory, the air was tense in Montreal. Montcalm had been in Canada only six months and already he and Vaudreuil were at loggerheads. No social life existed outside the governor's golden circle and Montcalm realized that he must grant perfect civility to the governor or live like a monk. "I entertain sixteen persons at table every day," Montcalm wrote to his wife. "Once a fortnight, I dine with the governor-general and with the Chevalier de Lévis – he has given three grand balls." The general found the cost of living exorbitant, commenting, "It is very expensive, not very amusing and often tedious."

Montcalm loved to eat. Much of what he craved was brought from France, so he had to be polite to Joseph Cadet, the man in charge of the king's transports. Cadet was willing to import anything for anyone who smiled and paid the price. A typical Montcalm shopping list included prunes, olives, anchovies, muscat wine, capers, sausages and confectionery.

4

Whispers at Court

"I am sure I can save this country and nobody else can."
— WILLIAM PITT, acting prime minister, London, 1757

England and France had been scrapping in North America since the seventeenth century and the latest series of outbreaks was referred to as the "French and Indian War." When war was officially declared in 1756, that name applied to battles along the American-Canadian border. But after the conflict ended in 1763, it became known as the Seven Years' War.

In the eighteenth century, nations fought over territory in Europe and vast areas much farther afield. Kings and emperors read the word "colonies" as "cash cows," seeing them as sources of taxes, diamonds, silk, spices, tea and slave labour. But in reality, colonies didn't always turn a profit. Louis XV poured millions of livres into New France and received little for his trouble except prestige and migraines. Yet the mystique of finding fantastic treasure still clung to foreign possessions and the land grabbing continued.

In England, Acting Prime Minister William Pitt had a grand vision: he would take the British show of power on the road and create a global empire; he would out-Caesar Caesar. Pitt was haughty, egocentric and difficult to know, riding roughshod over anyone foolish enough to stand in his way. Nothing dismayed him: not a Parliament deep in debt, not a slightly mad king, not even his own dubious popularity in the House of Commons. Nothing slowed him down.

Most of Pitt's colleagues distrusted him, as did the aging King George II, but after they dumped him as leader early in 1757 the government ground to a halt. No one seemed to know how to get things started again, and in a few short weeks the king and the cabinet convinced Pitt to return. He showed no surprise. At that time, in that place, William Pitt was indispensable. No one, including the king, could say him nay.

As Pitt saw it, the chief obstacle to his plan was King Louis XV of France, a man so out-of-date he still believed in the divine right of kings. It was easy for Louis to think he was the centre of the universe: Bourbons had ruled one part of Europe or another for centuries and, in the great world, no blood was bluer than his and no country more powerful than France. Pitt had a different view: he considered Louis a birdbrain in a gilded cage, ready to be knocked off his perch. When that happened, England would become the First Power in Europe.

William Pitt was born with a silver tongue, an iron will and enough energy to light up London. Although his family was influential, it was far from aristocratic, at least until Pitt himself became the first Earl of Chatham. But such an accolade was still a few years down the road. When king and cabinet reluctantly brought him back to Parliament in the spring of 1757, there was no such title as prime minister. The most powerful man in the majority party led the country as secretary of state or some other equally important cabinet post. The term "acting prime minister" was used because Pitt desperately needed to give guidance at a time when Britain's affairs were in a muddle. The word "acting" in the title was eventually dropped, and Pitt was referred to as the Prime Minister.

When Pitt came back to Parliament at the king's request, he was, in the eyes of his fellow politicians, just another hothead struggling to get his own way. His vision, energy and ability to get things done set him apart. He never forgot for a moment that Louis XV was a check to his ambitions. A major difference between Pitt the plebe and Louis the libertine became obvious every time one of them chose a commander to organize a war. Louis always picked a prince or a duke to fight his battles, a man from his own exclusive circle. Pitt was constantly on the lookout for a sizzling young patriot willing to do the impossible – to the devil with his ancestry.

Once Pitt was in charge again, he began looking for a coup that would prove his genius. What he came up with was a raid on the port of Rochefort: it would give the French a scare and impress his admirers back home. That summer, England's prestige abroad was close to extinction, and though the latest war with France was only in its second year, Britain already had suffered embarrassing defeats. An example was the loss of Minorca, an island so tiny the man on the street had never heard of it until a scandal broke. Minorca was a sheltered British naval base in the Mediterranean. The French attacked it and Admiral John Byng refused to defend it. The British government would not tolerate what they considered craven behaviour, and Byng was imprisoned, court-martialled and eventually shot – just the sort of ugly incident Pitt detested.

More bad publicity followed when, during a minor revolt in Calcutta, the nawab of Bengal defeated British troops. The nawab ordered his prisoners cooped up in a small airless room overnight. This space later became infamous as the "black hole," because the entire garrison suffocated. To blot out the public shame of these events and gain support for his schemes, Pitt needed a fast and stunning victory – and he didn't much care how he got it. The plan to capture a French coastal town germinated in this unsavoury compost.

Rochefort, on the North Atlantic coast of France, was tucked away behind a smattering of islands. As a naval arsenal, the town was considered a legitimate target. An attack had to be made from the sea – an action that would require cooperation between army and navy. Historically, such a partnership had never succeeded, but Pitt hoped to find leaders who would be sympathetic to his global aspirations. He was shocked to discover the breed was almost extinct, and was forced to settle for Admiral Sir Edward Hawke and General Sir John Mordaunt, a couple of oldsters well past their swashbuckling days.

And yet some good came of his choice. Mordaunt was a friend of James Wolfe, who had once been a suitor of his niece, Elizabeth Lawson. He knew James was bright, ambitious and admired in some military circles, so he appointed him quartermaster on the Rochefort expedition. Wolfe accepted without hesitation. To him, the raid promised a real fight and might even boost his career.

The Rochefort expedition got off to a rocky start. From the moment the fleet sailed, it was bedevilled by calm and fog; and when the ships came within striking distance of their target, the lower ranks had been confined below decks for two weeks. Rochefort lay behind Île de Ré and Île d'Oléron in the Bay of Biscay, and once the British ships passed these barriers they easily captured the tiny Île d'Aix, which lay close to shore. The fort surrendered in half an hour, and British luck appeared to have taken a turn for the better. Wolfe was seasick, but then he was *always* seasick. (He had once described himself as "the worst sailor in the world.") Yet he was a man who never allowed bad health to get in the way of duty and, green and dizzy, Wolfe landed on Île d'Aix with a small party of officers to take a closer look at Rochefort's defences through his spyglass.

Wolfe noticed a second fort protecting the town and, excited by his discovery, rushed back to tell General Mordaunt they must besiege this obstacle first. Much to Wolfe's disgust, Sir John ignored his advice. While Wolfe had been sizing things up, the general had decided to take no action. Wolfe was astounded. To him, such a decision showed a fear of failure; and fear was something he could not comprehend.

Admiral Hawke agreed with Wolfe. When he heard that the army refused to carry out the raid as planned, he threatened to sail home with or without them. General Mordaunt was infuriated by Admiral Hawke's high-handed attitude and reversed his decision; the army would land that very night! Some officers considered Mordaunt senile and didn't want to risk defeat, and while the leaders argued in comfort the miserable troops crouched in small boats on a dark and restless sea. In the end, the admiral and the general agreed to head back to England. In their opinion, it was too dangerous to attack Rochefort now or at any time in the future. Hearing this, Wolfe could barely contain his rage. And when he reached London he wrote a scathing letter that landed on Pitt's desk. Criticizing both Hawke and Mordaunt, Wolfe summed up his disgust: "We lost the lucky moment in war and were not able to recover it."

At the Court of Versailles, King Louis got wind of the raid before the British fleet left port and assumed the worst. "By this time," Louis told his advisers some days later, "the English are in possession of Rochefort and it will cost me more than thirty million livres to repair the injury they will do me." But this turned out to be incorrect – the English had turned tail and run for home. Word spread that the English had taken the trouble to sail all the way to Rochefort but hadn't fired a shot, and it struck the French as hilarious. Obviously, the British were all talk and no action! French courtiers took themselves seriously as supreme jokesters, and the Rochefort incident inspired a string of jokes the king found highly amusing. Louis had always enjoyed a good laugh at his enemy's expense.

In London, King George wasn't laughing. The Rochefort affair cost his government one million pounds and had achieved nothing.

He had never liked William Pitt, and this expensive failure made him detest Pitt all the more. When Pitt first read Wolfe's account of the business, he flew into a fury – not at James Wolfe's presumption (although in different circumstances it might have ruined Wolfe's career), but at the senior officers who dared ignore Pitt's own orders. *Did no one understand what he was trying to do for England? Did no one grasp the grandeur of his plans?* Pitt's moods rocketed from deep and silent gloom to fiery speeches in the House of Commons. A cloud hung over the Rochefort affair for a time, but Pitt was heartened by his own opinion of the young Wolfe. He had the makings of a hero.

The impatient Mr. Pitt urged the king to promote the new prodigy, but George was in no mood to give anyone a boost. Wolfe, he said, was too young to be a brigadier, and if he agreed to such a plan every brigadier in the army would expect to become a major-general overnight. George stalled, but the prime minister got his own way, as he always did. It was soon common knowledge in London's coffee houses and gin shops that Brigadier-General James Wolfe was to sail for Louisbourg the following spring under Major-General Jeffrey Amherst.

During the seventy-two-year reign of Louis XIV, his direct heirs had died off at an alarming rate. Strange accidents, exotic diseases, even hints of murder haunted the reign of the Sun King. During one eleven-year period, three dauphins died suddenly under mysterious circumstances. (In France, the dauphin was heir to the throne as the Prince of Wales was in England.) The man believed to be at the heart of the mischief was Dr. Guy Crescent Fagon, officially First Court Doctor and still active the day Louis XIV lay dying. Over the years it was noticed that when royal heirs passed away abruptly, the attending physician was always Fagon; and that he had just administered an emetic or a purge, with fatal results.

In the palace, courtiers whispered that Fagon had killed Marie-Thérèse, the first wife of Louis XIV. The queen died one hour after Fagon bled her. On another occasion, he managed to scald one of the king's illegitimate sons by the royal mistress, Madame de Maintenon: the child screamed for help and told his mother Fagon was responsible for his injury. Yet Fagon stayed on at Court, an ugly and charismatic man some courtiers found charming and others feared. When Louis XIV was on his deathbed in August 1715, Dr. Fagon ordered the gangrenous royal leg soaked in burgundy. Four doctors from Paris arrived in time to stop the treatment; they substituted ass's milk instead. The king died shortly afterward, in terrible pain.

Louis XV, the old king's great-grandson, was an orphan when he came to the throne, and it was only natural that concerns about his safety would linger on. As a toddler, Louis was bright, lovable and friendly. He was five when he became king, and his governess, Madame de Ventadour, was firm in her priorities. "First we must keep him alive," she informed the Duc d'Orléans, the appointed regent. The regent ruled in the little boy's place until he reached maturity, so he was a powerful person at Court. D'Orléans also happened to be little Louis' uncle and next in line for the throne. Given the situation, many courtiers harboured doubts about the duke's loyalty to the young king, but he stayed on as regent anyway. Madame de Ventadour offered little affection and no discipline of the kind found in normal family life, and d'Orléans was known as a "perfect rake." They were far from ideal models for a high-strung royal child.

Brought up in such an atmosphere, it's not surprising Louis turned from a lovable little boy into a self-indulgent, bored young man. His wild spending on elaborate masquerades, blooded horses and fine jewels and, when he was older, his failure to fix the creaking machinery of government hastened the bankruptcy of France. Costly wars with France's European neighbours completed the job. The Duc d'Orléans and Madame de Ventadour were the only "family" Louis knew for ten years, and though they protected him from physical harm he was ill prepared to rule in a sensible manner. From descriptions of his close relationships, Louis XV sounds dysfunctional.

Shortly after young Louis became king, the Duc d'Orléans and Madame de Ventadour moved him from the Court of Versailles to the Tuileries Palace in Paris because, they said, it would be safer. Exactly what they were shielding him from was never specified. In 1725, the Duc d'Orléans was banished to the country and a new regent, Cardinal Fleury, appointed in his place. Fleury promptly moved Louis XV back to Versailles for his personal safety, but it was still unclear what they deemed so dangerous. Louis grew into a tall, handsome teenager and it became obvious to Fleury that he must get married immediately. The alternative was a mistress, or he might turn to men. When a sudden fever befell the king, it shook Cardinal Fleury and everyone else in the royal circle. If Louis XV died, the Duc d'Orléans (his former regent) would inherit the throne – and there were many factions at Court that shuddered at the thought. Clearly, Louis XV must marry at once and produce heirs of his own.

Combing the lists of eligible European princesses, Cardinal Fleury settled on Marie-Thérèse Leczinska, daughter of the exiled king of Poland. True, she was seven years older than Louis, dowdy and devout, but all the other candidates were even less attractive. Much to the surprise of the courtiers, Louis met Marie-Thérèse and instantly fell in love: deep down, he was a romantic. On their wedding night the king made love to his bride seven times – all Bourbons were reputed to be vigorous lovers – and in nine months they had twin daughters.

For several years the marriage appeared to be a happy one, but eventually Marie-Thérèse tired of so much nuptial activity and hinted to one of her closest friends that the mere thought of sex was intolerable. The queen once remarked that she was always either in bed with the king making love, or in bed having one of his children. What she really wanted to do was pray, embroider altar cloths and gamble at cavagnole, an unfashionable game played with dice. The royal couple had ten children, three of whom died young. But at least there was a son, a dauphin, to carry on the line.

The Palace of Versailles was a daunting place in which to live, a collection of separate buildings so complex no one knew how many rooms there were. Its very size created special problems. The reception areas were drafty in winter and smelly in summer, on account of roaming dogs, flying birds and a variety of exotic pets on the loose. It was exhausting in any season to cover the great distances between one royal event and the next. One thousand nobles were tucked away in the palace, and hundreds more hung about begging for even the tiniest apartment. In French society, to give the Palace of Versailles as one's address was the *coup de maître,* the trump card. Once established, the freeloaders began badgering the king to upgrade their quarters. No one ever seemed satisfied, and residents waited for others to die so they could move into their space.

Court etiquette had become so complex that even the king, who had dealt with it all his life, was occasionally flummoxed. Trying to keep the peace among hundreds of bickering courtiers, all wanting something from him, strained the monarch's nerves. Louis grew tired of his placid wife and her dreary friends and, despite a series of aristocratic mistresses and young girls imported to Versailles for his pleasure, he became restless.

In the summer of 1745, all the women he'd loved, however briefly, were either dead or fatally ill. Since all Paris gossiped constantly about the king, it was known he was seeking a permanent lover, a woman fit to live in the palace. Dozens of beauties set their caps for him, not only because Louis was handsome and virile but also because the title of official mistress carried with it many valuable rewards for the holder and her family. The king usually gave all her relatives titles, property and high positions along the lines of General of the Galleys or Governor of Paris.

The future Madame de Pompadour was born Jeanne-Antoinette Poisson – Jane Fish. Her mother was beautiful and accomplished, her father worked for the Pâris brothers, bankers to the king. She married Charles Guillaume Le Normant d'Étioles, nephew of a highly placed government official. By the year 1745, she had lost a baby son and had a small daughter, Alexandrine. While the Poissons and their friends were rich and most of them owned huge town houses, they were *bourgeois,* which meant Reinette, as they called her, could never be presented at Court.

The d'Étioles bought a country place near Choisy, where the king owned a hunting lodge. Neighbours were allowed to follow the royal hunt and Madame d'Étioles often joined them, driving one of her own gaily painted phaetons. Within the family, she joked about loving the king and swore she would never leave her husband for anyone else but Louis. Her relatives thought this was just an attempt at wit. But the lady had a plan, and she stalked her idol by waiting in key positions along the route where His Majesty would be sure to spot her. The king was intrigued by these brief glimpses. Eventually, a meeting was arranged on the night of a masked ball given by the king to celebrate the dauphin's marriage. His Majesty came dressed as a yew tree. Madame d'Étioles appeared as Diana, Goddess of the Hunt.

People around the king said Madame d'Étioles would never learn the rules of the Court, that she was hopelessly middle-class. Her husband was beside himself with grief. But Madame d'Étioles moved into a small flat in the Palace of Versailles once occupied by a former mistress of the king. It was still connected to the monarch's room by a private staircase.

Most men thought Madame was pretty, and some women admitted she was tall and elegant. Her brother, Abel, swore no portrait did her justice because artists failed to catch the flash of her eyes. Dufort de Cheverny, a courtier who disliked her intensely, observed, "Not a man alive but would have had her for his mistress if he could." Very soon after Reinette moved into the palace, King Louis conferred upon her the title Madame de Pompadour. The reign of Jane Fish at the most dazzling court in Europe had begun.

5

Siege of Fort William Henry

"I sang the war song in the name of M. de Montcalm and
was much applauded."
— LOUIS-ANTOINE DE BOUGAINVILLE, July 1757

As events unfolded in France, Montcalm was struggling with his duties in the colony of Canada. Among the formal ceremonies he was expected to attend were certain feasts in Indian villages committed to the French cause. Speeches by the king's representative (Montcalm) were expected, along with sufficient roast oxen or boiled stew to feed a sizable crowd.

Three nations lived together at the Lake of Two Mountains: the Nipissings, the Algonquins and the Iroquois, each with its own cluster of dwellings. They shared a church and a large council house which, on the night of July 9, 1757, was jammed with war chiefs, women and warriors, all eager to hear Montcalm's message from the king and all sitting on the floor arranged in tribes. At the centre of the building, large kettles of meat hung at intervals, simmering in preparation for the evening meal.

The room was hot and airless and lighted by flickering candles, but the Indians seemed oblivious to discomfort. Colonel Bougainville, ever the student of people and exotic places, compared the meeting to a witches' coven. Among the crowd were many warriors with faces painted vermilion, white, green, yellow and black, their heads shaved, leaving only a tuft on top stuck with feathers and beads. Every young man was naked except for a breechclout, a large knife dangling on his bare chest and a collection of silver bracelets jingling on his arms. Montcalm had come to invite them to join him on the warpath and to spy for and guide the French in their fight against the hated English.

Governor Vaudreuil insisted Montcalm woo mission Indians, who professed to be Christians, because they were more dependable than their wilder brothers from the Far West. This was understandable since many tribesmen on distant lakes had never seen white people and still spoke in tongues no eastern interpreter could translate. Montcalm, remembering the cruelties at Oswego a year before, doubted that religion made much difference to Indian behaviour once their passions were stirred up. Yet he had come to agree with Vaudreuil on one issue: his army couldn't travel safely through the unmapped wilderness without Indian guides.

The night the French party arrived at the Lake of Two Mountains north of Quebec, Bougainville sang the war song in Montcalm's name. The chant was simple: *Trample the English underfoot, Trample the English underfoot* – over and over again, punctuated by loud cries from the audience. A war chief from each of the three nations gave a speech and Montcalm made graceful replies, assuring them he would capture Fort William Henry (a stubborn little foothold still in British hands) as soon as possible. This news was well received. One of the chiefs stalked around the room holding up a freshly severed bullock's head while he sang his war song. Montcalm took the first bite of meat from the nearest kettle and the feast began. For the general, it was a long and tiresome evening. Throughout the whole affair he thought about the high cost of three roast oxen, which appeared to be uppermost in his mind.

Next day the party paddled north to Sault St. Louis, where the performance was repeated and Bougainville again sang the war song. At twenty-eight, Bougainville was still looking for excitement, still curious about everything he saw in this strange land, and Montcalm was happy to let him do the chores. The young colonel's chanting won the Indians' approval, and they formally adopted him into the clan of the turtle. For the second night in a row, a village consumed three barbecued oxen and the warriors agreed to take up the hatchet for the French.

Montcalm left Montreal on July 12, with an army of seventy-six hundred men, including sixteen hundred Indians. To reach Fort Ticonderoga, which sat on a peninsula at the mouth of a winding creek between Lake Champlain and Lake George, his bateaux first had to navigate the Richelieu River. The French made camp several times along the way, usually to accommodate the Indians (who made their own camps, but were careful to stay close to Montcalm so they would be invited to dinner). The next three weeks brought many petty problems, usually from small groups of tribesmen who had joined the expedition without a chief and had no one to keep them in order. They expected Montcalm, whom they called "Onontio," or "Great White Father" (because he was acting for King Louis XV), to deal with every argument and insult. Instead of scouting the area to find out what the English were up to as they had promised at the outset, or doing necessary work, they took naps or played their favourite outdoor games.

Pushed to the limit (given Montcalm's impatience, that wasn't far) the "Great White Father" would summon his "children" and reprimand them in flowery speech. They had promised to gather information about the enemy, he said, and shouldn't take unnecessary risks by sniping at the English, since such actions posed risk but would not change the outcome of the coming battle. "The least among you is precious to me" was one of his better lines.

The Indians, who loved oration even when it was less than complimentary to them, listened carefully and promised to heed his words. But soon a new difficulty arose: they protested that Onontio did not consult them on military matters. In fact, he treated them like slaves. There may have been some truth in these complaints, because Montcalm was often infuriated by their tendency to jump in the lake whenever they felt hot or to vanish on ad hoc hunting parties. Bougainville, on the other hand, was amused by their playfulness and admired their skills at water sports, noting "they swim like fish, diving and remaining under water a long time."

In mid-July, after a tiring journey, Montcalm and his army reached Fort Ticonderoga, where he immediately began to make plans for the attack on Fort William Henry. The target was now only as far away as the length of Lake George, roughly thirty miles.

Bougainville, in his role as semi-scientific observer, watched Chevalier de Bourlamaque and his troops make the first portage from Ticonderoga to the north shore of Lake George. "One has no idea of the difficulty involved in moving artillery, 250 bateaux and food for six weeks for 1,000 men, without the help of horses or oxen. The hardships cannot be imagined," he noted in his journal.

Montcalm divided his army into two parts. The first, under Lévis, left Ticonderoga July 29 to hike down the western side of Lake George, depending for food on what they carried in their packs. Their destination was a small bay about nine miles north of Fort William Henry, screened from enemy sentinels by a spit of land. Three days later, Bougainville sailed with Montcalm and the remainder of the army, keeping close to the shore. Sailors made pontoons by fastening two boats together with a platform on top, and this construction enabled them to transport cannon mounted on their carriages. Once again, French officers were frustrated by their allies, who constantly criticized the food and demanded fresh meat. The chiefs apologized for the warriors' bad behaviour, blaming it on their youth. Only the Nipissings, Algonquins and Potawatomis didn't complain.

Two days later, Montcalm's division joined Lévis, who reported his men were exhausted from tramping through the bush, which he described as "hot as Italy." Clouds of insects and stumbles over fallen trees made the hike extremely painful. The men were given a couple of days to rest, but it was small comfort because now, within range of enemy scouts, they were allowed no cooking fires and no shooting, which meant no fresh game. Setting up a semi-permanent camp in the bush was back-breaking work.

Fort William Henry, the British post, was perched on the southern shore of Lake George, close to the water. The blockhouse was an irregular log square with four bastions resting on a gravel embankment. Just west of the main building, the English had planted a large vegetable garden and beyond that was a clearing and then the edge of a forbidding wilderness. To the east of the fort lay a marsh and an entrenched camp on top of a rocky rise of land.

That summer, the English garrison was twenty-two hundred strong and under the command of an experienced, courageous Scot, Lieutenant-Colonel George Monro. As well as the military complement, it sheltered several dozen men, women and children from the area, seeking protection. As usual when too many people congregated in too small a space, smallpox and other contagious fevers broke out. A military road slashed through the thick woods between the post and Fort Edward, fourteen miles to the south. When the French first put in an appearance on August 3, Colonel Monro had requested reinforcements from Colonel Daniel Webb, in command at Fort Edward. But Webb showed no signs of sending aid.

Montcalm established his main camp on the shore three miles north of Fort William Henry, screened from the British by steep hills and thick woods. Lévis positioned his troops on the military road, thus cutting communication between the two British forts. The Indians, according to custom, established themselves in the woods and fired at the fort throughout the day. This arrangement effectively surrounded the British. At three that afternoon, Montcalm invited Colonel Monro to surrender. The Scot declined.

The Indians had been told to stay with Lévis on the road where they might scout for raiding parties or intercept couriers from Fort Edward, but they had their own ideas. Attracted by the well-kept garden, they chose to lie among the beans and cabbages and take potshots at any enemy soldier foolish enough to stick his head above the ramparts. A few warriors amused themselves digging shallow trenches, imitating the French fighting style. They appeared to look upon the whole exercise as a game. On the afternoon of August 4, Montcalm, suspecting their cavalier attitude was brought on by yet another gripe, called a general council and asked what was bothering them. The Indians confessed they were eager to hear the cannon go off and begged to be allowed to point them. Montcalm promised they would get the chance once the guns were properly installed. After doling out gifts, he watched them head in the direction of Lévis' position on the road.

Two days later, at six o'clock in the morning, eight cannon roared into action and continued at intervals until the following day. By then, shots from a second battery echoed across the lake. The Indians were delighted with the noise and smoke. Inside the besieged fort, Colonel Monro was at the end of his resources. Montcalm had intercepted a letter from Colonel Webb saying that he could not send fresh troops. Three hundred of Monro's men were dead, sick or wounded and French artillery was doing heavy damage to the blockhouse. On top of that, smallpox was raging through the tightly packed community. Monro decided he was risking lives without hope of success. Early on the morning of August 9, he raised the white flag.

The terms of surrender allowed two thousand British soldiers to depart with the honours of war and march to Fort Edward with their baggage, under the protection of a detachment of French regulars. A hostage officer was to remain in British hands until the escort returned with news that all prisoners had been safely delivered. British troops agreed not to serve against France or her allies for eighteen months; and all French, Canadian and Indian prisoners taken on North American soil were to be returned. The British had to give up all their artillery, lake vessels and munitions with the exception of a single six-pounder to be presented to Colonel Monro as witness to the fine defence his troops had made at Fort William Henry.

Montcalm was careful to assemble the Indian chiefs, explain the terms and ask their consent before he signed. The chiefs agreed to everything and swore their young men would obey the rules. How much they actually told their warriors about the treaty was not recorded.

At noon, the fort itself was turned over to the French, and all English troops and civilians retreated to the entrenched camp with their belongings. After the English were gone, some Indians and Canadians rushed inside the blockhouse to scoop up anything that was lying around loose. Seventeen wounded soldiers, left behind because they were too sick to move, remained in the fort under the care of a British surgeon, Miles Whitworth. A French doctor was scheduled to take over and guards were to be posted outside the hospital huts.

Several hundred prisoners and civilians were marched to the entrenched camp and told to remain there until the following day when, at mid-morning, they would assemble and begin the long march to Fort Edward. A French escort was promised. Late on the afternoon of August 9, the same mob that had cleaned out the fort began prowling around the palisades of the entrenchment, threatening to break in. Colonel Bougainville, keeping an eye on the place for Montcalm, smelled trouble. He realized the Indians had good reason to be angry. When the French recruiters had visited their villages earlier in the year and begged them to fight against the English, they had promised the warriors scalps and plunder. Now the Indians were to get nothing for their trouble; the chiefs – by signing the surrender – had betrayed them. By early evening, the number of warriors inside the camp increased. Montcalm begged the chiefs to calm their men and promised more gifts. By 9 p.m. it looked as if order had been restored, but Bougainville wasn't so confident. "We'll be fortunate if we avoid a massacre," he noted in his journal. He meant, of course, in the camp they occupied at the time.

At ten o'clock, Montcalm made a decision that may have escalated the danger: he sent Bougainville to Montreal to inform Governor Vaudreuil of the French victory. Had Bougainville been on hand, he might have warned Montcalm in time to prevent the storm that was brewing. But that night he left by boat. Reaching Montreal in the late afternoon of August 11, Bougainville told Vaudreuil the good news and, as word spread throughout the town, a celebratory mood seized the citizens. In his journal Bougainville wrote, "The news I brought caused a sensation."

But joy soon turned to anger. Questions were asked. Why were no prisoners taken? Why had Montcalm not pressed on to Fort Edward and seized that, too? Why not Albany, as well? Bougainville suspected Vaudreuil and his supporters deliberately stirred up the dissatisfaction because this second victory for Montcalm was hard for the governor to swallow. Bougainville knew perfectly well why Montcalm had stopped with the surrender of Fort William Henry. The general had barely enough provisions to feed his own troops, let alone hundreds of English prisoners. Luckily, Indians from the Far West were already starting for home; he couldn't have sustained them much longer. Yet if he'd mounted an attack on Fort Edward he would have needed every man available: French, Canadian and Indian. It was a relief to know that once the settlers and British soldiers reached Fort Edward, they would become Colonel Webb's problem.

In Montcalm's view, it was madness even to consider marching on Fort Edward. His regulars were exhausted and the militia and mission Indians were eager to go home and harvest their crops. The order to fight again might have caused a mutiny. In any case, Montcalm didn't have enough ammunition to besiege Fort Edward, or enough oxen or horses to drag his heavy artillery over fourteen miles of rough road. According to Montcalm's spies, Colonel Webb had at least twenty-five hundred men in a well-fortified position and a supply line that stretched to Albany. Only a fool would have invaded Fort Edward in such circumstances.

The seventeen wounded men left in the fort the day before were still in their huts when the nightmare began at 5 a.m. A handful of Indians and their European trapper friends dragged out the sick and applied the tomahawk. The British doctor, Miles Whitworth, still on duty, tried to stop them; but they ignored him and scalped the patients while French guards stood nearby pretending not to see.

Having accomplished their first goal, the wild ones rushed to the entrenched camp, broke in and forced the prisoners to surrender their baggage. A few soldiers hung onto their muskets, but since they had no ammunition it was just a gesture. Fear spread through the camp and, although the promised escort had not yet appeared, soldiers, farmers, women and children gathered on the military road and formed a loosely organized double line. Someone said there was an advance detachment of French regulars up ahead, so they shuffled forward, hoping for assistance. The raiding party, sensing French aloofness to the situation, ran beside the marchers, snatching at caps, weapons and anything else the captives were carrying.

Suddenly a war whoop shivered through the cool morning air. The Indians and their allies struck down settlers at the edges and tail-end of the column. Within seconds, women were screaming, babies bawling, men cursing. The ground grew soggy with blood.

Montcalm, Lévis and Bourlamaque all hurried to the scene and tried to stop the attack, but they had left it too late; the killing went on. Some terrified settlers stumbled forward, trying to reach the French guards. But when they succeeded, all they got was advice: *run into the woods!* Colonel Frye, a captured British officer, had his uniform ripped off. An officer in a Massachusetts regiment was stripped of all his clothes but managed to get away, hide in the marsh overnight and eventually reach Fort Edward. Jonathan Carver, a colonial volunteer, said French officers standing nearby refused to help when two Indians grabbed him and threatened to tomahawk him. When he asked a nearby sentinel for help, the man called him "an English dog." Carver managed to get away and, like many others, lived to tell his story.

Father Robaud, who had accompanied the Abenakis throughout the expedition, saw the massacre and reported forty or fifty corpses on the road. Lévis said fifty were killed, not counting the seventeen patients in the fort hospital. At least six hundred prisoners were kidnapped by the Indians. Montcalm himself recovered four hundred of them, leaving two hundred unaccounted for. It was believed they were taken to Montreal and sold to residents for cash or brandy.

For Montcalm, the siege of Fort William Henry fell far short of the victory he had prayed for so earnestly. Sickened by the murders as they unfolded before his eyes and, later, enraged at Governor Vaudreuil's accusations that he ought to have attacked Fort Edward, Montcalm once again considered resigning his commission.

6

Ticonderoga: Montcalm's Stunning Victory

*"Never was General in a more critical position than I was.
God has delivered me. His be the praise."*
– LOUIS-JOSEPH, Marquis de Montcalm, at Ticonderoga, July 1758

Montcalm and Bougainville were in Montreal when they heard that government storekeepers at Fort Chambly, Fort St. Jean, Crown Point and Ticonderoga had been fired for "thefts too glaring." A well-meaning priest explained to Bougainville that most penitents believed stealing from the king was only a petty offence and that every Easter Louis made them a present of what they had taken. Bougainville, for one, didn't see how this rule would apply to men in charge of the king's stores and was delighted to hear the culprits had been punished.

By late spring, conditions in Canada were fast deteriorating. The food shortage was critical for everyone except the rich. Bad weather had prevented *les habitants* from planting seed grain distributed by the government on time, and a late harvest was predicted. Unrest among Indians west of Lake Michigan was marked by the murder of a French family, although the French settlers believed all tribes were French allies. They also suspected that the Ottawas had evil designs, and the Potawatomis were strangely uncooperative. Closer to home, the Five Nations warned Governor Vaudreuil that spies had told them the British meant to rebuild on the ruins of Fort William Henry and begged for protection. Bougainville wondered if this were possible. "What can we do? We who are dying of hunger?" he asked himself dramatically. "Many people keep alive only by fish, and fast when they catch none." A rumour was going around that Quebec's poor had been reduced to eating grass.

The colony waited eagerly for the first ships of the season, believing they would be loaded with provisions. Nine ships in the first convoy arrived safely, but the remainder had been captured or sunk by the English. Two more ships anchored in the Quebec Basin, bringing the total to eleven, and it was calculated that the combined cargoes would feed a pound and a half of bread and meat to twelve thousand soldiers for 130 days. Civilians weren't taken into account.

Troops in outlying garrisons suffered more than those closer to the capital. On June 2, a boatload of supplies managed to reach Fort Chambly on the Richelieu River, where the inhabitants were "in the last stages of famine." Poor crops were responsible to some extent, but commanders selling foodstuffs on the side to make a profit for themselves – what nowadays is called a black market – were also to blame. Bougainville, alluding to officials who ignored hardships inflicted on army privates, asked, "Why have they not sent oxen and wagons for the portage at Chambly which must be made by all troops?" In other words, why were they using the rank and file as pack animals? Because, he answered himself, providing oxen and horses didn't produce profit for Bigot and his crowd. Bougainville, with his scientific bent, suggested to authorities that if they built a canal on the site, it would shorten travel time between Montreal and Fort Chambly. No one took his idea seriously.

When Montcalm asked Vaudreuil how many men he could expect to command at Ticonderoga, the governor said five thousand. In the officers' mess they were saying Vaudreuil planned to send sixteen hundred Indians under the command of his brother, Rigaud, and sixteen hundred colonial troops under Lévis, to level British forts along the Mohawk River. Such an expedition would mean using troops Montcalm needed to defend Ticonderoga.

Hearing about Vaudreuil's plan, Bougainville scoffed, "This is what the Marquis de Vaudreuil believes should come about because he doubts nothing, but which will not happen." On June 23, Vaudreuil further provoked Montcalm by giving him two orders worded in a way that guaranteed the general would be blamed no matter how he acted if Ticonderoga were attacked, or how things turned out. Montcalm refused to sign such a document. Bougainville sided with Montcalm. To Montcalm he wrote, "I admit that he [Vaudreuil] should have done it [kept Montcalm informed], that the position, the successes, the reputation of the Marquis de Montcalm, the orders of the king, required it. But as he [Vaudreuil] never consulted him about anything, had never informed him of the news, nor of his plans, nor of his measures, the Marquis de Montcalm has positively declared that he will never allow this preamble to stand as a monument against his reputation." As late as the summer of 1758, Montcalm was still taking orders from Governor Vaudreuil and still resenting it.

But Montcalm was stubborn and forced the governor to change the wording. While this matter was being settled, Vaudreuil heard from his Indian friends that the British were about to attack Ticonderoga, the French post deepest in disputed territory. According to these informants, Major-General James Abercromby, Brigadier Lord Howe, a regiment of Scottish Highlanders and five companies of Rogers' Rangers were building a fort on the ashes of Fort William Henry. When it was completed, thousands of British regulars would join them and the army would sail north. For once, the governor acted swiftly; within days, Montcalm and Bougainville were assigned thirty-six hundred men and sent on their way.

The quality of the troops already posted at Ticonderoga made Montcalm nervous; the eight battalions of French regulars were weakened by the addition of ill-trained colonial troops, militia and Indians. On July 1, the day after Montcalm and Bougainville arrived, the garrison had only enough food for nine days and an emergency ration of thirty-six hundred biscuits. Colonel Bourlamaque, in command until the general arrived, had already sent a courier to Governor Vaudreuil reporting the crisis and begging for more provisions. So far, there was no sign of fresh food. Was it simple incompetence or a deliberate attempt to undermine Montcalm? Was Vaudreuil so eager to discredit Montcalm that he would risk defeat?

"The enemies [of Montcalm] may well get him [Vaudreuil] to announce he will come here himself," Bougainville wrote to Montcalm. "Let him come. Let him see, and I will add with all my heart, let him win!" Then he added several complaints: "The small number of Indians, realizing the need we have for them, are extremely insolent. This evening they wished to kill all the general's hens. They forcefully take away barrels of wine, kill the cattle and we must put up with it. What a country! What a war!"

On a clear day in July, after threatening for more than a year, the British sailed for Ticonderoga with great fanfare. General Abercromby, now commander-in-chief of the British Army in North America, and Brigadier Lord Howe, his second-in-command, had mustered fifteen thousand men and a thousand boats on the south shore of Lake George. A new stronghold stood on the ashes of Fort William Henry, sharing the ground with the resident ghosts of murdered men, women and children. It was renamed Fort George.

Abercromby was described by his contemporaries as "heavy," "aged" (he was fifty-two) and "infirm in mind and body." Certainly he had more political clout than he had military smarts. But William Pitt expected very little from him, so what did it matter? Pitt relied instead on his latest protégé, Lord Howe, one of those rare young men who live under a lucky star. Howe had courage, brains, good looks and an astonishingly egalitarian view for a British blueblood.

Everyone loved Lord Howe, from educated senior officers to illiterate privates, from Pitt the prime minister to Howe's American hostess, Mrs. Schuyler, who actually wept when he went off to battle. Pitt himself had infected England with the idea that if anyone could stop Montcalm's mad march to glory, it was Lord Howe. No one examined the why or the how of it too closely. Enough that m'lord was a hero.

The British fleet, packed with men in bright uniforms and accompanied by flags flying, trumpets sounding and drums beating, pushed off into the brilliant sunshine that bathed Lake George. There wasn't a single hitch in the arrangements, but then, Lord Howe was an expert on organizing expeditions. Within hours, the surface of the lake was thick with boats for a distance of three miles. Men chanted, chattered and cheered, completely confident, a touch arrogant. All day the glittering mass moved majestically in a northerly direction.

Months before, Lord Howe had taken time to study wilderness warfare with Major Rogers and his Rangers – living as they lived, relying on the land for food, water and shelter. A hand-picked group of his own men accompanied Howe on the adventure and he did not hesitate to consult the Rangers who in the past had survived extraordinarily harsh conditions. The British soldiers were there to learn. At Major Rogers' suggestion, Howe ordered his men to throw away their lace cuffs, cut their hair short, wear leather leggings as protection against briers in the forest and cover the barrels of their muskets with mud or foliage. One of his officers commented, "Regulars as well as Provincials [colonials] have cut their coats so as scarcely to reach their waists. No officer or private is allowed to carry more than one blanket and a bearskin." And, most telling of all, he added, "No women followed the camp to wash our linen. Lord Howe has already set an example by going to the brook and washing his own."

While Howe's junket with the Rangers prepared him for *some* obstacles, it wasn't a substitute for years of experience in the bush. His own common sense made him ask John Stark, a veteran Ranger, where to land his troops. Stark advised setting his men ashore beyond the second narrows, near the lake's outlet. As the boat carrying Lord Howe and Major Rogers came abreast of the dark slab of Rogers Rock, they caught a glimpse of enemy soldiers crouched on top. It was Sieur de Langy and his men, trained to operate in hostile country. Langy sent a runner by a little-known Indian trail to warn Montcalm, who was camped at a sawmill a couple of miles away. Then, as the body of redcoats disappeared into the gloomy forest, the French began to shadow them, a game that was one of their special talents.

Fort Ticonderoga sat between Lake George and Lake Champlain. From his own scouts, Howe learned that Montcalm had destroyed the bridge across the creek; he had to find a roundabout route. Again he consulted John Stark, who said a primitive road running along the western bank of the creek would lead him to a clearing just north of the fort. Howe, with Rogers, two hundred Rangers and a battalion of colonials mixed with British regulars, started on the overland march in a confident frame of mind. The Rangers were the recognized authority on this part of the country. After a short march, however, the trail vanished and the men found themselves pushing their way between giant trees and thickets of scrubby vines and tangled bushes.

On the lakeshore it had been sunny, but deep in the forest the trees had grown a canopy of leaves that cut off the light. Men could scarcely see three feet ahead in the dim, damp shadows. The air was hot and motionless. Buzzing insects stung their hands and faces. Curtains of dense underbrush had to be hacked away before the men could take a step. Huge fallen trees got in the way, breaking up the lines and separating soldiers from one another and from their officers. It was oddly silent: no whinnying horses, rattling cannon or echoing shouts.

Men began to flounder and tempers rose, although Howe himself remained calm. When Major Rogers admitted he was just as mystified as anyone else, he shattered Howe's confidence. How could the invincible British Army be lost in the woods? All the brigadier could see in any direction were thick tree trunks, curtains of matted branches and spurs of moss-covered rock. If Lord Howe could have observed the scene from above, it would have looked like a giant board game on which two armies were playing "Who will find the enemy first?" Although it seemed the British were alone, Langy and his party were close behind.

Standing helplessly in a prison of trees, Lord Howe and Major Rogers were incoherent with rage: Rogers, because territory like this was his bailiwick; Howe, because he was frantic to spring his troops from an unnatural trap. As the two men sized things up, a sharp challenge cut the puzzled silence, *"Qui vive?"* A quick-thinking Ranger answered, *"Française!"* But the French, knowing the British must be somewhere close, were not deceived and began firing at random. Shots ricocheted off tree trunks, were swallowed by tangled bushes and even hit a few British soldiers. Without warning, the worst thing that could happen to the British, happened. Lord Howe took a musket ball in the chest and dropped dead.

After an hour or so, the skirmish rattled to a stop and the British, without their idol to lead them, milled around helplessly. (It came to light later that the British had managed to take 148 prisoners. Fifty Frenchmen had melted into the trees and the rest were either killed or drowned while trying to cross the rapids on the creek.) The British discovered by questioning their prisoners that they had just clashed with the detachment under Langy, who had seen them from his perch on Rogers Rock. But no amount of information could change the fact that the episode had ended badly for both sides.

British officers kept their men under arms all night for no good reason. Next morning, the hot, bitten, hungry men and their equally miserable prisoners were rescued by a search party and led back to the landing place. General Abercromby, now truly in charge of the expedition, sat down to study his choices.

Montcalm abandoned his main camp at the sawmill on the creek and moved all his troops into Fort Ticonderoga. The regulars stationed there under Bourlamaque were constructing an abattis (a breastwork of logs and tree branches) along the fort's north side. General Montcalm decided to make his stand behind this extraordinary wall. His scouts told him the British force would soon be upon him in thousands.

It was now July 6 and, at the landing place on Lake George, Abercromby consulted his senior officers about what to do next. At noon, he decided to send Colonel John Bradstreet with a large contingent of regulars and colonials to occupy the camp Montcalm had abandoned. Such a takeover would save an enormous amount of time and effort.

At mid-morning, the weather was tropical. Montcalm, in his shirt-sleeves, summoned every man fit to work and he, himself, helped strengthen the abattis. A row of regimental colours waved brightly along the top of the barrier, an attempt to inspire the confidence that no one felt. The pointed ends of new-cut trees bristled like giant quills. One officer said the structure looked like "a forest laid flat by a hurricane." Despite all the sweat, the general entertained only the frailest hope of driving off the British; but if by chance it happened, he felt it would be more because of Abercromby's recklessness than his own strategy.

Montcalm pondered Abercromby's plan of attack. The barrier, nine feet high, dictated the use of heavy artillery. Would the British general occupy the heights of Rattlesnake Hill overlooking the fort and train his big guns on the inside of the breastworks? In that event, the defenders would be wiped out immediately. Or would he cut off the French supply line from Crown Point, a slower, less bloody approach? But when the moment arrived, Major-General Abercromby seemed not to consider any options open to him. Instead, he prepared to storm the breastworks with muskets, completely ignoring the heavy artillery he had hauled so many miles.

As Montcalm waited for Abercromby, he was aware his ammunition and food supplies were dangerously low and he wasn't sure when Lévis would arrive with reinforcements. But on July 7, Captain Pouchot, a topnotch officer from the Béarn Regiment, reached Ticonderoga with three hundred regulars and news that Lévis was close behind. Within hours, Lévis arrived and gave his blessing to all Montcalm's arrangements. At daybreak on July 8, having been warned the British were about to sweep down upon the fort, the French beat drums and their troops formed in order of battle. Montcalm commanded thirty-six hundred soldiers; the British numbered thirteen thousand, a large portion of them held in reserve.

At 9 a.m. the Indians under Sir William Johnson began a scattered fire on the fort while the French, pretending nonchalance, continued to work on their abattis. At noon, a volley from the north signalled the English were driving in the French pickets. Montcalm's regulars lined the platform behind the log wall, leaving only the crowns of their black hats showing. The British marched across the clearing toward the barrier, first the Rangers, Light Infantry and colonials, then the regulars in their stiff scarlet columns.

Unlike Wolfe at Louisbourg or Howe in a skirmish deep among the trees, Abercromby directed the battle from a distance. In relative safety, he ordered his troops to attack the breastwork with bayonets. The first line met with a deadly barrage of musket balls and grapeshot, but the men struggled on – madly trying to penetrate the logs and matted branches without being impaled. As they scrambled and cursed, the defenders poured down a murderous fire and the British fell back. Given the news, Abercromby ordered them to attack again. As Francis Parkman, an American historian, put it, "masses of infuriated men who could not go forward and would not go back, straining for an enemy they could not reach, firing on an enemy they could not see." Rounds of shot from behind the formidable wall killed British soldiers by the dozen and they fell, spread-eagled on the ground or hanging in strange attitudes among the branches.

Montcalm, still commanding with his coat off, directed the defence from the centre of the barrier, astonished at how many times the British charged. Near the end of the afternoon, he hurried to the spot where the enemy were pounding the hardest, bringing some reserves with him and thinking this must surely be his last effort for the day. But the British came on again and again – seven times, Montcalm later declared. The Highlanders were unstoppable; even when wounded they fought on, although most of their impetuous assaults ended in death. French soldiers were equally determined not to give in and, when flames broke out among the logs and branches, they formed lines and passed pails of water to douse the fires. Toward the end, the action came from the British as they covered those bringing off the wounded and others who were making an orderly retreat.

When darkness fell, it was all over. Silence descended on the smoky forest. For the British, the toll was terrible: Abercromby lost 1,944 – killed, wounded and missing. The French lost 375. Bourlamaque was badly wounded and Bougainville grazed by a bullet. Lévis' hat was shot through twice.

Montcalm felt an enormous sense of relief. Once the British had disappeared, he walked along the lines thanking his soldiers for their courageous fight and ordered beer, wine and food for everyone. Although Ticonderoga was Montcalm's most stunning victory so far, the danger was far from over. The colony now called Canada was beset by problems that prevented him from waging an aggressive war – lack of food supplies and ammunition, too few soldiers – but the next day a curious Lévis combed the road to the landing place and found evidence of a headlong flight. The English had left barrels of provisions, baggage and even shoes stuck in the mud. French officers were at a loss to understand why their enemy had panicked. Still, they were grateful for the lull, however brief.

After three victories in three years, none of them *earned* by Montcalm if one listened to the governor, the little general allowed himself a moment of exultation. "The army, the too-small army of the King," he wrote to his superiors, "has beaten the enemy. What a day for France! What soldiers are ours!"

Abercromby had fled to Fort George, taking his troops and heavy artillery with him. What a difference a day made! The glorious pageant that had set sail so confidently two days before was now a beaten army. Despair, confusion and shame settled over the English camp like an invisible cloud.

Soon news of the disaster reached the Thirteen Colonies. A young colonial officer from Massachusetts dashed off a letter to his uncle describing the lemming-like departure of Abercromby and his troops from the scene of the fighting. "The best part of the army is unhinged," he reported. "I have told you enough to make you sick." And from that small beginning, the word "defeat" flashed from town to town: Abercromby had run away! British poltroons, aided ineptly by colonials, had had the temerity to lose a battle against an insignificant force behind a makeshift barrier and then flee.

In the aftermath of Ticonderoga, every scourge known to a huge army camp appeared and multiplied at Fort George. Bad relations between British regulars and American colonials grew worse under the strain of defeat, causing an increase in brawls, thefts and drunkenness; the whipping post was in constant use. Filthy conditions and bad food killed more men than enemy bullets. Morale was at a low point. The British still commanded thousands of soldiers on the American continent, but they were without an effective leader. The death of Lord Howe was felt daily. Abercromby seemed frozen in time.

Conditions at Fort Ticonderoga improved slightly after the victory, but Montcalm didn't have sufficient resources to challenge Fort George or Fort Edward as his personal enemies so enthusiastically suggested. Instead, he was reduced to sending out small parties under the partisan fighter St-Luc de La Corne to terrorize enemy outposts. Abercromby responded to these hornet-stings with similar attacks on the French by the ever-willing Rangers. But such sideshows didn't make any difference to the central struggle.

In early September, Lieutenant-Colonel Bradstreet (the colonial officer who earlier had delivered supplies to a starving Oswego) came up with a daring plan. He proposed to take Fort Frontenac, a key French post at the mouth of the Cataraqui River, directly across the lake from Oswego. It was the only remaining fort the British needed to monopolize control of Lake Ontario.

Two years before, Montcalm had mustered his forces at Fort Frontenac for the siege of Oswego and won. But the French had never taken advantage of their prize because they lacked the men and money to maintain it. Using British colonists, the ambitious John Bradstreet now saw a chance to use the abandoned Oswego ruins as a launching pad for his attack on Fort Frontenac, the last important fur post in the French system. There was a touch of poetic justice in Bradstreet's notion.

Fort Frontenac was built by the French in 1673 to protect Montreal from hostile Indians. Later, it acted as a check on English troops and fur traders operating out of Oswego. In the present conflict, Bourlamaque had reinforced Frontenac, but the garrison was still poorly manned and provisioned. Colonel Bradstreet had first proposed his scheme to Loudon in 1757; the commander accepted the proposal, but did nothing. Early in 1758 Bradstreet approached Abercromby, who turned it down. After the defeat at Ticonderoga, however, a hastily summoned council of war forced Abercromby to change his mind, and the dithering commander at last gave

Bradstreet his blessing along with three thousand men (most of them colonials), and ordered him to seize Fort Frontenac.

Bradstreet, an efficient organizer, soon had his expedition moving along the Mohawk to Lake Oneida and what was now a desolate Oswego, the point from which he planned to launch his attack. Having accidentally picked up a handful of Oneida warriors looking for action, the colonel crossed Lake Ontario in a fleet of whaleboats and bateaux. On the night of August 26, he was lodged within two hundred feet of the fort walls. The next morning, without a shot having been fired, the French commander, Noyan, surrendered.

It was, indeed, a small garrison: 110 soldiers and a handful of labourers and prisoners were handed over. Still, the plunder was impressive. Bradstreet's men seized nine armed vessels – all that was left of the French naval force on the lake – a large quantity of munitions and a variety of goods intended for Indians in the western regions. The fortifications were dismantled and British ships loaded with stores the victors considered valuable.

No battle meant no scalps and the Oneidas were more than a little disgruntled. To soothe them, Bradstreet turned over most of the provisions. The British burned a number of small boats and leftovers no one wanted to carry off and then burned anything the enemy might find useful should they return in the future, a common practice in those days. Whatever Bradstreet may have thought about the waste, he had no orders to preserve any boats, goods or tools that he couldn't transport.

The loss of Fort Frontenac hit the French hard: it left them without a port on Lake Ontario, thus cutting their link with trading posts in the Far West. The capture of the fort not only made the British supreme on Lake Ontario but also encouraged many tribes to desert France, either to remain neutral or to become allies of England.

7

Unrest in the Colony

*"How could it happen that small-pox among the Indians cost the King
a million francs? What does this expense mean?"*
– Minister of Marine NICOLAS-RENÉ BERRYER,
Court of Versailles, 1758

Back in Britain, the taking of Quebec, the absolute necessity to
subdue and occupy it, had become an obsession with Prime Minister
Pitt and the war hawks who supported him in Parliament. Over the
centuries, France and England had seldom agreed on anything, but
on one point they saw eye to eye: if England conquered Quebec,
France's influence on the American continent would come to an end.

Quebec, linked to the sea by the great St. Lawrence River, was the
very heart of France's network for importing and distributing supplies to its settlers along its banks and trading posts in the west, on
the Ohio River. If France should lose this natural stronghold, how
could it service these outlying forts? Fur traders and settlers in need
of supplies and protection would turn automatically to the Thirteen
Colonies and they, forever pushing their boundaries westward,
would be happy to accommodate. France still owned Louisiana, but
so far had extracted little of value. When the king's advisers told him

it was impossible to defend Canada and Louisiana as a joint action, Louis lost interest. Most politicians at Court sighed with relief. They viewed Canada as a boundless forest that swallowed money, and Louisiana as a million acres of bug-infested swamp.

With the war entering its third year, life for Canadian peasants and labourers was harsher than ever. Ordinary people lived in harsh conditions at the best of times, but the upcoming winter of 1758–59 promised to be particularly long and bitter. Drought during the summer had caused a sweeping crop failure. Landowners who had produced enough vegetables and meat animals to feed their families watched helplessly as Intendant François Bigot scooped it all up "for the army." Word spread that the thickest cream and fattest chickens ended up on the tables of the rich, not in the stomachs of the troops. People were becoming more and more resentful. Theoretically, they could buy grain from the government warehouse, but who could afford the exorbitant prices? The bread shortage in the Quebec area was so acute even soldiers felt the pinch.

Since the art of public relations was seemingly unknown to rulers in the eighteenth century, it never occurred to Quebec officials to hide their extravagant lifestyle. The poor couldn't help noticing that their "betters" were still sitting down to tables laden with food while they, the workers, were sick and starved. Hatred of Bigot simmered just beneath the surface.

Colonists with *some* resources were forced to take soldiers into their homes. The fifteen livres a month per head included bed and board and, in some cases, debauched daughters – one reason why French regulars were so disliked by Canadians.

Vaudreuil was partly responsible for these conditions, since he had the power to correct them if he had deigned to interfere. Regrettably, he was a man famed for looking the other way when anything shady was afoot. Despite suspicions about the governor's part in profitmaking schemes, French settlers apparently forgave him simply because he was a Canadian. At least for the moment, they could blame Bigot;

he set prices on all items sold in the government store. People believed he was using his position to line his own pockets and those of his friends. They had their villain.

In the mid-eighteenth century, Canada was a trackless, mysterious domain stretching from Hudson Bay to the Gulf of Mexico. Colonists travelled mostly by water and, as a matter of convenience, the choicest Canadian farms were ribbons of land with a narrow frontage on the St. Lawrence River. Many *habitants* lived miles from the nearest village, but there was always a church within reach, and priests traditionally supported government policies. Most Canadians were steadfast churchgoers and in the present crisis, parish priests harangued the faithful from their pulpits: *If you love your king and country, you must fight!* Of course the people loved King Louis, probably more than did the relatives they'd left behind in France, but to stay alive they were forced to eat the very grain they should be hoarding to plant next year's crop. In the grip of winter they worried about spring, a time when all fit young males would be forced by law to join the militia, leaving women, children and old men to tend the fields. Defending their country had lost much of its appeal.

No one in power seemed to notice the growing disenchantment and unrest. The colony was on the brink of ruin, but greedy officials paid little heed to the mood of ordinary citizens. Bigot, Vaudreuil and their flunkies were not about to sacrifice pleasure and profit just because there was a war on. If anything, high society stepped up the pace, held more lavish dinners, indulged in more wife-swapping and skimmed more off the tax revenues than ever before. In fact, they were beginning to think the unthinkable: England might conquer Canada! If that happened, colonial rulers would be shipped back to France and forced to live on whatever money they had managed to send to their agents in Bordeaux.

Graft among government officials wasn't new. Throughout colonial history officers of the king stole large amounts of money – millions of livres – a practice the authorities in France took for granted.

When a colonial governorship, an intendancy or some lesser post was handed out, the recipient had to tear up his roots and live in a "primitive society," often without his wife, children or mistress. How was a king supposed to attract brilliant men to serve in remote places (any location outside France was considered remote) unless he offered them bait? When a man accepted a political plum in the hinterland he expected to make a small fortune as a reward for slugging away in dark and grungy places, running the risk of being eaten by a lion, attacked by a tropical disease or scalped by a native; to say nothing of the horrors of ocean travel – long voyages on leaky ships, bad food, wretched cabins shared with questionable companions.

What sane man would willingly moulder in one of these dark holes unless it was for gain? History tells us there were very few. The two generals who would clash on the Plains of Abraham were exceptions. Wolfe was eager to die a hero and Montcalm was a slave to duty. Neither man expected to make a fortune out of his career, which only renders their stories more poignant. During that last winter, Montcalm heard from his friend Colonel Bourlamaque, who described conditions in Fort Duquesne (which later became Fort Pitt and, eventually, Pittsburgh). The colonel wrote, "[There's] mutiny among the Canadians who want to come home, the officers are busy making money and stealing like mandarins." From reports like this, the General knew perfectly well that some of his best officers were corrupt. But what was he to do?

Montcalm took no bribes, nor did he steal from the king. He was an honest patriot. But in most cases, if the king wanted candidates with brains and courage to go out and rule the colonies, carrots had to be dangled. The hope of making extra money on the side was one of those carrots. At the same time, His Majesty expected discretion – not barefaced piracy. The French Court's objections to the frauds perpetrated in Canada during this period were not based entirely on the crime; it was the bold and reckless lifestyle of the thieves that stung the Court.

Madame de Pompadour got wind of Bigot's larcenies as early as 1756, but she and the king, living in the splendid isolation of Versailles, believed a few threatening letters would straighten him out. However, Bigot was addicted to his feasts, masquerades and gaming, to the gold and crystal ornaments and rich oriental carpets that adorned his "palace." Ironically, the marquise herself had appointed Bigot, and at first she had assumed he was "her man." Over time, when Bigot showed no signs of reforming, Pompadour became enraged.

In the winter of 1758 the Marquise de Pompadour discovered Bigot had salted away millions of livres belonging to the king, at the very time she was selling her diamonds to help Louis reduce the national debt. The fact that she had never cared much for diamonds was beside the point; it was the principle of the thing. The war between France and England was still ravaging Europe, and France was near bankruptcy. Secretly, the marquise and the king were selling tons of their private silver to jewellers and silversmiths to keep the ship of state afloat and – it was unspeakable! – out in the boondocks called Canada, Bigot and his merry men were making themselves rich.

As a result of her findings (she had managed to install a spy in the midst of Bigot's staff), Pompadour ordered Nicolas-René Berryer, minister of marine and in charge of Canada's affairs at the time, to make frightful accusations in his letters to Bigot. (The idea was to frighten him into honesty.)

"The ship *Britannia*," Berryer wrote, "laden with goods such as are wanted in the colony, was captured by a privateer from St. Malo and brought to Quebec. You sold the whole cargo for eight hundred thousand francs. The purchasers made a profit of two million – two hundred thousand more than the price for which you sold the whole. With conduct like this it is no wonder that the expenses of the colony become insupportable."

Bigot ignored these warnings and forged ahead with his illegal schemes. Perhaps he felt the Court was too far away to enforce the law. Perhaps he didn't care. Ordinary people were plunging into debt just to stay alive. High food prices were bad enough, but Bigot had instituted a questionable system of finance that was just about to crash. For some years, currency in the colony had consisted of playing cards and even scraps of paper signed by Bigot to be redeemed later for money from the royal treasury. Suddenly, Minister Berryer refused to pay up when the chits were offered to him – automatically rendering the fake money valueless. Again, it was the poor who suffered.

The colony had even deeper problems. Because of the chummy way Quebec officials wined and dined one another, gambled together and passed around their wives, an onlooker might have assumed they were of one mind about running the country. Such was not the case. There were two factions during these crucial years. The governor-general (Vaudreuil's full title, although he was usually addressed as governor), Intendant Bigot and Commissary-General Cadet had one agenda (to make money for themselves) while General Montcalm and his favourite officers had another (to defend Canada against England, or any enemy that threatened). From the very beginning, when Montcalm first arrived, the governor had detested him. Vaudreuil imagined himself a military expert and wanted to be in sole charge of the defence – perhaps he would emerge from the war a hero. So he was jealous of Montcalm. The general, an experienced campaigner, naturally resented having to defer to an amateur like Vaudreuil. The king had intended to create a unified command with the governor clearly in charge but, when he sent an honest and experienced soldier like Montcalm, he achieved the opposite result.

In the fall of 1758, before Bougainville left for France, he was involved in a routine prisoner exchange between the French at Fort Ticonderoga and the English at Fort George. An English captain presented Bougainville with a basket of Bristol beer and Bougainville returned the gesture with a basket of Pacaret wine. "A good example to set in this barbarous country," Bougainville explained.

The two men met at the north end of Lake George, and the Englishman was also able to give Bougainville the latest news from Europe. France, he said, was in trouble. Her navy was almost wiped out, there was no discipline in the army and she had no more able generals. As for the others, the Dutch were on the verge of joining France as an ally, the Turks were threatening to invade Russia, and Denmark was ready to attack Sweden.

Bougainville, saddened by his country's plight, concluded, "Talent, understanding, resolution, virtue, wise and decisive undertakings, France knows you no longer, she owes her safety to some luck of chance."

Part Two

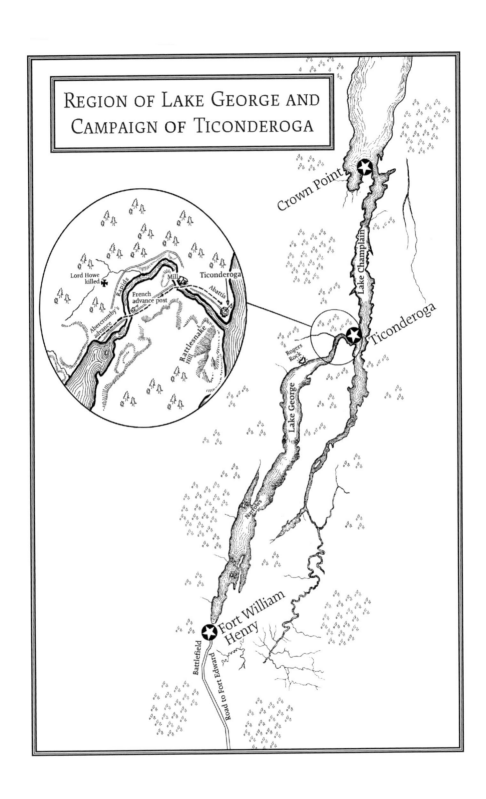

REGION OF LAKE GEORGE AND
CAMPAIGN OF TICONDEROGA

Crown Point

Lake Champlain

Lord Howe killed

Rapids

Mill

Ticonderoga

French advance post

Abatis

Abercromby's advance

Rattlesnake Hill

Ticonderoga

Rogers Rock

Lake George

Narrows

Fort William Henry

Battlefield

Road to Fort Edward

8

The Walls of Louisbourg

"We are gathering strawberries with seeming indifference about what is going on in the rest of the world."
— JAMES WOLFE, Louisbourg, 1758

Legendary Louisbourg! France's strongest fortress in North America. French citizens might forget the names of outposts scattered through the northeastern wilderness, but not Louisbourg. It was a source of great pride. Perched on Île Royale (called Cape Breton Island by the British) and facing the Atlantic, it was believed to be impregnable. Of course, the English had captured the fortress in 1745, but the French looked upon that loss as a fluke.

When the two countries signed the Treaty of Aix-la-Chapelle three years later, England returned chilly Louisbourg to the French in exchange for the steamy port of Madras. Both sides considered it a bargain. By the time General Jeffrey Amherst planned his attack in 1758, the French had controlled Louisbourg for ten years and the king had poured enormous quantities of gold into its defences. His people talked about it with pride, but his engineers, sent to examine it around this time, took a much gloomier view.

The wall overlooking the harbour was "adequate," they reported, but the works on either side were crumbling, probably owing to poor-quality mortar and stone used in the original construction. Privately the king told his cabinet the great fortress was damaged goods but they agreed among themselves not to make a public disclosure. It would be just one more thing for Parisians to carp about, and they had plenty already. There was a distinctly antiroyal feeling in the air.

People were saying privately that if the king would show less interest in sex and more in running the country, these problems would disappear. In wine shops, customers were more apt to blame the continental war for the woes of France, an ongoing horror that ate up munitions, men and money. In the current conflict with England, King Louis was so short of money he was eager to rid himself of every possession that drained his revenues. Madame de Pompadour endorsed this feeling: North American colonies, she remarked, were more trouble than they were worth. When Pompadour said no to sending enough troops and provisions to save Louisbourg, she became partly responsible for its loss.

General Amherst knew little about politics at the Court of St. James in England or the Court of Versailles in France. He had a job to do and, in his plodding way, he set about doing it. When Pitt made Amherst commander-in-chief of the British Army in America, Admiral Edward Boscawen was put in charge of transporting the expedition. It sailed from Portsmouth in the spring, with thirty-nine ships carrying twelve thousand soldiers, four thousand sailors and 554 guns. One of Amherst's brigadiers was James Wolfe, a man he knew only slightly.

After three months on a tempestuous Atlantic Ocean, the old sea dogs aboard the flagship *Princess Amelia* declared it was the worst voyage of their lives. Brigadier-General Wolfe lay in his cabin from February 19 to May 8, scarcely able to keep down water. The few times he managed to rise, he worried more about his precious redcoats jammed below decks than himself, deprived as they were of air, exercise and decent food. Only the sailors were more miserable, and their case was doubly sad because the majority had been kidnapped by "press gangs" in the alleys and gin shops of England's ports. Captives of the navy, ill-fed and ill-clothed, they risked their lives every day, manhandling frozen sails and shinnying up icy yardarms.

When the fleet finally sighted Nova Scotia, Admiral Boscawen and General Amherst agreed it was in no shape to take on Louisbourg. Ships and men were in pitiable condition – they needed at least two weeks in Halifax harbour to recover. Officers could use the time to hold a council of war on a most important matter: where should they land the troops? It was not an idle question. Thirteen years before, the British had opted for Gabarus Bay, found it vulnerable and scored the victory that gave them Louisbourg. Amherst, the arch-conservative, favoured a repeat performance. It had worked for England once, so why not again? But Wolfe, a more imaginative strategist, felt the key to success was surprise; and since the French expected them at Gabarus, it was sure to be a death-trap. He preferred Miré Bay.

Miré Bay was large enough to accommodate the fleet and, if the maps were accurate, the overland route to Louisbourg would be about the same distance as that from Gabarus Bay. Wolfe felt uneasy. Unless the French were idiots, he argued, they would never leave that spot unprotected as they had in 1745. But Amherst was determined to stick with the familiar, and Boscawen fell in with his plan. Gabarus it would be. At the end of May, when the fleet sailed north from Halifax harbour, Amherst hinted that he saw himself the hero who took back Louisbourg for England. Wolfe, still fuming and fearful, stopped trying to change the commander's mind.

The two-week stay in Halifax allowed the British rehearsal time for the amphibious action about to begin, and Wolfe used it to drill his men. A military observer, James Cunningham, wrote to Lord George Sackville, then master-general of the ordnance, describing Wolfe's behaviour: "Some military operations were daily carried on. They frequently landed in the boats and practised in the woods different manoeuvres they were likely to act on the Island of Cape Breton. Gen. [*sic*] Wolfe was remarkably active. The scene afforded scope for his military genius."

Wolfe, writing to the same Lord Sackville (his old colonel in the 20th Regiment, and a friend), had much to say about a great many things. He was highly critical of some arrangements, pleased with others. While in Halifax he discovered the original roster had been reduced by a total of three thousand men owing to wounds, sickness, desertion and death, and he demanded reinforcements. However, he approved of the Highland regiments, an addition to the British Army Wolfe himself had inspired during his service in Scotland. "The Highlanders are very useful soldiers and commanded by the most manly corps of officers I ever saw," he wrote to Pitt. His opinion of Rogers' Rangers, tough volunteers from the American colonies, was quite the opposite: They were "little better than *la canaille*"; in other words, riff-raff. This was a first impression. Later in the campaign Wolfe changed his mind about the Rangers and was grateful for their assistance, but meanwhile, Wolfe's estimation of his own officers wasn't much higher: "I believe no nation ever paid so many *bad* soldiers at so high a rate."

It wasn't only the quality of the fighting men that drew bitter complaints from Wolfe. There was a shortage of pickaxes, and too many muskets were faulty. The uniforms were unsuitable for the climate. His list to his superiors in London went on and on: "Our clothes, our arms and accoutrements, even our shoes and stockings are all improper for this country … the army is undone and ruin'd by the constant use of salt meat and rum … so your lordship may rest assured that the enterprise of Louisbourg will cost a multitude of men." He might have added it would cost a lot of money. In the end, the imperial grant from the war chest amounted to twelve million pounds sterling.

For the worried citizens of Louisbourg, there was a mixture of good news and bad news. Five French ships of the line and five frigates had escaped the British blockade and slipped into the harbour loaded with much-needed supplies. Governor Augustin de Boschenry de Drucour was an experienced commander and a royalist who had spent much of his own money in the king's cause. Inside the fortress, soldiers and civilians claimed they were eager to join him in the fight, and a small band of Indians promised to act as scouts. Madame Drucour, the governor's wife, was courageous and popular. And Drucour, unlike his predecessor in 1745, had fortified the shores of Gabarus Bay with his best soldiers and sturdiest cannon.

But the bad news was very bad indeed. The walls of Louisbourg were full of holes and, despite the governor's efforts, there was a break in the line of shore defences. Only the year before, a watch-tower had been erected beside the inlet on Freshwater Cove and a sentry who was posted on top could see four miles along the coast. Now, when it counted most, the tower was left unguarded.

Throughout the fort's history there had been hostility between snobbish regulars and unsophisticated colonials who resented being treated as bumpkins. One quarrel ended in murder: it was an open secret that a colonial officer called Langy had killed a regular officer, De Caubet, though no trial or punishment followed. Such lax discipline and endless bickering weakened the morale of the community. An epidemic of smallpox infested the town. At the crucial moment, the Indians and Acadians reneged on their offer to scout for Drucour. But even with so many disadvantages, the defenders of Louisbourg might still have beaten Amherst's army during the ill-conceived assault on Gabarus Bay. It was Wolfe's last-minute decision to land at Freshwater Cove in the face of heavy French fire that gave the British the edge.

But when the British fleet first sailed into Gabarus Bay on June 2, a fierce storm burst over the coastal area and raged for eight days.

Troops suffered almost as much in that short time as they had during the turbulent Atlantic crossing. By dawn on June 8 the skies had cleared. Officers on the wind-battered warships could see enemy guns, most of them entrenched in strong earthworks and at least one that poked through masses of cut evergreens. Amherst had divided his army into three sections. Wolfe led the main assault on Coromandière Bay, a rocky arc cut out of the larger crescent of Gabarus. Brigadier-General Edward Whitmore and Brigadier-General Charles Lawrence slipped east to distract the enemy near White Point, closer to the fortress.

The French held their fire until Wolfe's party was within range and then almost blasted them out of the water. Boats were shattered. Geysers of icy spray shot men into the air, and many drowned in the heavy surf. A lucky few were rescued by sailors who dragged them out of the sea. Wolfe had just signalled his flotilla to sheer away from the deadly French bombardment when he spotted three young officers of the 35th Regiment – Thomas Hopkins, Thomas Brown and Allan Grant – disappearing behind the rocks of Freshwater Cove. They'd found an opening between two gun emplacements and drifted or rowed toward the spot. Edging onto the shore, they managed to lead a handful of men to safety. Wolfe saw a minor miracle and turned it into a major one.

Reversing his earlier signal and waving his walking stick like an avenging conjurer, Wolfe leaped into the crashing breakers and ordered the boats behind him to follow. Although dozens more men drowned in the surf or were wounded, those who reached land stumbled over the narrow beach to join the vanguard. Wolfe ordered a flank action on the French batteries to his left and right, flushing out the defenders. More troops arrived to support Wolfe's first contingent and, after a sharp skirmish, the invaders drove the defenders northeast toward the fortress. Four hours later, the shoreline was clear of French troops and the British were digging trenches on the high ground overlooking their target. The siege of Louisbourg had begun.

For the next three weeks the British pounded away at the shaky walls until great chunks of masonry came crashing down, creating larger and larger gaps. And still the defenders hung on grimly. According to one British soldier who had been taken prisoner earlier, the French considered surrender only when their food supplies ran out. Eventually a shell hit the roof of the officers' quarters, setting fire to nearby casemates where women, children and wounded men were hiding. On July 26, aware he couldn't hold out much longer, Governor Drucour capitulated

It was the second time in thirteen years that the white flag had gone up over the Dauphin's Bastion. Tales of Wolfe's dashing adventures soon reached London, and Englishmen all over the country began toasting not only the capture of the fortress, but also their latest hero. In Louisbourg, the victors spent two weeks cleaning up the mess and burying the dead. As usual, Wolfe found peace a bore and longed for a bloody good battle. He began to dream of capturing Quebec this season – there was still time to sail up the St. Lawrence and take Montcalm by surprise! Whenever he thought of Montcalm, Wolfe remembered the atrocities at Oswego and Fort William Henry (although he had not been in either battle) and anger overwhelmed him. "Montcalm has changed the very nature of war and has forced us to a dreadful vengeance," he wrote in a letter to General Amherst.

Since Amherst seemed preoccupied with other plans, Wolfe appealed to his friend Lord Sackville back in London, who had Pitt's ear. "If we are carried directly to Quebec," Wolfe wrote to London, "I am persuaded we will take it." But no one was listening. In a postscript to Lord Sackville, Wolfe had the grace to admit he hadn't known all the facts when he urged they sail quickly for Quebec. It had just come to his attention, he wrote, that "Admiral Boscawen needs provisions and the anchors and cables of the transports have been so damaged in Gabarus Bay that an expedition up the River St. Lawrence is now impractical." Realizing this, Wolfe understood why

Amherst had refused to proceed to Quebec, but still regarded him as something of a tortoise.

In Wolfe's next letter to Amherst, he omitted Quebec from his plans and suggested a small convoy could carry a brigade to Boston or New York, or even closer to the place where he was now stuck. Joining with colony troops, they could attack the French at some point along the east coast.

"With the rest of the troops, we might make destructive war in the Bay of Fundy and the Gulf of St. Lawrence." Wolfe continued, "I cannot look coolly upon the bloody inroads of those hell-hounds, the Canadians; and if nothing further is to be done, I must desire leave to quit the army."

Amherst informed Wolfe that he intended to take five or six regiments to Boston by ship and make his way to Lake George to assist General Abercromby. At the same time, he begged Wolfe to keep writing to him expressing his views. He refused to consider Wolfe's threat to leave the army. "I know nothing that can tend more to His Majesty's service than your assisting in it," Amherst wrote encouragingly. Wolfe replied that an offensive war would awe the Indians and ruin the French. (In this, he was later proven to be right.) "If you will attempt to cut up New France by the roots, I will come with pleasure to assist." But Amherst, bound for Fort George by way of Albany, was not to be swayed from his course.

Meanwhile, Wolfe spent the month of September terrorizing fishing villages along the Gaspé Peninsula. His orders came directly from General Amherst, and he had no choice but to obey. Still, he was openly contemptuous of what he considered to be cruel and useless operations. In a letter to his father, Wolfe wrote, "Sir Charles Hardy and I are preparing to rob the fishermen of their nets and to burn their huts. When the great exploit is at an end (which we reckon will be a month's or five weeks' work) I return to Louisbourg and thence to England, if no orders arrive that oblige me to stay."

The phrase "the great exploit" has been cited by Wolfe's detractors as proof he enjoyed inflicting cruelty on the powerless population. Admirers familiar with his letters to family and friends know he was addicted to sarcasm and often sent news of himself and his career in exaggerated terms. If he was harsh at times, it usually signified he was in one of his tempers.

Once the Gaspé raids were over, Wolfe reported directly to Amherst in a remarkably outspoken letter. "We have done a great deal of mischief – spread the terror of His Majesty's arms through the whole gulf; but have added nothing to the reputation of them." This was his way of telling Amherst he considered it foolish to punish the fishermen. With surprising aplomb he offered advice to his superior officer about the future assault on Canada, although Wolfe himself had not been assigned to the Quebec campaign: "If you do business up the river, the St. Lawrence, you must have small craft and a number of whale boats, two at least to each transport. Pilots are easily had for sloops and schooners, every fisherman in the river can conduct them up." He even nailed Amherst for not turning a profit: "If you had sent two large empty cats [catamarans] I could have loaded them with 30,000 pounds' worth of the finest dried cod you ever saw, but you won't make money when it is in your power, though there are such *examples* before your eyes." Amherst seems to have taken the criticism calmly.

Early in October, Wolfe sailed for England without waiting for Pitt's orders. His health was poor and he needed the healing waters of a good spa. It was also an advantage to hitch a ride with Admiral Boscawen on the flagship *Namur* – the larger the vessel, the less likely it was to be tossed about. Wolfe could never forget the terrors of seasickness. The *Namur* arrived at Portsmouth on November 1 after a difficult passage, and Wolfe sent his first message to his mother, saying he was safe.

In late October, Amherst, in his usual slow and methodical manner, sailed for Boston with six regiments and eventually reached General Abercromby at Fort George. After discussions concerning a second attack on Ticonderoga, the two officers agreed it was too late in the season to launch such a project. Perhaps they would organize a raid next year. After having moved his troops by land, river and lake to isolated Fort George, Amherst reversed the process and escorted them to winter quarters near Albany. Two weeks after Amherst's departure, a deserter brought word that General Montcalm was about to depart from Ticonderoga, taking the bulk of his army with him. Abercromby and his dispirited troops left Fort George for their own winter quarters and, except for the rare appearance of a scouting party, ice and snow ruled lonely Lake George for the next few months.

Once he was in England, Wolfe reverted to the rank of colonel of the 67th Foot; "brigadier" was valid only for the time it took to capture Louisbourg. Nonetheless, he received a wild welcome each time he appeared in public. His originality and mad risk-taking made him a star while Amherst, who had commanded the siege, came in a poor second. After a few days with his regiment in Salisbury, Wolfe went home to Blackheath. While dining with his friend Lord Sackville at White's, a London coffee-house later to become an exclusive men's club, he discovered that Pitt's letter ordering him to remain in North America had crossed his path in mid-ocean. Dashing off a note to the prime minister, he described his poor health and claimed he needed medical care, adding, "I have no objection to serving in America, particularly in the river St. Lawrence." The sabbatical was granted.

Still in low spirits, Colonel Wolfe wrote to his friend Captain Rickson: "I offered my slight carcass to Pitt to do with as he likes. I am in very bad condition both with gravel [kidney stones] and rheumatism." Hoping the waters at Bath would relieve his condition, Wolfe took lodgings at Queen Square and, overnight, became the season's most popular guest at dinner parties. On one of these dressy occasions, so much a part of Bath's lifestyle, he noticed a pretty young woman he had met the winter before. For a while at least, his depression vanished.

Katherine Lowther was the daughter of Robert Lowther, a former governor of Barbados, presently visiting Bath with her mother, now a widow. Katherine's brother, Sir James Lowther, later Earl of Lonsdale, was very rich and very unpopular. Horace Walpole described him as "equally unamiable in public and private." Katherine had large, dreamy eyes, dramatic hair and a rather long nose. As heiresses went in London, she was a good catch. Her family approved of the sudden romance, though it may have been Wolfe's celebrity that drew them; it certainly wasn't his fortune. Wolfe's mother, Henrietta, was against the match from the beginning, but James took care to keep his growing passion to himself. He had learned not to confide in Henrietta about his love life after their quarrel over Elizabeth Lawson.

James and Katherine spent Christmas at Bath, where they became engaged. On January 5, 1759, in the midst of their courtship, Pitt summoned Wolfe to his country house, Hayes, just outside London and offered him command of the Quebec expedition. For the remainder of the month Wolfe divided his time between seeing Katherine and preparing for his departure. Katherine commissioned a miniature portrait of herself, small enough to fit into a locket her lover could carry with him. Wolfe sat for a large portrait wearing a wig, no hat and a crimson frock coat with generous sleeves. While his expression is severe, his slim figure makes a nice change from the paunchy portraits of his contemporaries.

9

The Worst Posting in Canada

"A good fire and indifferent fare are much more acceptable to us than a turtle-feast without fuel."
– JOHN KNOX, Fort Cumberland, February 1759

Fort Cumberland was the worst posting in all of Canada, described by those who lived in it as a mean log square and smaller blockhouse perched on a bald hill between two vast swamps. From the ramparts, an approaching enemy could be seen for miles across the marshes. Conversely, French Nova Scotians (Acadians) and their Indian friends (Mi'kmaqs) could hide safely in the forest and spy on every scarlet-clad figure who ventured outside the walls.

Originally, back in 1751, the French built the fort on the isthmus linking Nova Scotia to the mainland and called it Fort Beauséjour – "beautiful place." In a wild rugged way the area *was* beautiful, but it was hard to provision. Violent storms and defiant ice floes often prevented ships from reaching the top of Chignecto Bay, so the spot remained a barrier between British and French territory rather than becoming a centre of trade. When the British captured Beauséjour in 1755 they named it Fort Cumberland after the Duke of Cumberland, one of the king's sons; but even that didn't change anything. Although both French and English were willing to fight and die for this miserable outpost, neither bothered to upgrade it and, two years into the present conflict, Halifax bigwigs made only sporadic attempts to send food and ammunition.

Weather on the isthmus was a constant aggravation: hot and buggy in summer, cold and foggy in winter, with no pleasant season in between. Captain John Knox, posted there with the 43rd Regiment in December 1758, kept a journal that might aptly have been called *Stormy Weather*, since his wails were always about sub-zero temperatures, gale-force winds and blinding snow. Phrases like "temperature inconceivably severe" and "it froze hard last night" are sprinkled throughout the text. On days when the sun *did* manage to shine, an armed party from the fort crossed the snowy marshes to cut firewood or shoot game for the cooking pot. Indians, who huddled in communal houses when the big storms blew, emerged the minute the weather improved and were on hand to torment the intruders. Rumour had it that the French were threatening to recapture the fort or destroy it by fire. So when Knox's regiment appeared as reinforcements, the garrison greeted the arrivals with rousing cheers.

Because the snow was so deep, British privates tried to master the art of walking on snowshoes – but the slow pace only exposed them to frostbitten noses, chins and foreheads. In Fort Cumberland, getting cold feet was a reality, not a turn of phrase. Army footwear wasn't designed for Canadian winters, so many soldiers wrapped coarse woollen cloth around their shoes while others resorted to wearing moccasins. When it rained and then froze, the marshes turned to glass. To avoid falling and breaking their bones, the men strapped "creepers" to the soles of their shoes – little metal cleats that gripped the ice. Even the hardy American Rangers, sent to Cumberland to train the British in wilderness survival, complained about the harsh conditions. And they were said to be the toughest of the tough.

In summer, mosquitoes ate men alive (it was no consolation to discover the Indians were immune to insect bites either naturally or with the application of a smelly lotion they concocted); and in winter the drafty buildings and unhealthy diet destroyed all hope of creature comforts. Because they got so little fresh air, the men were bored. In January and February it was impossible to drill outdoors or to hunt, fish, skate or repair the walls. Many took to gambling to pass the time and, when they could get their hands on it, drinking too much rum.

Even army camps in friendlier spots could be a trial to a private in the eighteenth century: he had to cope with ice, lice, mice and dice. The first was seasonal, the second ubiquitous, the third gnawed his greased hair while he slept and the fourth stripped him of his money. If a soldier had sex with a prostitute (and there were always women attached to camps, although historians tended to call them laundresses), he risked catching an infectious disease. When a soldier stood sentinel duty, snipers took aim at him. On the march, he had a rifle slung over one shoulder and a backpack and tools hanging from his belt – a total of sixty pounds. If lucky, he shared a tent with five others, although he might find himself out in the rain with no shelter at all. At times, flatboats moved him from camp to camp, but on other occasions he walked for miles in shoes that didn't fit – along paths that barely existed. Even in Wolfe's headquarters at Montmorency Falls, the quartermaster had been known to run out of fuel, food, ammunition and drinkable rum.

A general fared better than his men, of course – horse-drawn wagons hauled his baggage, including such items as silver plate, personal bedding, wigs and wine. A chef prepared delicacies to tempt his palate and a medical man kept watch over his health. Even a general might get rained on or feel the cold, but he wore a warmer coat, slept in better digs and had a flunky to light his fire. Many generals, governors and other high officials left journals filled with their own heroic deeds, brutal battles and rough conditions on the campaign trail, but they hadn't any real grasp of life below the salt. Senior officers didn't see soldiers as individuals but as a means to an end, like dogs, horses or cattle. The notion that war at the top was more comfortable than war at the bottom would never have entered their minds. General Wolfe and Brigadier Lord Howe were exceptions.

In the early spring of 1758, a ship loaded with provisions tried to anchor in the bay nearest Fort Cumberland; in fact, a message arrived to say the vessel was close by. But even as the marooned men cheered, thick ice in Chignecto Bay forced the ship to turn around without delivering its cargo and to seek shelter in milder Annapolis. Captain Knox had heard this chilling story; but when he was based in Cumberland the following winter, he feared Acadian snipers more than starving to death. "I am credibly informed that there are not any enemy settlers nearer than sixteen miles and yet these skulking wretches never pass one day without scouring the environs of this fortress," he wrote.

In mid-March 1759, when he was set to leave the place, Captain Knox made a depressing entry in his journal: "The men are living on thin pea soup spiked with a bit of salt pork. Our constant drink has been spruce beer or bad cider or bad rum. We have almost forgotten the flavour of wine."

Knox had no sympathy for the Mi'kmaqs because he had seen first-hand how cruel they were to their prisoners. One day in deepest winter, four soldiers and a Ranger left Fort Cumberland to fetch wood and were attacked, wounded and scalped alive. Next morning they were found dead in the snow, their faces contorted in agony, frozen like marble statues.

John Knox began keeping a diary long before he joined Wolfe's army and continued to do so long afterward. Pernickety about details, diligent about dates, low in morale, desperate to get out, he still had energy to record his observations. His fellow soldiers had been living in darkness for five months when word arrived that the 43rd was slated to join Wolfe's expedition on the St. Lawrence. Wretched and ragged though they were, the men raised a cheer.

Actually, they would have gone anywhere and faced any danger if it got them out of Fort Cumberland. Although he was desperate to leave, Knox still took time to jot down notes about the colonials from New England who arrived to replace his regiment: "A mean-looking set of fellows without any kind of discipline." Their officers, he allowed, were "sober, modest men who talk very clearly and sensibly and make a decent appearance in blue, faced with scarlet." Privates, by contrast, had no uniforms but wore their own shabby clothes.

One of the first things Knox spotted in Louisbourg harbour was the British flag floating over the ramparts. Then, it was called the Union Flag and consisted of the white cross of St. Andrew on a blue ground topped by the blood-red cross of St. George. It was 1801 before the cross of St. Patrick was added and the flag became known as the Union Jack.

The forest of masts Knox saw in the harbour meant the fleet was in. Even as he scribbled his first impressions, thick fog rolled across the bay, blotting out the scene. Later, when it cleared, he was fascinated by the risks some men took to get back to their ships, "stepping from one ice patch to another with boat hooks or setting-poles in their hands. I own I was in pain while I saw them for, had their feet slipped from under them, they must have perished." Once ashore, Knox chatted with his brother officers and learned he had missed General Wolfe's review of the troops. Disappointed, since he already considered James Wolfe a hero, he noted a remark by Wolfe that was already going the rounds. When a junior officer apologized to Wolfe for not having taught his men a new exercise, the general huffed, "Poh! Poh! New exercise! New fiddlesticks! If they are otherwise well-disciplined and will fight, that's all I shall require of them."

Wolfe knew from experience that bickering between the army and navy was death to a campaign – his scathing denouncement of the Rochefort fiasco two years earlier had made him Pitt's darling. As early as December 24, 1758, Wolfe wrote to the prime minister, "I will

add from my own knowledge that the second naval officer in command [he was referring to Rear-Admiral Philip Durell] is vastly
unequal to the weight of the business and it is of first importance to
the country that it does not fall into such hands." Exactly what Wolfe
knew about Durell isn't recorded, but on this point, at least, Pitt listened to his protégé and made Vice-Admiral Charles Saunders – a
man who was experienced and unflappable – the commander of the
fleet. When it came to blockading French transports in the Gulf of St.
Lawrence, however, Pitt (directing things from London) put Durell
in charge. Wolfe was alarmed. French ships were certain to be carrying provisions crucial to Quebec's survival, and Wolfe believed that if
the Canadians were starved out, it would save many British lives.

Originally, Pitt's plan had called for the fleet to collect at Louisbourg
by May 7. It was to consist of twenty-two ships of the line and twenty-
seven smaller vessels, the whole mounting a total of 1,944 guns. But
the weather refused to cooperate and, at the end of April, the
Louisbourg harbour was blocked by a huge ice field stretching down
to Canso on the tip of Nova Scotia. The fleet sailed farther south and
Wolfe and Saunders, both aboard the *Neptune,* arrived in Halifax
harbour on April 15. After a quick inspection, Wolfe dashed off a
glowing report to Pitt about advance preparations. However, he had
barely landed when he received news of his father's death. Personal
matters took precedence, among them a request to his uncle, Major
Walter Wolfe, to assist his mother. Since Henrietta had not been on
friendly terms with her own relatives for some years, she couldn't
expect support from that quarter.

Thrusting family matters aside, Wolfe discovered that preparations for the advance upon Quebec weren't quite as complete as
he'd first thought. Admiral Durell was still dallying around Halifax
instead of heading straight for the Gulf of St. Lawrence to stop
French transports before they entered the river. Wolfe was anxious
to succeed in this particular scheme, but Durell didn't seem to
grasp why time was precious. Certainly, his excuse to Admiral

Saunders was limp. He claimed he didn't know whether the ice was out of the gulf.

Wolfe fumed but managed to hold his tongue and even sent two hundred and fifty additional soldiers to Durell under the command of Colonel Sir Guy Carleton. He also issued a general order supporting Admiral Durell's authority: "Troops are to be obedient to the Admiral's commands and attentive to all his signals. When weather permits, the men are to be as much in the open air as possible and eat on deck. Cleanliness in berths and bedding and as much exercise as the situation permits, are the best preservatives of health."

But it wasn't in Wolfe's nature to forgive easily and, after a short time, he confronted Admiral Saunders with Admiral Durell's laxity. He even hinted that Durell was gun-shy, a remark so insulting that in some circles it would have called for a duel. Naturally, Saunders took exception to Wolfe's criticism and, although the two commanders eventually left Halifax together on the *Neptune,* their relationship had chilled.

By the end of May, Wolfe discovered a company of American Rangers was "missing" from the roster. More mysterious was the disappearance of several transports carrying provisions and small boats Wolfe would need in the coming campaign. He found no explanation for the discrepancy and concluded it was due to theft. In Louisbourg, Wolfe noted that he had no cash with which to buy Canadian supplies or hire workmen for much-needed repairs on the ships. Pitt hadn't provided him with money and Amherst, commander of the British Forces in North America, had turned down his request. Wolfe was frustrated and humiliated. Here he was, in charge of the greatest expedition England had ever mounted against the French in America, and he didn't have a pound in his pocket! Before he sailed for Quebec, there was still another blow. The equipment for three regiments had vanished completely, and he was forced to borrow from stores in Louisbourg to make up the loss.

Wolfe understood how important it was for the men to be well shod. His orders on May 25 read, "It is particularly necessary for the service of this campaign that the regiment be provided with a very large flock of shoes before they sail, as any supply hereafter will be uncertain."

Despite disappointments and frustrations, Wolfe found time to request fresh beef for all regiments arriving in Louisbourg and ordered a large quantity of spruce beer to be put aboard the transports. Hooks and lines were issued to all soldiers so they could add to the supply of fresh food. But his best idea was the creation of a "hospital-ship," where patients with infectious diseases could be kept separated.

In Louisbourg, fog, rain and cold winds continued to plague the expedition. Knox, living on board the *Goodwill,* a catamaran of 340 tons, admitted the accommodations were better than he had expected. The price of mutton and beef in the town was high – twelve to fifteen pence per pound – important to him because officers paid for their own food and wine. Listing improvements made in the uniforms and gear of the Light Infantry, Wolfe wrote, "The hat has become a cap with an ear-flap and button. When the flap is down there is enough cloth to reach under the chin and keep the soldier warm. It hooks in front and is made like the old velvet caps in England."

The *Goodwill* sailed June 5 and everyone aboard, army and navy, was in good spirits, happy to be on their way to Quebec at last. The popular toast among officers was "British colours on every French fort, port and garrison in America." The fog continued, but eventually the skies lightened and the first section of the expedition reached the mouth of the St. Lawrence in twelve days and waited for the other ships to catch up.

On June 18, the entire fleet was upriver, some as far as Bic Island off Rimouski, where two companies of Rangers who had walked overland were taken aboard. The *Prince of Orange* was waiting for them with a message from Durell: he had reached Île d'Orléans, anchored offshore, but had not attempted to capture it. Earlier, he had seized three enemy ships bound for Quebec and loaded with food and ammunition. This was all good news, but Wolfe was edgy. Never a patient man, he left the cumbersome *Neptune,* boarded the faster *Richmond* and passed the *Goodwill* with Knox aboard. Wolfe waved to the crew as if he were royalty, and the troops cheered. It took very little to please men in those days.

"We saw an immense number of sea-cows rolling about our ships today," the indefatigable Knox wrote in his journal, "white as snow. Fired on them but the shot bounded off as if upon a stone." French and Indians, he learned, ate parts of these animals and boiled the rest to make an oily substance they used to cure skins collected on the traplines.

A French pilot put aboard the *Goodwill* to guide her through the dangerous Traverse, the channel between Île d'Orléans and the mainland, was noisy and boastful. Knox quoted him as saying, "Canada will be the grave of the whole army and the walls of Quebec will be ornamented with English scalps!" Only the admiral's intervention saved the fellow from physical abuse.

James Cook, then a thirty-year-old petty officer, had taken soundings in the Traverse so accurate that English ships sailed through with no trouble at all. Vaudreuil, angered by the fact that French pilots had pretended it was a difficult task, complained in a letter to the Court of Versailles that Cook "knew more about the river in a few days than local pilots had learned in a century and a half. The enemy passed 60 ships of war where we had hardly dared to risk a vessel of 100 tons." The reference was to the same naval officer who, as Captain Cook, would explore the South Pacific from 1768 to 1770.

On the morning of June 27, Wolfe and the first brigade landed on Orléans. The general was now opposite Quebec, although he would have to march to the northwest tip of the island to actually see the famous fortress. The second brigade followed at 7 p.m. that night and the third was poised to land on Point Lévis, on the south shore of the St. Lawrence River, when a wild storm erupted over the area, driving several ships ashore and destroying a number of small boats. The next day, the wind was still so strong that several ships broke loose. According to Wolfe, "At night, the enemy sent fire ships at the fleet but [our] seamen prevented them from doing any harm."

Wolfe had just arrived, but the weather was already getting on his nerves. He was itching to see Quebec clearly, but two more stormy days passed before Colonel Guy Carleton, one of his aides, could escort the general to the western point. Until Wolfe actually gazed across the narrow stretch of water that separated him from his target, the fortress of Quebec had been a fantasy. He studied the rocky promontory, saw the stiff row of guns along the barricades that stretched as far downriver as Montmorency Falls and knew it would be foolhardy to attack the French along this line. He would have to scrap all his plans and come up with a new one.

Admiral Saunders asked Wolfe to seize Point Lévis to protect the fleet, now moored in the Quebec Basin; and Wolfe ordered Brigadier Robert Monckton to do so immediately. Although it had been part of his plan to take the point, he listened attentively as Saunders explained that if Montcalm established heavy artillery there, he could blast the British fleet to bits. In fact, said Saunders, he was astonished the French hadn't fortified that part of the south shore long before the British fleet arrived. What were they thinking? Monckton and his brigade established a camp between Point Lévis and Pointe-des-Pères, with very little opposition from French guns across the water.

Planting his cannon on Point Lévis was Wolfe's first brilliant move in the campaign. Unfortunately for the British, it would be his last for quite some time.

10

The King and His Mistress

"An empire is like a tree. If the branches spread too far
they drain the sap from the trunk."
– CHARLES SECONDAT, Baron de Montesquieu, 1755

It is doubtful if Canadians understood why King Louis XV left his North American colonies to fend for themselves. Ordinary citizens were far from the heart of world affairs and even Quebec officials were unaware of France's empty coffers, the king's insidious weariness or Pompadour's failed attempts to inspire heroic efforts in her generals. In the great world, France was still perceived as the richest nation in Europe. Her enemies had no idea money was as tight for her as it was for them. Although King Louis knew that if he lost his foothold in America it would diminish his prestige, he feared an invasion by the English more than he feared his own loss of face.

Outsiders saw the Court of Versailles as a magical place; insiders knew the extravagant goings-on were mostly a sham. For beneath the dazzle and sycophancy, the king and his mistress were desperately short of cash. The Court's palmy lifestyle was the envy of every monarch in the civilized world, yet France herself was close to bankruptcy. Louis picked his advisers from a pool of aristocrats who may have had a talent to amuse him or to win a battle. But they had no idea how to fix the antiquated tax system.

In earlier times, the clumsy government structure worked fairly well. It always seemed to turn up one or two politicians capable of steering the king in the right direction. But in the 1750s, all the king's men were lazy, silly or ham-fisted. One court wag, describing Mirepoix, the newly appointed ambassador to England, quipped, "It's a good appointment. He can teach the English to dance."

If only Louis' incompetent ministers were his worst problem! But the blunderings of cabinet shrank in comparison to the damage done by his mistress, the Marquise de Pompadour. She had the king's ear, mind, heart and just about every other part of him, but she *would* meddle in politics. By 1759, her hold on him was as tenacious as ever, but based on a whole new set of values. In the first few years of her reign, it was lust with him and love with her although, ironically, the lovers were far from being sexually compatible. In fact, Pompadour worried about her cool response to the royal kisses right from the start and once consulted a wizard specializing in aphrodisiacs, who suggested Madame change her diet to chocolate, truffles and celery with a daily dose of an elixir, his secret recipe.

Pompadour took the doctor's advice but soon became so feverish that her maid-companion, Madame du Hausset, thought she was dying. Du Hausset discussed Pompadour's health with the Duchesse de Branca, who then had a word with the marquise. Pompadour burst into tears. Madame du Hausset, who seems to have spent much of her time eavesdropping on her mistress, heard Pompadour say, "I'm afraid of losing the king's heart. Men set great value on certain things and I have the misfortune to be of a very cold temperament."

The clever duchesse assured the mistress it was all in her imagination, whereupon a distraught Pompadour confessed that one night after making love, the king had slept on the sofa, blaming the hot weather. Pompadour felt sure he no longer loved her and that's why she had resorted to the diet and the horrible potion. The duchesse grabbed the vial off the dressing table, sniffed it, cried "Fie!" and threw it in the fire. She then told Pompadour to accept the king's lovemaking as enthusiastically as possible and time would do the rest. "The chains of habit will bind him to you forever."

Unlike former mistresses, who relied solely on sexual games, Madame de Pompadour came to understand that Louis' chief problem was not sex but boredom, and she switched from *fille de joie* to ringmaster. For the remainder of her years as the official mistress, Pompadour dedicated all her waking hours to keeping the king amused. A talented actress and musician herself, she organized an in-house theatre, musical recitals, afternoon picnics, epicurean banquets and masked balls with original themes. Together, the couple shopped for diamonds, horses, sculpture and paintings and built several tiny jewel-box houses where the king could play cards in private with friends who amused him. This was accomplished largely by selling old "toys" to buy new. There was always someone ready to buy the king's treasures, always someone to extend credit, for a time at least.

It is revealing that even when Pompadour first came to Court and the king's passion for her burned brightest, he took other lovers. Louis believed he must have sex every day; more often, if possible. There was also the problem of rivals for Madame's position: she had to be constantly on guard. A series of close calls, times when ambitious beauties almost seduced the king into replacing Pompadour, made her tolerant of the pretty young things His Majesty kept at the Parc-aux-Cerfs. Better these fleeting fancies than the installation of a new mistress and her own banishment.

By the mid 1750s, descriptions of the Parc-aux-Cerfs ranged from a private brothel for Louis and his friends, to wild orgies with dozens of innocent young girls on tap. Originally, the Parc-aux-Cerfs was a game reserve near the village of Versailles. When the stags disappeared, it was turned into a suburban development of small houses, well-tended gardens, a square, a marketplace and a church. The deed for a modest house located behind the hostel for the king's guards was signed by the king's intermediary in 1755, but it's possible Louis had been testing its usefulness for two years before buying the property. The house had four rooms on the ground floor and four above, providing space for only two or three live-in girls at a time and servants to look after them.

Beautiful young women of "low condition," which meant they were the daughters of peasants, were searched out by men the king trusted. Despite the girls' dimples and other charms, they were destined to marry labourers or farmers, a hard life. It's not surprising that when these young women were invited to become mistresses to a mysterious rich man, they accepted. In their position, it wasn't a disgrace; it was a bit of luck. The king visited Parc-aux-Cerfs incognito and his lovers were unaware of his identity, or pretended to be. When Louis tired of a girl or she became pregnant, his servant would find a husband for her in some distant village and she would receive a pension of one hundred thousand livres and a yearly allowance of ten thousand livres for the child. Although the gossips claimed that Pompadour helped find girls for the king, it's more likely that the marquise was in the same position as the queen: she simply ignored the whole sordid business and went on with her life.

If Madame de Pompadour's relationship with King Louis had remained purely sexual, her influence probably would have vanished long before 1759. But the hold she had over him was more enduring. To retain her power and prestige as official mistress, she needed to keep the king amused every minute he was with her. The marquise once confided to a woman friend that loving the king was worth any amount of pain and suffering and, as she aged, it became apparent that she needed all her willpower to survive. When crucial decisions were being made about the fate of Canada and Louisiana, Pompadour was thirty-seven, considered rather old for a king's mistress. Her health was deteriorating. She had an irregular heartbeat, overwrought nerves and internal injuries from too many abortions. The Marquise de Pompadour, at the peak of her good fortune, had family responsibilities: a young daughter, Alexandrine, and a brother, Abel, who was still trying to establish his position at Court and needed her help.

Louis XV was not a man who improved with age. Even when Pompadour was ill, he insisted she attend dinners and soirées, just as his great-grandfather Louis XIV had done with his mistresses. Bourbon kings made no exceptions for ladies who were feverish, pregnant or recuperating from a birth; they had to make long journeys in jolting carriages in any kind of weather, if that was the royal wish. Louis grew more difficult and there were times when Pompadour endured his mysterious sulks, bursts of violent exercise, even drunkenness. It took all her sweet songs, witty remarks, delicious gossip and shaky political views to hold his interest. Every year it became harder to make him laugh or spring a delightful surprise that would light up his face.

Over the years, the king and his mistress had created a model farm where they pretended to work. The marquise set up a china factory at Sèvres and a carpet factory at Aubusson, projects that not only interested the king but also gave employment to locals. Only a few years before, the flashiest couple in the world often sallied out to purchase costly ornaments and toys they didn't need and might never look at again. By 1759, however, money was hard to find and buying baubles had ceased to be a game.

When 1759 dawned, Louis was middle-aged and fretful. He was stung by critics who begged him to wage a more rigorous war against England and by others who screamed for peace. Those close to him said he'd lost his zest for life. Money was so short that both he and Pompadour sold off personal possessions to help pay government debts; she, her jewels and he, his horses. Despite the apparent sacrifice, the king had no grip on reality: after one sale, he was heard to complain that he had only a thousand horses left in his stables.

Some of his ministers suggested that if the king really wished to restore his popularity in France, he needed to loosen the purse strings and save Quebec. But no one could tell him where to find the money for such an enterprise. As for Canada the colony, he was fed up. Where was the promised treasure? Where were the revenues? Instead of pouring gold into his coffers, his ice-bound prize had cost him millions of livres! And what did he get in return? His representatives were stealing him blind. The governor, the intendant and the commissary-general were lying, cheating and making a fool of him. He wanted love from his subjects, not betrayal.

How innocent *les habitants* were, then, to expect a crusading army from a king who was totally disenchanted with their homeland.

11

Hoping for Another Miracle

"We shall save this unhappy colony, or perish with it."
– LOUIS-JOSEPH, Marquis de Montcalm, 1759

Pompadour's blood would have boiled if she'd seen the procession that jingled its way through the streets of Quebec one February morning in 1759. The roomy red and blue sleighs bound for Montreal were filled with the likes of Intendant Bigot, his staff officers and his current mistress, Madame Péan, all snug under silver fox fur blankets. Bringing up the rear were several smaller, drabber vehicles stuffed with chefs, valets, maids and a major domo to keep track of all the others – occupants who weren't quite so warmly bundled up as their masters and who shared space with crates of champagne, caviar and other delights. Bigot, famous for his hearty appetite, was taking no chances on the simple cookery *les habitants* might offer him along the way. He risked no discomfort as a guest in the governor's mansion because his personal bedding, silver tableware and fine wines had been sent on ahead the week before.

As the bright parade wound down the snowy slope to the river road, townspeople lined the route. But by this time, they no longer cheered. They hated Bigot, blamed him for all their woes and resented his thievery. How different it was for them! If an ordinary citizen stole so much as a loaf of bread it meant jail, the whip or even death. The latest bit of gossip had Bigot lending Major Péan enough money (the king's, of course) to buy a huge quantity of grain, which was held until Bigot raised the price; then Péan quickly sold it and made fifty thousand crowns on a single transaction. And this was only one of the schemes Bigot had set up for himself and friends over the years.

The intendant wasn't being philanthropic when he helped Péan. He was paying for services rendered by the major's wife, Angélique – she and Bigot were having an affair while her husband conveniently looked the other way. Eventually Bigot looked in the direction of his business partner's wife, Madame Pénisseault, "a woman of taste" according to one contemporary author. She was also ambitious, a characteristic proven by her move up the social ladder from Péan's bed to Bigot's and, near the end of the war, that of Lévis. But there was nothing unusual in such liaisons. Many army officers formed attachments to local women and, since the number of beauties was limited, there was fierce competition in the lists of love. In Quebec society the appearance of an attractive new face was always good news for the rakes.

When Governor Vaudreuil's guests first reached Montreal they seemed more concerned with roast beef dinners than with plumping up Quebec's weak defences, although the governor managed to send a circular letter to all the parishes urging men to join the militia "to defend your religion, women, children and goods from the fury of the heretics" – meaning the British. Pontbriand, Bishop of Quebec, was just as enthusiastic in his efforts to recruit for the militia. "On every side, dearest brethren," the bishop pleaded, "the enemy is making immense preparations. His forces, at least six times more numerous than ours, are already in action. Never were we so destitute, or threatened with attack so fierce, so general, so obstinate." It was smoothly put, but not quite accurate: with militia and colony troops, the French had twice as many men as the British. Still, the bishop could be forgiven – he was dying of cancer and faithful to his duties as he saw them.

During these years, Montreal was little more than a link in the chain of French trading posts that stretched inland along the St. Lawrence River and dipped down into the Ohio Valley. Certainly there were many different opinions about life in the colony; but most people agreed that while the elite led a lively social life, it wasn't Paris.

That February the Bigot party, ensconced in the governor's mansion, spent several days playing cards, dancing and drinking before devising a scheme to repel the British. The populace believed the fortress was impregnable because it sat on a rocky promontory and was protected by the St. Lawrence River on one side and the St. Charles on the other. The nobs who gathered in Montreal that winter knew better: their capital had been declared indefensible by a range of experts.

Quebec's appalling lack of security went back to the year 1740 when, after a century of French occupation and enormous expense, the overall construction of her fortifications was deemed inadequate. In 1744 the king appointed an engineer named de Léry to examine the ramparts and make a report. De Léry said Quebec was "incapable of defence and essentially unfortified," and the king promptly hired him to design and build a stone wall around the town. It was to be supported by earthen banks, but there was no mention of a moat. The records show the work was completely paid for in 1749 and yet, ten years later, Montcalm was fussing over the same problem.

"If the enemy reaches the foot of the walls," Montcalm told the assembled officials in 1759, "we must capitulate," adding, in his caustic style, "De Léry robbed the king like all the others." Later the general scribbled in his journal, "The city's fortifications are so bad that it would be taken as soon as besieged." During the same session, Bigot and Montcalm were of the opinion that more cannon ought to be installed on the western bastions; but despite Bigot's support, nothing came of the suggestion.

The council discussed setting up a strong battery at Point Lévis on the south shore, directly opposite Quebec's wharves. Cannon installed there would be in a position to fire on British ships should they anchor in the Quebec Basin. Here at last was a clear and practical plan, and yet no steps were taken to carry it out. But, when it came to establishing a line of batteries along the north shore, Vaudreuil, who owned property there, pressed ahead eagerly as soon as the weather improved. Montcalm's main camp was near Beauport, midway between Quebec and Montmorency Falls, and the enemy had to be prevented from landing there. If they crossed the St. Charles River and attacked Quebec on the undefended northeast flank, it might end the struggle in England's favour.

After the meeting ended, Vaudreuil and his party slapped each other on the back and hastened to another liver-destroying dinner. But before they disbanded that night, Montcalm confronted the governor with bitter words: "*You* have sold your country. But while I live *I* will not deliver it up!"

Montcalm knew what he was talking about. Two years earlier, he and his aide Bougainville had toured the riverbank east of the capital and concluded that four big guns and two mortars ought to be installed on Cap Tourmente, a jut of land overlooking the eastern tip of Île d'Orléans. From that position, the French could fire on the British fleet long before it reached Quebec. The plan was never executed.

In the same report, Montcalm advised establishing at least two redoubts (small v-shaped works that protect isolated gun positions) on the shore below the cliffs at Beauport. They were to be placed where they could be covered by musket fire from the fort. (The western redoubt was to contribute to Wolfe's first defeat.) Montcalm and his officers also favoured a fortified line on the west bank of the St. Charles River stretching from the General Hospital to Lower Town, to be supplemented by a second line from the same hospital and angling west along the Côte d'Abraham. But, like most of Montcalm's suggestions, they were ignored. The row of batteries along the north shore between Quebec and Montmorency Falls came to be known as the Beauport lines.

While their masters were in Montreal, presumably occupied with the safety of the colony, the people put their trust in God and begged for a miracle. Everyone understood that the king's ships, loaded with guns and provisions, had to arrive ahead of the British fleet if they were to be of any use. By April, work began on the Beauport lines and all was hustle and bustle. In early May, word came that a mighty armada was in the Gulf of St. Lawrence – and everyone assumed it was the British navy. Officials panicked on the ramparts, peering down the St. Lawrence and hoping against hope they would spot their own flag. The townspeople still relied on earnest prayer.

At the first sign of sails, colonists swarmed over the wharves. A huge sigh swept through the crowds when they recognized the elegant fleur-de-lis. Men threw their hats in the air and screamed, "*Vive le roi,*" and women danced recklessly to the tune of a local fiddler. For a few hours, most people believed Canada had been saved.

It wasn't long before the truth leaked out. As the French ships docked and began to unload their cargo it slowly became apparent that there was no magical army, avalanche of food or limitless supply of ammunition. The king's ships brought four hundred regulars, just enough to replace the sick and the dead in battalions already posted in Canada, along with a few engineers to shore up existing batteries, along with an unspecified number of cannon. Cadet's private transports were loaded with rich foods and wines, laces and velvets, mirrors and fashionable outfits from which he expected to make a good profit. Most of the goods were too expensive for commoners. For once Montcalm didn't rant when he discovered the Court's miserly contribution, but he merely remarked, "A little is precious to those who have nothing."

Montcalm's philosophical mood was short-lived. After riffling through papers Bougainville had brought from the Court of Versailles, he discovered he had been promoted to lieutenant-general. The news ought to have cheered him – in the military sense, he ranked higher than the governor – but there was no official letter stating that he, General Montcalm, must approve every major military decision. He was virtually in the same position he'd been in three years earlier, when he had landed – unless he confronted Vaudreuil about his promotion.

Vaudreuil continued to behave as before, assuming he had the last word in major military decisions. As a result, problems no one had foreseen threatened to engulf Montcalm. For example, the governor stubbornly insisted Canada must defend the eastern peninsula, Nova Scotia, when he didn't have enough first-class troops to protect the capital. The Court of Versailles' blithe warning that General Wolfe had sailed from England with eight thousand well-trained soldiers did nothing to boost Montcalm's morale; it only made him worry. The loss of Fort Frontenac and the fact that they had failed to take advantage of his first victory at Oswego meant the French no longer controlled Lake Ontario.

Worse, perhaps, for a man of Montcalm's volatile nature, there was talk that he was treasonous. Montcalm, on the advice of Bougainville, had suggested that if all else failed, the government might move officials, the army and all willing inhabitants to Louisiana. By doing so, went the argument, France would retain a toehold in America. But Vaudreuil pretended to be horrified by the idea and hinted darkly that the proposal was subversive. Montcalm, it was whispered, wished to be governor of the colony. Bougainville, returning from France a colonel and with permission to use the prestigious "de" before his name, was astounded at Vaudreuil's duplicity. He had long criticized the governor, but now he was even more convinced that Vaudreuil would stop at nothing to discredit Montcalm.

As for Montcalm's personal life, Colonel Bougainville brought sad news from Paris: one of Montcalm's daughters was well-married, but the other was dead. Bougainville had received the message as he boarded ship and there was no time to discover any details. Montcalm was crushed. "I think it must be poor Mirête," he said, "who was like me and whom I loved very much." The marquis never did find out which of his daughters had died, but in a dispatch from Maréchal de Belleisle, the minister of war, he learned in the coldest terms that the king meant to abandon Canada to her fate. "If we sent a large reinforcement of troops," Belleisle explained, "there would be great fear that the English would intercept them on the way, and as the king could never send you forces equal to those which the English are prepared to oppose to you, the attempt would have no other effect than to excite the Cabinet of London to increased efforts for preserving its superiority on the American continent."

This must be one of the best-documented examples of political gobbledygook any government minister ever offered for his shady shenanigans. Belleisle went on to explain that the English intended to attack Canada on all sides at once, so Montcalm must limit his defence to the most essential points, and added that if France lost the colony entirely it would be impossible to regain it.

"The king counts on your zeal, courage and persistency to accomplish this objective and relies on you to spare no pains and no exertions. Impart this resolution to your chief officers, and join with them to inspire your soldiers."

How could the king possibly believe such an insensitive message would inspire either Montcalm or his men? The general was expected to battle on without adequate reinforcements, food or ammunition while saddled with a governor who was constantly trying to undermine him. Even King Louis, not a particularly perceptive individual, ought to have realized that Montcalm's new rank as lieutenant-general could not compensate for such a cold-blooded betrayal. Montcalm was a caring man and found the Court's attitude hard to bear. For a time, he was in an emotional slump and barely able to function. Across the St. Lawrence, General Wolfe, too, was almost paralyzed by depression and a physical condition described by the catch-all word "fever." It seemed likely that both leaders, so different in most ways, were looking at a bleak future. The cataclysmic battle for Canada might be fought without either general leading his troops.

Meanwhile, the Court had written to Vaudreuil saying he must check all future military decisions with Montcalm. Upon reading this instruction, the governor was outraged. He decided not to reveal the contents of the letter to his associates and instead began looking for loopholes that would permit him to act as he liked. No one knows when, if ever, he passed this crucial message to Montcalm, because the general continued to consult Vaudreuil on major issues affecting the troops; and yet there was no sign of a détente between them.

Cadet brought one piece of riveting news: the British fleet was right on his tail. If Wolfe hadn't stopped at Louisbourg to pick up additional troops, Cadet assured his listeners, he would have reached the Gulf first and the colonists would have lost *all* provisions sent by the king.

But that first night, before people discovered the truth, they danced and sang and made merry, filled with hope for the future. Halfway up the rocky road to Upper Town, François Bigot gave a dinner honouring Joseph Cadet. Ten years earlier, when Bigot served his first term as intendant, he had transformed a huge stone and timber brewery into a palace with a dual purpose. The building embraced a richly furnished home for Bigot and an intimidating courthouse where he handed out justice and administered the civil affairs of the colony. Arriving in 1756 for his second term, Bigot moved back into this "palace," making no attempt to hide his lavish dinner parties and drunken gambling sessions. In fact, he was renowned for his generous hospitality and, when he felt particularly cordial, invited a few peasants to watch the dancing and feasting from a gallery constructed for the purpose.

The night the French fleet moored at Quebec, Bigot played host to his friends in the main salon with its glittering chandeliers and thick Turkey carpets. Cadet and friends draped themselves around the long oak dinner table while courses were served on gold-plated platters: butter-fried trout, suckling pig stuffed with apples and sage, slabs of roast beef, fresh asparagus and ripe strawberries grown in the intendant's glasshouse garden.

The serving valets filled brimmer after brimmer with the best burgundy and talk centred on how cleverly Cadet had outwitted the British navy. Bigot soon grew tired of hearing his flunky praised and pushed his plate away impatiently. It was high time Cadet offered a few choice details about Pompadour's frame of mind, the latest news on the continental war and any juicy gossip he had picked up in Paris. Bigot signalled the valets to remove the remains of the meal, leaving on the table platters of fruit and nuts and huge pitchers of wine. Then he ordered the doors closed; if he really *was* in disfavour at Versailles, no word of it must leak out by way of talkative servants; it would undermine his power in the colony.

Bigot had good reason to stew. On scanning the official documents Cadet had brought him from Pompadour, he found they had a nasty edge. There was even a hint that Pompadour had planted a spy among his personal staff. Despite these concerns, Bigot put a good face on it. At last he rose, faced the larger-than-life portrait of the Marquise de Pompadour hanging at the far end of the room (given him by the lady herself in happier days) and raised his glass in a toast. His guests followed his example. "To Madame de Pompadour! Long may she reign!"

Laughing, they drained their glasses so fast ruby rivulets trickled down their chins. After still more wine, Cadet admitted he'd detected some hostility at the Court of Versailles not only toward Bigot and his friends, but to Canada as well. It soon became clear that Cadet had failed to worm his way into the confidence of anyone important. And yet it was Cadet who galvanized the drunken party with his announcement about Wolfe. "He was right behind me!" Cadet insisted loudly. "Right behind me!"

The governor was still in Montreal when the banquet occurred, but his response when he heard of Wolfe's approach was prompt. Battalions of regulars wintering at the outpost were shipped back to Quebec. Women, children and animals living on isolated farms without garrison protection were advised to hide in the woods when the enemy fleet appeared. British prisoners of war held at Quebec now found themselves carted off to distant Trois-Rivières where Vaudreuil thought they'd be less likely to come in contact with British invaders and leak dangerous secrets. As another protective measure, navigation markers were removed from the Traverse – the main channel all large ships used to navigate the St. Lawrence River between Île d'Orléans and Quebec. No point in giving guidance to British ships; let them run aground and good riddance! As a double precaution, Bigot bought several old ships from Cadet (at great expense to the king) with the intention of sinking them in the Traverse to stop British ships from reaching the Quebec Basin.

On May 24 Governor Vaudreuil arrived in Quebec and enthusiastically supported Montcalm's orders to speed work on the north shore batteries. But even in the present emergency he couldn't resist grabbing the spotlight. From now on, Vaudreuil announced, he would hold a meeting every evening to issue orders for the next day, a move that left Montcalm sulking in the wings and foreshadowed the modern press conference. As if that weren't activity enough, he had five hulks converted into fire ships, a trick the French liked to pull when they wanted to set somebody else's navy ablaze. As well, he had a "floating battery" installed on the Beauport bank three miles downriver from the capital that was capable of firing on approaching enemy ships.

In early June, Vaudreuil and his advisers made a decision they would later regret: they sent several frigates loaded with army provisions fifty miles upriver "for safety's sake." No one believed British ships could get past Quebec's big guns, and removing the supplies was hailed as clever. When Montcalm heard that the Traverse was too wide to be blocked by sunken wrecks, he was angry with the French pilots who claimed to know all there was to know about the river. Montcalm announced publicly that the river men were a disgrace. Privately, he faced the possibility that the British fleet *might* get past Quebec's big guns. If they did, it would put his supply line to Montreal in grave danger.

Before long Montcalm had a more urgent problem. His well-trained regulars formed the backbone of any defence he might throw up against Wolfe should he decide to assault Quebec. But his Indian allies reported that Wolfe's superior officer, General Jeffery Amherst, was planning to attack Ticonderoga. If this was true, Colonel Bourlamaque, the present commander, would desperately need reinforcements. Additional troops were also needed at the rapids near the head of Lake Ontario. Montcalm was frantic with worry as he dispatched hundreds of his best soldiers to defend a string of isolated forts he considered worthless.

Montcalm, striding around his headquarters near Beauport, was at his lowest point. The autumn before, fresh from his victory at Ticonderoga, he had written to his wife, "Can we hope for another miracle to save us? I trust in God. I wait the news from France with impatience and dread. Adieu, my heart! I believe that I love you more than ever." He had driven off an army three times the size of his own, but he knew it was coming back in thousands and he doubted even God could save Canada for France, this time.

Montcalm still longed for Provence and his close-knit family. If only he could sail for France, wipe out all memory of this ill-fated colony, this hell that even the rulers of France despised! But he could not bring himself to break his promise to the king. He would do his duty, even if it killed him.

12

Bitter Exchanges: Townshend and Wolfe

"Oh, when shall we get out of this country? I think I would give half of all that I have to go home. O Bon Dieu! Brulez ma lettre!"

– LOUIS-JOSEPH, Marquis de Montcalm, Quebec, 1759

Montcalm was standing on the ramparts of Quebec when he first caught sight of Wolfe and his sappers on Point Lévis, beavering away with shovels and axes. Montcalm couldn't believe his eyes: his arch-enemy, a lanky boy in a huge black hat, was directing the work with a walking stick! Of course the British were mad, everyone knew that. But really, this was too much. He sighed. It was difficult for an old campaigner like himself to take a jumped-up general like James Wolfe seriously, but bemusement turned to anger when he realized that Quebec soon would be under the gun. Even after Montcalm's artillery fired on the diggers, killing several of them, the stubborn redcoats refused to stop.

It was one thing for Montcalm to deem the British crazy, another to watch the danger to Quebec grow steadily each day. Montcalm's fury mounted. *None of this was necessary.* Hadn't he suggested establishing batteries on Point Lévis as long ago as last February? And hadn't that pompous ass of a governor ignored him? Even after the British fleet anchored in the Quebec Basin, thumbing their noses at the fortress, Montcalm was certain he could hold the point with four thousand trusty *troupes de la terre* (French regulars); but it had to be done quickly. Now, it was almost too late. He was still taking orders from Vaudreuil to avoid a confrontation and the governor's solution was to leave six hundred ill-trained volunteers and a handful of Indians to defend the point! In less than a day, British troops had driven them off – and look at the result. The enemy was setting up cannon half a mile from the wharves of Quebec, defying the shells Montcalm lobbed at them. Soon they would be bombarding the town at will.

From Montcalm's viewpoint, things rapidly grew worse. Two weeks after Wolfe landed, Vaudreuil ordered two frivolous military actions, one little more than a joke. And this was from the man who had boasted in a letter to the minister of war, at Versailles, "I expect to be sharply attacked … there is no ruse, no resource, no means which my zeal does not suggest to lay snares for them, and finally, when the exigency demands it, to fight them with an ardour and even a fury which exceeds the range of their ambitious designs."

˙The first fiasco was typical of Vaudreuil. After buying eight decrepit ships from Commissary-General Cadet at an exorbitant price, the governor had them loaded with tar, explosives and flammable rubbish and aimed at the British fleet moored in the Quebec Basin. The leader, Captain Lelouche, lit the fuse half an hour too soon, forcing him and his men to save their own skins by jumping overboard. The rest of the armada followed his example and, in no time, every contraption they had assembled exploded – long before they endangered the enemy. As for the British, a few quick-thinking tars threw themselves into small boats and towed the "fiery monsters" to shore, creating "the grandest fireworks that can possibly be conceived." General Montcalm, once again infuriated by the governor's idea of warfare, lamented, "I am afraid that they [the ships] have cost us a million and will be good for nothing after all."

Once the danger was over, each British sailor was rewarded with a tot of rum for fast response to the crisis. The final score was England, no casualties; France, seven dead. It ultimately turned out that the expedition to the south shore had cost the French king one million livres.

Vaudreuil's second brainwave was even more farcical. By mid-July civilians in Quebec were alarmed when they saw enemy cannon pointed directly at the town. If the army couldn't get rid of the British, the reasoning went, they'd do it themselves – and civilians began pestering Governor Vaudreuil to organize a group of volunteers. Montcalm's role in this charade isn't clear. The governor had never consulted Montcalm about his military projects but if he did so on this occasion, the general must have refused to take part, because a Vaudreuil protégé, Adjutant-General Jean-Daniel Dumas, of the colonial troops, led the raid.

On the night of July 12–13, a party fifteen hundred strong left Quebec in a fleet of canoes: a mixture of militia, merchants, schoolboys from the seminary and the usual smattering of Indians. The adventurers landed a good three miles from the British position on Point Lévis, scrambled up the slope and disappeared into the woods. Unable to see one another in the dark and fearing the British were upon them, they began firing at random and killed seventy of their own men before tumbling down the bank and into the boats. It was a mighty sheepish group that paddled back to Quebec. If Vaudreuil had hoped to emerge from the adventure a hero, he must have been disappointed. The citizens decided the less said about the affair, the better.

That same night, Wolfe bombarded Quebec for the first time. While the French blundered about in the forest, the British were too busy firing their cannon to worry about a sneak attack. Wolfe's destructive show was to last a month, ruin most of Lower Town and damage dozens of buildings in Upper Town. Vaudreuil's "raid" on the point was so trivial that Wolfe didn't hear about it for five days.

Montcalm had set up his headquarters in a stone manor house close to Beauport, a village on the heights midway between Quebec and Montmorency Falls. Like a spider, he crouched in his web of earthworks and big guns, patiently waiting for Wolfe to make his move. That summer Montcalm commanded eight battalions drawn from the regiments of Béarn, Berry, Carignan-Salières, Guienne, Languedoc, La Reine, La Sarre and Royal-Roussillon. Intendant Bigot claimed the entire Canadian force was sixteen thousand strong, including 2,900 regulars, colonial troops, militia, Indians and soldiers in the town garrison. Montcalm's strategy was simple: he would stay within the Beauport lines until Wolfe sailed back to England. Since a large portion of the French army was made up of bush fighters and farmers who fought best in a protected environment, Montcalm was determined to avoid warfare in the open. If he could hunker down until the first signs of winter sent the young British upstart and his army scuttling home, Canada might be saved for another year. Time was on the side of the colony.

Both Vaudreuil and Montcalm were convinced that Wolfe would strike somewhere along the north shore, probably just east of Quebec, where the British landing boats could bypass mud flats close to the mouth of the Beauport River. While he was still at sea, Wolfe had considered landing there, but he also gave a great deal of thought to assaulting Quebec's western side – where his maps showed a good-sized field called the Plains of Abraham, a mile or so from the west wall. If he adopted this plan it meant relying on the navy to shuttle thousands of soldiers to a hostile shore in the dead of night. Wolfe's past experience with the navy hadn't been encouraging; he had witnessed Admiral Hawke's comic opera at Rochefort and, more recently, Rear-Admiral Durell's wimpish blockade in the Gulf of St. Lawrence. With such bad memories in the back of his mind, he wondered if it might be safer to assault the French fortifications along the north shore – near Beauport – where the navy's part in the action would be minor. Montcalm, trying to read Wolfe's mind, had guessed the right place for the wrong reasons.

In early July, Wolfe ditched all his carefully considered plans and, for the next three weeks, came up with a flurry of fresh ones. Each time he prepared to attack, he changed his mind at the last minute – and his fidgets got on the nerves of his senior officers. Brigadier George Townshend had a small talent for drawing and Wolfe became his chief target. The mean and often vulgar cartoons – one had Wolfe sniffing at latrines to see if they were clean – were passed around in the mess, where officers with complaints against the general had a good laugh at his expense.

Wolfe spent his free time studying the French works through his spyglass and could make out a strongly fortified camp on the west bank of the Montmorency River, close to the edge of the cliff where the Montmorency Falls poured down to the St. Lawrence. The French had thrown up two redoubts on the beach below. To Wolfe's eye, these two guns appeared to be out of range of French musket fire from above. All he had to do, he figured, was land a large body of troops on the beach near the western redoubt, seize it and hold on until his reinforcements arrived. At that point, they would all storm up the steep bank and take possession of the French fort. On paper, it looked remarkably simple.

Wolfe was itching to act. Dysentery and a painful bladder made him irritable, but somehow he kept on the move between Point Lévis (where Brigadier Monckton was posted), the main camp on the western tip of Île d'Orléans, and Admiral Saunders' headquarters on board the *Sutherland*. Before attacking the French battery, however, Wolfe decided he had to establish a strong camp on the east bank of the Montmorency River, directly across the falls from his target. Once installed in the new fortification, he would be free to study the strength of his enemy and, equally important, seek a ford where his men could cross the river to attack the French fort from behind. As a first step Wolfe landed a party of Grenadiers on the north shore of the St. Lawrence, about two miles downriver from Montmorency Falls, and ordered his men to drag their guns and gear up the cliff. There was surprisingly little action from the French. Wolfe's advance party was already setting up at the top of the steep bank when Townshend's brigade arrived. By the time the brigadier stepped ashore, Wolfe had vanished, leaving all the first division's baggage unattended on the beach. Furthermore, Wolfe had left no specific orders for Townshend. The self-important Townshend had been ignored! An aristocrat, accustomed to people jumping at his every command, the brigadier had a temper tantrum.

Actually, his resentment had been simmering for a month; he despised Wolfe's methods. The creation of a camp so close to the French fortification was, in Townshend's opinion, a tactical blunder. Nevertheless, he was a professional soldier and intended to carry out his end of the operation. As the brigadier's cursing troops dragged cannon and equipment up the bank, Montcalm's Indians began firing on them, and Townshend was inspired to build a palisade of wooden logs for their protection before setting out to find General Wolfe and give him a piece of his mind.

As it happened, Wolfe was on his way to confer with Admiral Saunders about moving two thousand men across the St. Lawrence to the new campsite. Townshend found him on the beach waiting to be rowed over to the *Sutherland*, moored close by. In Wolfe's view, Admiral Saunders took precedence over Brigadier Townshend, so when the latter suddenly appeared and began to rant, Wolfe gave him short shrift. The two men exchanged hot words: Townshend accused Wolfe of negligence, and Wolfe said Townshend was "consumed with self-concern." Adding to the insult, Wolfe criticized the rough palisade Townshend had thrown up, saying it was in the wrong place and facing the wrong way, and that he must move it immediately. Townshend had no choice but to obey. The rift was a sign of deeper rifts to come.

It was early in the game for Wolfe to be having a nasty disagreement with a senior officer. After all, Wolfe himself had chosen two brigadiers for the Quebec campaign. Pitt had picked the third, and back in January it looked as if they would all get along famously. But the hostility between Wolfe and his brigadiers was rooted in the very nature and status of each of the four men involved. Wolfe was from a middle-class family, the other three were upper class, and one, Townshend, was not only rich but also connected with powerful politicians. Wolfe was younger than all three brigadiers, a fact that had caused problems when he was appointed colonel of his regiment in Scotland. James Wolfe wasn't in the habit of appointing officers just because he liked them; he wanted men he could rely on, men who had shown courage and dependability in battle.

The Honourable Robert Monckton, head of the first brigade, was Wolfe's choice. Monckton was the second son of the first Viscount Galway and had reached the rank of colonel by the time Wolfe invited him to join the Quebec expedition. Wolfe had first encountered Monckton at the battle of Dettingen, when Monckton was a lieutenant and Wolfe was training to be an adjutant. Later, Monckton was given the unpleasant task of expelling the Acadians from Nova Scotia, and in 1755 he was appointed lieutenant-governor of that province. Three years later, he fought at the siege of Louisbourg.

Wolfe considered Monckton a "conscientious and loyal officer," but far from brilliant. He recommended Monckton as first brigadier on the Quebec expedition but was thought to be less than enthusiastic. It was said at the time that he was drawing from a very small pool of good candidates. Perhaps Monckton looked good when compared with some of the others.

The Honourable George Townshend, Pitt's choice for second brigadier, had a checkered military career. He was aide-de-camp to the Duke of Cumberland (the king's son), but the two men quarrelled and Townshend resigned from the army. Townshend came from a rich family – he was the son of a viscount and the nephew of a duke – and didn't need a career in the army. If he chose, he could have idled away his days like many a young aristocrat. But George had a taste for adventure and a hope of glory. When the Duke of Cumberland no longer headed the army (his father had fired him for incompetence), Townshend rejoined as aide-de-camp to the king.

George's friends thought he was being condescending to Wolfe when he agreed to go to Quebec, but Wolfe's reply to Townshend's acceptance letter was cordial, even unctuous. "Such an example in a person of your rank and character," Wolfe wrote, "could not but have the best effects upon the troops in America and indeed, upon the whole military part of the nation." And in the same letter: "I persuade myself that we shall concur heartily for the public service." Wolfe couldn't have been more wrong. Townshend wasn't about to agree with Wolfe or anyone else.

Contemporaries described George Townshend as sarcastic, showy and given to ridiculing friends and enemies with doggerel verse and unflattering portraits. In the days following the angry scene on the beach, his vicious cartoons of Wolfe caused yet another bitter exchange between the two men. Townshend passed the drawings to his officers, undermining Wolfe's authority. Wolfe went so far as to say he would "have satisfaction" (which meant a duel) when the war was over.

The third brigadier, James Murray, was the son of Lord Elibank. A small man with a jutting chin and a violent temper, he, too, had fought at Louisbourg. Wolfe was said to have great confidence in him, though Murray's contemporaries weren't quite so flattering. Some considered him a "dangerous man, both on the field and off it" and "eaten up with ambition" (a description that might have been applied to Wolfe himself). Notes left behind by an officer on Wolfe's staff at Quebec accused Murray of being "seditious, envious and ambitious." Murray's conduct at the siege of Louisbourg made up for all his faults and Wolfe forgave him. It soon became obvious that Murray did not forgive Wolfe.

It can be seen from all this that the choices made by both Wolfe and Pitt were not destined to create harmony in the upper ranks of the army.

13

Montmorency Falls: Wolfe's First Major Defeat

"Experience shows me that pushing on smartly is the road to success."
— JAMES WOLFE, 1757

When Wolfe set up his third camp at Montmorency Falls, directly across the river from the French, it was the act of a boy sticking out his tongue at the school bully. Lévis was anxious to get rid of the redcoats, but when he asked Montcalm if he should attack the British before they dug in, the marquis waxed philosophical: "Drive them away and they will give us trouble," he said. "While they are there they cannot hurt us. Let them amuse themselves." Each man had his own view of the event: Lévis thought having the English camp so near was dangerous, Wolfe considered it logical and Montcalm dismissed it as trivial.

Wolfe took over a two-storey stone farmhouse large enough to provide an office for himself, quarters for his senior officers, a kitchen and a mess. It wasn't long before the British works were as formidable as the French and the two armies settled down to watch one another across the rushing water. During the rest of July, the pressure on Wolfe increased. The warm weather wouldn't last long, and so he needed to engage the French soon. The question was *where* should he attack? The expedition had cost a staggering amount of money already, millions of pounds sterling, and it was mounting daily.

Wolfe remembered from the siege of Louisbourg how maddeningly slow Amherst was to make a decision. Back then, Wolfe was the one urging action. But he could afford to be cheeky because it wasn't his show, and blame for any mishaps would fall upon Amherst. Now that Wolfe was in charge, he found the responsibility nerve-racking. When he had met with Pitt in London, Wolfe assumed that Amherst had been ordered to mop up French forts in the Lake Champlain area first and then press on swiftly to help Wolfe subdue Montreal. As summer wore on, Wolfe was beginning to suspect Amherst had a different scheme in mind.

Whether or not there was a misunderstanding over Amherst's role, Pitt expected, and the people of England expected, great things of General James Wolfe. And if he didn't produce a miracle soon his growing reputation was bound to shrink. Wolfe knew, too, that he could not afford to make a mistake. With this scenario playing over and over in his head, Wolfe danced around every decision. Often he was physically ill; Canada's climate didn't agree with him. Belgium and Scotland hadn't agreed with him either, but he was younger then and had managed to shrug off the fevers and bouts of crippling rheumatism.

Writing to his mother in the midst of those earlier campaigns, James alternated descriptions of his ailments with assurances that he felt amazingly well. In the summer of 1759 he seldom had a good-health day. Heat and humidity often overwhelmed him, and knowing his senior officers were maligning him behind his back only added to the strain. Brigadier Townshend was an exception, of course: *he* ridiculed Wolfe to his face. The rank and file still trusted him, though, and often asked for advice about their personal problems. Wolfe was sympathetic and helped whenever possible. He was keenly aware the men were eager for action – they felt that any plan, however lunatic it might appear, was preferable to suffering constant insect bites and boring drills.

Among the many plans bubbling in Wolfe's mind, one kept rising to the top: was there a way to land his army on the river *above* Quebec and draw Montcalm out on the Plains of Abraham? He mulled this over in July, tossed orders up in the air like confetti and then blew them off so fast his staff never knew what he meant to do or when he meant to do it. Even his most loyal supporters showed signs of doubt. The bombardment of Quebec that began on July 12 lasted for weeks and continued to do terrible damage to the town, but it had little effect on the French army because the bulk of Montcalm's troops were safe inside the Beauport lines.

Wolfe finally threw in his lot with Admiral Saunders, begging him to push a portion of his ships upriver, knowing there was a risk of serious damage from Montcalm's guns. Saunders agreed to make a run for it on July 16, but bad weather caused a delay and Wolfe exploded – going so far as to suggest the Admiral and his sailors were cowards. His ferocious temper seemed to erase all memory of the lesson he had learned at Rochefort – the army and navy must cooperate fully if the expedition was to succeed. When Wolfe calmed down, common sense returned and the two men mended the break. Fortunately, Wolfe and Saunders had one thing in common: they both loved a good fight. The admiral was just as eager as the general to attack Quebec.

On July 18 the long-awaited migration began. The *Sutherland* (ninety guns), the *Squirrel* (twenty guns), two armed sloops and two armed transports with soldiers aboard safely passed the fortress and reached Cap-Rouge, fifteen miles upriver. Only the *Diana* was put out of business by French artillery, and she was sent back to Boston for repairs. Despite the successful movement of ships, Wolfe's journal contained a sour note: "Reconnoitred the country immediately above Quebec and found that if we had ventured the stroke that was intended we should probably have succeeded." The "stroke ... intended" meant landing enough troops to swoop down on Quebec. Why didn't he go ahead with his plans once the ships were safe above the town? Perhaps the bad feeling between Wolfe and certain naval officers made such a move hazardous; perhaps it was because his own brigadiers had sneered at every plan he had offered up to this point. Then again, it might have been the weather. It had poured for days, a condition bad for morale and Wolfe's rheumatism.

On July 20, as Wolfe watched from the deck of the *Sutherland*, Colonel Guy Carleton led a raiding party against Pointe-aux-Trembles, where the enemy stored sizable quantities of ammunition and a group of wealthy citizens had taken refuge. Wolfe had been told these folk might give up valuable information. Carleton was opposed by a handful of Indians who killed three of his men before vanishing, whereupon the British occupied the small settlement. As previously rumoured, a few wealthy Québécois were in residence there, but no valuables were found and the genial prisoners told the British only what they knew already: Quebec was desperately short of food.

As Wolfe saw it, the assault was merely a distraction. On board the *Sutherland* he hosted a dinner party for the gentry, exchanged jokes in French (which he spoke fluently), drank a considerable amount of claret and gave his autograph to anyone who asked for it. After these pleasantries, one hundred and fifty men, women and children, with assorted cattle, horses and sheep, were loaded on flatboats and transported to Quebec under escort. At this point, Wolfe was still returning civilian prisoners to their homes. As the boats prepared to leave, a posse under Adjutant Dumas arrived, fired at the British and disappeared into the forest, leaving the village at the mercy of roving Indians. When the boatloads of refugees reached Quebec the bombardment was suspended while Wolfe restored them to their families.

On the surface, the river affair seemed chummy and almost futile. But the confirmation of eleven armed ships on the upper river was a blow to Montcalm. It meant his supply line from Montreal was compromised. The French made one last attempt to destroy British ships still at anchor in the Quebec Basin, using a variation on the burning-ship caper. This time they built a contraption seven hundred feet long and consisting of huge logs, small boats and larger vessels stuffed with rubbish, ammunition and flammable tar. This time the French officer in charge came within twenty feet of his target before setting the monstrosity alight. Saturated logs spit, hissed and sent up fiery showers that might have done considerable damage if British sailors hadn't once again taken to the small boats, grappled with the burning debris and towed the whole flaming mess ashore. After the "all's well!" sounded, the seamen were given an extra ration of brandy and everyone was satisfied – except, of course, the French.

During July, hostilities erupted on several fronts. The invaders began harassing farmers over a large area, seizing livestock, burning homes and barns and taking prisoners. Sometimes they procured meat for the army and sometimes they raided to punish the locals for killing or maiming British soldiers. When Wolfe first landed on Île d'Orléans at the end of June, he warned that if civilians fired on his ships or ambushed his men they would pay dearly. If they remained neutral he would protect them. As early as July 5 he had issued general orders to his own officers concerning their behaviour when dealing with civilians: "No churches, houses or buildings of any kind are to be burned or destroyed without orders. The persons that remain in their habitations, their women and children, are to be treated with humanity. If any violence is offered to a woman, the offender shall be punished with death."

Canadians were caught in a trap. Vaudreuil had told them to harass the invaders or he would set the Indians on them. Most citizens tried to stay out of the conflict, but there were some who feared the Indians would burn their buildings and take their livestock if Vaudreuil gave the order. British soldiers had no quarrel with the farmers; when they burned and killed, they were merely following Wolfe's orders.

American Rangers were a different breed altogether. Many had been born along the ever-changing border between Canada and the Thirteen Colonies. Over the past twenty years, French troops and their Indian allies had committed hundreds of atrocities against American settlers at the behest of French officials. Rangers, often the sons of parents who had been captured or killed, their livestock stolen, their houses burned to the ground, had not forgotten. Rogers' Rangers weren't like ordinary militiamen: they were volunteers specially trained in wilderness survival and Indian warfare. Their exploits were the stuff of legend. Often, their motive was revenge.

The massacre at Fort William Henry two years earlier was still fresh in the minds of Rangers in the summer of 1759. They could scalp and kill with the worst of them and, although they were attached to Wolfe's army, the general detested their unfettered style. Rangers were rough, ready and freewheeling, but Wolfe dared not dismiss them because he needed them as guides and spies.

Wolfe was responsible for waves of blind destruction during the Canadian campaign, and it reflects badly on his record. However, in the eighteenth and nineteenth centuries, it was usual for an occupying army to live off the land. Wolfe had sailed from Louisbourg to Quebec without funds, a situation neither General Amherst nor William Pitt ever admitted or rectified. At times, Wolfe had no money to buy supplies or have repairs made to the ships supporting him. The human factor entered the picture in terms of the day-to-day behaviour of occupying troops: some officers of the day were principled, and others had no qualms about stealing food and wine or raping women.

Wolfe's behaviour could be erratic. He sometimes contradicted his own orders against pillage, especially if he'd just heard reports that French farmers had shot at his men. How much of his anger was due to his bad health and his natural impatience is debatable. Off duty, James Wolfe was a civilized man who demanded civilized behaviour from friends and troops alike. When he was reasonably healthy, he lived in the style expected of an army commander, travelling with valet and chef and enough silver and china to set a decent table. That he could be gallant, even theatrical, was revealed one day when a young Scottish captain declined an invitation to dine with his fellow officers by saying, "You must excuse me. I am dining with Wolfe." A sassy subaltern chided the Scot for not referring to him as *General Wolfe*, and the Scot replied, "Sir, we never say General Alexander or General Caesar." Wolfe acknowledged the compliment with a sweeping bow from the waist.

Wolfe's obsession wasn't food, wine, gambling or women: it was fighting. By midsummer his health was swiftly deteriorating and his plans were crumbling as fast as he could make them, yet he was still determined to meet Montcalm in battle. On July 26 he took two thousand men up the east bank of the Montmorency River in an effort to find a ford that would allow his troops to cross the river and take up a position behind the French fort. He discovered the ford all right, and made camp as nonchalantly as if he were holidaying at some popular English resort. An experienced bush fighter would have ordered scouts to flush out snipers and then posted guards before settling down for the night; but Wolfe was new at the game and had no idea that one hundred Indians and a Canadian captain were lying in wait for him. The French officer who discovered the British camp quickly notified Lévis and asked for permission to attack. Receiving no reply, impatient allies descended on the sleeping redcoats with war whoops and tomahawks and killed or wounded one hundred and fifty before the British were fully alert.

Wolfe ordered a withdrawal to base camp and sent Brigadier Murray to the ford with fresh reinforcements. The brigadier lost forty-five men in the ensuing skirmish and drove off the Indians before scurrying back to headquarters. It wasn't a glorious day for England. Nonetheless, Wolfe had learned it was impossible to take the French post from behind. He had to launch a frontal attack from the St. Lawrence River.

By now, half the summer had expired. In two months the British fleet must return to England, taking Wolfe and his army with it, and the French forces would retire to winter quarters. Everyone knew the rules: a gentleman's agreement had long existed in the western world not to conduct war in winter if it could be avoided. Wolfe took stock of his situation.

A large part of his army and artillery were now located on the east bank of Montmorency Falls, encouraging Wolfe to believe that if he landed troops on the shore below the French works, his men could scale the cliff – even in the face of enemy guns. From his main camp on Île d'Orléans, Wolfe had seen the two French gun positions on the shore three weeks earlier and, somehow, got it into his head that they were totally unprotected. This dangerous piece of misinformation lay at the heart of his plan. Wolfe had studied the tide and knew it ebbed at five in the afternoon, leaving a muddy stretch of ground at the base of the falls. Putting his observations to use, Wolfe devised a pincer movement. From the river, he would lead boatloads of Grenadiers onto the beach, capture the western gun position and hold it until Townshend brought his brigade down the cliff on the east side of the falls and across the temporary ford to support the Grenadiers. The dyspeptic brigadiers, who had sneered at all Wolfe's suggestions so far, protested this tactic as well. The general scheduled the assault for July 31, in spite of them.

Wolfe himself offered the clearest description of the debacle at Montmorency Falls in a September dispatch to Prime Minister Pitt:

> The Admiral had prepared two transports – drawing but little water – which could be run aground to favour a descent. With the help of these vessels, which I understood would be carried by the tide close in shore, I proposed to make myself master of a detached redoubt near the water's edge and whose situation appeared to be out

of musket-shot of the entrenchment upon the hill. If the enemy supported this detached post, it would necessarily bring on an engagement, which we most wished for.

But nothing was as it seemed. The first wave of small boats crammed with Grenadiers and a body of Royal Americans (regulars from the colonies and Swiss mercenaries) rowed toward the shore near the cannon Wolfe had chosen as his target. The general himself was in the *Russell,* which got caught on a long rocky shelf just below the surface of the water. Captain James Cook – the same Captain Cook who had recently discovered the secrets of the Traverse and who would eventually circumnavigate the world, explore Antarctica, rediscover the Sandwich Islands and be killed by natives in the Hawaiian Islands – took the soundings. But on this occasion, he was in error. The rocky shelf was much longer than it appeared and the boats following the *Russell* ran aground. They instantly came under heavy fire from the French on the heights. General Wolfe realized that the key to his plan, to take the gun position and hold it until reinforcements arrived, was impossible.

In his dispatch to Pitt, Wolfe admitted, "I observed that the redoubt was too much commanded [protected by musket fire] to be kept without great loss [Wolfe's mistake]. The two armed ships could not be brought near enough to cover both with their artillery and musketry [Cook's mistake]."

It was double trouble. With the *Russell* once more afloat, Wolfe and a handful of naval officers approached the beach looking for a better place to land. Behind them, seamen struggled to get the remainder of the boats off the shelf. Because the assault troops were in chaos, Wolfe sent an order to his brigadiers to stop the march across the muddy flats. Still, he believed he could succeed if only he could rally the Grenadiers to carry out his original plan. In the same dispatch to Pitt he explained:

The thirteen companies of Grenadiers and 200 of the Royal American battalion got on shore. The Grenadiers were ordered to form themselves into four distinct bodies and to begin the attack supported by the corps of Brigadier Monckton and Brigadier Townshend as soon as they passed the ford and were at hand to assist. But whether from the noise and hurry at landing, or from some other cause, the Grenadiers ran on impetuously toward the enemy's entrenchment in the utmost disorder and confusion without waiting for the corps which were there to sustain them.

The French abandoned the gun position on the beach and the Grenadiers and Royal Americans took shelter in it, coming under hot fire from above. Realizing his error, Wolfe tried to call them off so they could form up behind Monckton's and Townshend's brigades, but the men paid no attention to his commands. By now the afternoon was dark with storm clouds. A mischievous fate (it always seemed to be hanging about in the wings during this campaign) suddenly took a hand and flooded the area with sheets of rain. Neither side could keep its powder dry, and the grassy slope leading up to the French earthworks became so slippery the British couldn't scale it. The ford was now a sea of mucky potholes that made marching almost impossible and, finally, the tide turned – which meant the ford was about to vanish. Wolfe, fearing his whole army would drown or be wiped out, called off the attack. According to his journal, 210 were killed and 230 wounded. Those figures included 31 officers.

It was Wolfe's first major defeat.

Montcalm, on the other hand, had spent a very satisfactory day. Around noon he watched a fleet of British boats hover uncertainly just off the Beauport shore, but couldn't figure out where Wolfe intended to strike. At two o'clock, he rode his charger toward

Montmorency Falls, cheered along the way by cries of "*Vive nôtre général!*" For a commander who had survived months of criticism, isolation and scorn it was a sweet moment. He felt so confident that he left Lévis to conduct the defence and returned to headquarters at Beauport to eat his dinner.

By late afternoon (according to historian Francis Parkman, who said *he* got it from a French source), twelve thousand men were gathered between Beauport and Montmorency Falls. Wolfe was unaware of the overwhelming odds against him.

The raid was later described to Montcalm in graphic terms: a deafening roar from British artillery, the barking of French guns and the answering rattle of musketry from the British. Then, as the impetuous Grenadiers struggled up the cliff under a shower of bullets, came thunder and a torrent of rain. From the heights the French could see the British dead and wounded rolling down the hill; they could hear Wolfe sound the retreat and watch their enemy flee, some in boats heading for Point Lévis, others for Île d'Orléans. A great many soldiers escaped before the ford sank beneath the tide. Wolfe himself led the Highlanders up the eastern side of the waterfall to the safety of British headquarters.

For Montcalm, July had been a long, dark month, but on the last day he basked in a brief and brilliant success when his own vision triumphed. That evening he broke out the champagne. The marquis was no braggart but he preened a little for the benefit of his Indian allies. "You see we have beaten the English. We drove them away. We defeated them. We conquered them."

A canny chief replied, "Conquered them? We will never believe that until you drive them back to their ships. Are they not still firing against Quebec?"

Vaudreuil was, of course, his usual fatuous self. After the affair he wrote to Colonel Bourlamaque, "I have no more anxiety about Quebec. M. Wolfe, I can assure you, will make no progress."

14

General Wolfe Is on the Recovery

"From the heights of Beauport, the rock of Quebec or the summit of Cape Diamond, Montcalm could look down the river and watch each movement of the invaders."

— FRANCIS PARKMAN, *Montcalm and Wolfe*

After Wolfe's stunning defeat at Montmorency, Vaudreuil boasted and Montcalm basked, each man feeling vindicated because events had proven Wolfe to be vulnerable. Vaudreuil accepted the victory at face value: Wolfe, he said, had been defanged. Montcalm, more cautious, admitted he wasn't a magician – just a good campaigner who knew a thing or two about strategy.

Before the Montmorency Falls disaster, General James Wolfe was looked upon as an invincible warrior. Afterward, descriptions of his military prowess became more modest. At Quebec, he was handicapped by the fact that any preparations for an attack would be hard to conceal. From the rock, Montcalm could monitor every boat trip Wolfe took, every cannon he transplanted, every splendid hat he wore. But when it came to any future shocks Wolfe might have in mind, the Frenchman was at a loss. He hadn't the slightest idea what the Englishman was thinking.

Deeply loyal to King Louis, Montcalm had very different feelings about the cabal that was running Canada. Even if he defeated Wolfe, he had no plans to remain in the colony. He loved Candiac, and that's where he meant to spend the rest of his days. If, by some miracle, Canada remained French, Bigot and his friends would continue to rule – and Montcalm was incapable of adopting their wicked ways. Writing to his good friend Bourlamaque that summer, the general put it this way: "I should like as well as anybody to be Marshal of France but to buy the honour with the life I am leading here would be too much."

Carefully, Montcalm began to review his strategy. There was a chance Wolfe might blunder a second time and Montcalm might defeat him, or perhaps – and this seemed more probable – the French could hold off the enemy until winter itself shut down the country. In Montcalm's opinion, the foolish assault on Montmorency Falls had stained Wolfe's image and, if he had any sense, he'd lie low until it was time to go home.

Montcalm's best hope was to play the waiting game. He knew only what *he* would do in a given situation; he couldn't imagine what a man like Wolfe might dare. And this same narrow view prevailed throughout the French hierarchy. Neither Governor Vaudreuil nor Intendant Bigot had an inkling of Wolfe's obsessive nature. Not one senior officer suspected the existence of his personal demons.

On the evening following the Montmorency raid, Wolfe withdrew to his farmhouse headquarters wrapped in gloom. He desperately needed to be alone to think things through, but a sense of duty drove him to walk from tent to tent offering words of comfort to the wounded. Wolfe himself had been nicked by musket fire and his cane had been knocked from his hand, but such near misses only excited him. Never fearing for his own skin, he strode about under enemy fire as if he wore invisible armour.

After the defeat at Montmorency, Wolfe was tormented not by bleeding scratches or steamy weather but by familiar aches and pains from his rheumatism. In his view, sickness was tedious and even humiliating; only a wound suffered in battle was a badge of courage. He barely managed to struggle through dinner with the handful of officers who had limped to his table and, even then, he fell silent and picked at his food.

Seeing Wolfe despondent, his friends wondered if his brilliant career was over. They worried about his mood, not his appetite. Food and drink had never been as comforting to him as they were to some men. He hated excess and often expounded on its wickedness. "Gaming, eating and the pox are the vices of the effeminate and flatigious and have loosened the morals and ruined the constitution of half our countrymen" was a typical Wolfe remark. Those who knew him best were concerned about the dead look in his eyes.

After the meal was cleared away, after the port, the general climbed the stairs to his room and sat down to prepare a manifesto to be read to the troops the next morning. It included a sharp reprimand directed at the soldiers who had rushed up the hill without waiting for orders: "The check which the Grenadiers met with yesterday will, it is hoped, be a lesson to them: such impetuous, irregular and unsoldierlike proceedings destroy all order, make it impossible for their commanders to form any disposition for an attack, and put it out of the general's power to execute his plan."

Next morning Wolfe wrote a letter to Brigadier Monckton, making his position clear: "This check must not discourage us, the loss is not great." This was the party line: the British had not been defeated, nor had they retreated; they had simply met with a check.

By August 2 Wolfe looked so sick that some officers thought he had tuberculosis. But others shrugged it off as the same old fevers that had always plagued him. Whatever the cause, Wolfe was so fatigued that it was an effort just to get out of bed, let alone hoist himself into a boat so he could visit camps on Point Lévis and Île d'Orléans. Dozens of problems churned in his head. He had created the catastrophe at Montmorency, and he alone was to blame. He admitted that impatience and, yes, a lust for glory had blinded him to the truth. Sly Montcalm was not so easily drawn from his cover, and another way must be found to lure him out. Wolfe had lost 443 men dead and wounded, along with some of his lustrous reputation – and *it was all for nothing.*

During a campaign, boredom always hovered in the wings. Professional soldiers were trained to fight and perhaps die but not how to maintain their spirit between battles, and it was common for an army to lose its cutting edge. Men drank, gambled away their money and slept with women who were apt to infect them. Looking for relief from drudgery they took unnecessary risks. The average soldier earned sixpence a day, wore an ill-fitting uniform (which he had to pay for, eventually) and ate dry bread and hard cheese washed down with watered rum. Wolfe's notion that his troops needed meat and vegetables every day was unique, and he often thrust the task of finding such provisions on unwilling privates. Even Wolfe couldn't guarantee a healthy diet at all times. Much depended on the attitude of the officers who, if sympathetic, might look the other way while soldiers stole food from civilians. To a hungry man a squawking chicken was a potential feast, and it was hardly surprising if he wrung its neck and cooked and ate it.

And then there were the women. Wolfe, like most commanders, found the women hanging about his camps a constant aggravation, and yet he was helpless to get rid of them. Every army had its camp followers: they were sometimes wives, but more often they were prostitutes or gypsies. A few women were sutlers, that is, traders who sold clothing, food, tobacco and liquor to anyone with cash, or they became chips when men were gambling. Some of these unfortunate creatures had stowed away on army transports leaving British ports; others had attached themselves to the expedition in Louisbourg and Halifax and a few had drifted north from the Thirteen Colonies, while still others were local women. Now, in the middle of nowhere, they were adrift and no one was responsible for their welfare.

The first days of August teemed with rain and the men living under canvas had no way of drying their clothes or getting outdoor exercise. Ferocious bolts of lightning threatened them (one soldier was actually killed by lightning while he was in camp), and violent winds uprooted their tents. Humid weather bred fevers; freezing weather encouraged head colds; and an inadequate diet left everyone vulnerable to scurvy, which could be fatal. Symptoms ranged from bleeding gums, loss of teeth, aching muscles and running sores on the skin to large, ugly swellings filled with blood. Sailors had been prey to scurvy since the beginning of sea travel, but by the middle of the eighteenth century it was understood that an ill-fed land army was also a target.

Scurvy is mentioned in the records of the Crusades and, later, in the fifteenth century when long voyages of discovery became popular with greedy European rulers. In fact, it was the chief cause of death at sea until 1747, when James Lind, a British naval surgeon, noticed that sailors who ate two oranges and one lemon every day appeared to be immune. Those fruits quickly became standard fare on British ships and eventually, when the authorities substituted limes, the word "limey" came to mean a British sailor.

European explorers borrowed the recipe for spruce beer from North American natives, believing it had the same properties as citrus fruit, and discovered that it cut the scurvy rate by about fifty percent. Brewed from West Indian molasses and the tops of spruce trees, it sold for half a penny a quart. Although Wolfe's own health was shaky, he always found time to fuss over the welfare of his men and he made an effort to keep them constantly supplied with spruce beer.

Most of the time Wolfe adhered to rules of war accepted in the mid-eighteenth century, but in an army of seven thousand men, a few were bound to behave badly. The most infamous officer during the Quebec campaign was thought to be Captain Alexander Montgomery of the 43rd Regiment, the man responsible for a frightful incident near the village of Ste-Anne-de-Beaupré. The curé, Robineau de Portneuf, had gathered thirty of his parishioners to repel the raiders, and for a time the little band managed to hold off the British by sheltering in a stone farmhouse. Finally, they were forced to come out. But instead of taking prisoners, Captain Montgomery ordered them shot in cold blood. Montgomery's fellow officers were disgusted by the captain's part in the affair and, later, he was severely reprimanded by his superiors. The gruesome story took on a life of its own and is still cited as an example of Wolfe's cruelty.

Montcalm wasn't the only general on Wolfe's mind that summer. He thought often of Amherst. So far, Wolfe had received one letter in five weeks from his commanding officer, and it had told him very little about Amherst's situation. Dared he hope the major-general was trying to boot Colonel Bourlamaque's battalions out of Fort Ticonderoga? And if he succeeded, would he continue north to the St. Lawrence and sail downriver to Quebec? Wolfe wasn't surprised by Amherst's silence, of course. He had fought under him at Louisbourg and remembered the methodical, almost dreamlike quality of Jeffery Amherst's decision-making. But Wolfe *was* worried about the man's tactical skills. When Wolfe and Pitt had talked in London (how long ago it seemed now!), the prime minister was vague about distances in the wilderness, lumping Fort Oswego and Fort Duquesne together as if they were neighbours. Furthermore, Pitt hadn't the faintest idea about the difficulties of travel in a country where there were few roads and rivers were the only highways. What if Amherst took the same approach?

Actually, Wolfe needn't have worried. Before Amherst left Albany, he had shown considerable savvy by dispatching Brigadier John Prideaux to Fort Niagara and Brigadier John Stanwix to Fort Duquesne, in two distinct missions. It was a pity he hadn't bothered to communicate any of this to his man in Quebec. Wolfe, hearing only rumours, felt abandoned.

Perhaps Amherst wasn't *trying* to avoid Quebec, but his behaviour postponed his arrival indefinitely. Even with seven thousand men at his command he rambled about the territory near Lake Champlain without making any real progress. On May 22 he was on Lake George picking out the site for a new fort to replace Fort William Henry, now a ruin where the wharves had been totally demolished. Amherst lingered on Lake George and made several sorties to check British camps along the Mohawk River, but failed to find any of his enemies.

François Bourlamaque, recently promoted to brigadier, was still in command of Ticonderoga, the scene of Montcalm's victory the summer before, and he was expecting an attack by Amherst any day. But nothing happened. It was as if the war had come to an end and nobody had announced it. The truth was, Amherst, instead of tackling Ticonderoga, had begun new works on the south end of Lake George near the camp he had created the year before, keeping the name Fort George. For a month, white tents flowered on the slopes while soldiers bathed, fished and took woodsy walks to gather herbs for the cooking pots. Daily drills, target practice and scouting parties were organized. The walking wounded paraded to the surgeon's tent for checkups and down to the lake to wash. Spruce beer was plentiful, and the troops were encouraged to drink it.

But for all its rustic charm, the site remained a British army camp and for hundreds of soldiers there was plenty of hard work: tree-cutting, log-sawing, earth-digging, boat-lugging and all around sweating in the sun. Amherst had a huge labour force to draw on, and the men were assigned to build roads along either side of Lake George. The number of courts martial rose alarmingly, mostly owing to desertions and theft. Floggings increased and occasionally an offender was hanged as a deterrent.

By the middle of July, scouts reported that Bourlamaque had fled to Crown Point. This apparently inspired Amherst to make his first move north. When Amherst's troops arrived at Ticonderoga they found the outside trenches empty and took them over, saving themselves a lot of digging. Bourlamaque had left a small band of soldiers inside the fort with orders to stall Amherst as long as possible. When these stragglers fired on the British, inflicting a number of casualties, it irritated the phlegmatic Amherst so much that he brought up his artillery to teach them a lesson. Seeing the big guns, the French soldiers realized they couldn't survive a siege and quickly waved the white flag.

True, the fort was empty, but there was a catch: the French prisoners warned Amherst that Bourlamaque had lighted a slow match in the magazine that was set to blow the place up. No sooner had Amherst been warned than a loud explosion, followed by a rain of wood and metal, destroyed one bastion. In the uproar, a British sergeant rushed into the flames, grabbed the French flag and brought it out as a trophy for General Amherst. The English then moved inside the works and Amherst pondered his next move. Should he chase Bourlamaque and drive him out of the fort at Crown Point? Or should he remain at Ticonderoga and repair the ruined bastion? After thinking things over, he decided to stay and, once again, the march to Montreal drew to a complete halt.

Amherst left a body of men to continue the restoration of Ticonderoga while he ambled on up to Crown Point on Lake Champlain. Long before he reached his destination, scouts reported that Bourlamaque had abandoned Crown Point too, and was now on Île-aux-Noix, a secure little compound situated on the Richelieu River. General Amherst was so animated by the fact that he had captured two forts with no effort that he actually talked about rushing to Wolfe's aid. In a fit of patriotic fever he wrote to Brigadier Thomas Gage, "We must all be alert and active day and night. If we all do our parts the French must fall." His ardour soon cooled and he set about repairing the battered fort at Crown Point, adding three small satellite blockhouses to support it. Clearly, his motto this year was "make forts, not war."

Meanwhile, Brigadier John Prideaux established himself in the ruins of Oswego, which, in English hands, would secure Amherst's safe passage to Montreal should he ever decide to go in that direction. Prideaux left Colonel Haldimand at Oswego with two thousand men to repair the works Montcalm had destroyed earlier and turned his attention to Fort Niagara, an outpost tucked between the Niagara River and the south shore of Lake Ontario.

Niagara was commanded by Captain Pierre Pouchot of the Béarn Regiment, one of the "regulars" so detested by Governor Vaudreuil. Pouchot was a first-class officer with six hundred men and enough provisions to sustain a good fight. Much to his joy, several hundred friendly Indians from a small garrison on the Niagara River suddenly landed on his doorstep. Fate seemed to be smiling on the fleur-de-lis, a feeling that deepened when Pouchot heard the news that his enemy Brigadier Prideaux had been killed instantly by one of his own cannons. While Prideaux's troops were firing on Fort Niagara, the gun exploded and a flying fragment of metal smashed the brigadier's head to pieces.

The British troops took Brigadier Prideaux's death as a bad omen, but things brightened up when the command fell to Colonel Sir William Johnson, a dashing Irishman who for some years had managed his uncle's vast estate on the Mohawk River. Johnson had recently been made a baronet (a hereditary British title one step above a knight and one step below a baron) as a reward for having wooed so many Mohawks to the English cause. Johnson was a Gargantua in buckskins who lived in an enormous log mansion and offered hospitality to anyone who happened to pass by, a man common enough to make merry with his Indian friends and refined enough to drink champagne with stuffy European officials. The first chatelaine to rule over Sir William's manor house was a Dutch woman whom he eventually married. After she died, he took up with a Mohawk woman (there is no record that he married her), a union that automatically strengthened his ties with the tribe. Johnson was heaven-sent to besiege Fort Niagara, and his troops dug in for an excellent adventure.

After two weeks of firing back and forth, the defenders ran out of food and ammunition, one rampart was breached and the men were so exhausted that it was only a matter of time before they collapsed. Pouchot, one of those leaders who magically appear in every war, kept up his men's spirits with promises of relief. No one knew whether he believed them himself but, sure enough, on July 24 the sound of firing in the forest nearby signalled the arrival of a ragtag army. It was made up of colony regulars, fur traders, bushrangers and Indians. About a thousand men in all, they had walked and canoed to the rescue.

The trick now was to filter the newcomers through the British lines and inside Niagara's thick stone walls, where they would do the most good. For a time, things seemed promising for the French because the English suddenly ceased fire and the trenches looked empty. A few volunteers staggered out of the fort to investigate, and the British sprang out of the earth like great red weeds, slashing madly in all directions. Pouchot and his officers put up a courageous fight, but most of the men were killed and the captain reluctantly surrendered. The British now occupied Fort Niagara as well as Fort Oswego and, if Amherst ousted Bourlamaque from his island fortress at Île-aux-Noix, his path to Montreal would be clear. Had Wolfe known about these victories, the news might have cheered him in his blackest August hours. On the other hand, if Amherst had written in detail, Wolfe might have seen through his ramblings about building roads and restoring forts and realized his superior had no intention of making the long journey to Quebec. Not this year, anyway.

On the Richelieu River, where it flowed out of Lake Champlain, wet summer slipped into cool autumn. Given a choice, Bourlamaque would have preferred to fight Amherst immediately. He was tired of roughing it and longed for any scrap of social life that might still linger in the capital. Referring to General Amherst, he wrote, "I wait his coming with impatience, though I doubt if he will venture to attack a post where we are intrenched [sic] to the teeth and armed with 100 pieces of cannon." Bourlamaque had thirty-five hundred men on his little island, water protected him on two sides, and the exposed northern tip of the island was spiked with cannon. He felt very secure and very bored.

Amherst had mixed feelings about attacking Île-aux-Noix. At the beginning of August, he noted, "The enemy is trying to have a superior force by water. I sent to Capt. Loring to come to me that I may build a sloop as soon as the Brig is finished and that everything may be prepared as fast as possible." By August 16, scouts told Amherst, "Mons. Bourlamaque is making an intrenchment [sic] all around and has 100 cannon and four ships, one a schooner and one a sloop." Obviously, the longer Amherst hesitated, the stronger Bourlamaque's position became.

Back at his headquarters, Wolfe knew nothing of Amherst's fortunes. His main concern was to prove he was still in business and, to do that, he had to draw out Montcalm. In early August he sent Brigadier James Murray on a raiding expedition above Quebec to test the French defences. Murray marched twelve hundred men along the south shore to rendezvous with Admiral Charles Holmes near the Etchemin River. Flatboats and armed vessels were on hand to transport them upstream. Wolfe usually relied on French deserters for information about Montcalm's deployment of troops and frequently got it wrong. His sources now claimed Colonel Bougainville's patrol along the north shore was two thousand strong. Murray's expedition was expected to come up with an accurate count.

Murray made two attempts to land at Pointe-aux-Trembles and was driven off both times with a considerable loss in dead and wounded. At Deschambault, a post farther up the river, he made a third try and finally got ashore. His men burned a storage depot and a large quantity of spare baggage belonging to the French regulars, a sad loss for soldiers who were already on half-rations and hadn't received any pay for weeks. When Montcalm learned of the assault, he rode toward Deschambault but turned back when he was told the English had already departed. What Montcalm would have done if he *had* met Murray in the village isn't clear. One wonders why the British didn't try to block French transports regularly carrying supplies from Montreal to Quebec; the British had enough armed ships in the Cap-Rouge area to make such attacks feasible. Brigadier Murray apparently didn't consider using his gunboats to fire on French wagons that were hauling badly needed provisions along connecting roads.

By this time, Montcalm regretted the council's earlier decision to send armed frigates and supplies upriver. It's impossible to be sure who first suggested it – Montcalm or Vaudreuil – but if the French frigates had been within range of Deschambault, they might have fought off Admiral Holmes' squadron and prevented the British troops from landing. In any case, neither side treated the action as a serious attempt to gain ground. They looked on it merely as a fact-finding mission.

So far, Amherst had made no attempt to bypass Île-aux-Noix near Lake Champlain because he feared French armed vessels in the area. In early August he finally sent Wolfe an encouraging word about the victory at Fort Niagara, via Ensign Hutchins, an American Ranger. The courier had promised to carry the letter by "a long and circuitous route," an idea supported by the length of time it took the missive to reach Wolfe's camp. Montcalm (whose side lost Fort Niagara) learned of the French defeat on August 9, but Wolfe (whose side won it) didn't hear until August 23, when Brigadier Murray returned with the balance of the British army. The arrival of Amherst's letter was anticlimactic.

Apart from Amherst's failure to communicate and Murray's less than dazzling performance on the upper river, Wolfe had another urgent problem. Fever and dysentery were thinning the ranks so rapidly that if he didn't act soon he wouldn't have enough men fit to fight a skirmish, never mind make an assault on a fortified town. Then, on August 19 came the real catastrophe: Wolfe took to his bed. He could no longer move around the farmhouse, much less sit in meetings or deliver pep talks. Word spread that Wolfe was dying. He lay prostrate in a haze of pain and fever and, fast running out of hope, begged his surgeon for help: "Make me up so that I may be without pain for a few days and able to do my duty. That's all I want." The doctor probably gave him laudanum since that was the drug of choice in those days. An uncertain week passed while the spirits of the British expedition sank steadily and the men whispered among themselves, "There'll be no great victory this season!"

But on August 25, the world turned once again. Captain John Knox, who happened to be stationed in the Wolfe camp, made the following entry in his journal: "His Excellency General Wolfe is on the recovery to the inconceivable joy of the whole army."

The sun shone. The British camp sprang to life. Wolfe's pain was under control and his strength slowly returned; and Murray had returned with the remainder of the army. For the invalid, it was now or never: he dared delay no longer. Major-General James Wolfe swallowed his pride and, with some difficulty, dictated a letter to his three brigadiers asking for their opinion on the best place to attack Quebec.

Captain Knox, sent from the main camp on Île d'Orléans to Wolfe's headquarters beside Montmorency Falls to pick up orders for his brigade, was disappointed to discover Wolfe was too sick to see him. "This is the first opportunity I had of being in that camp, where no pains have been spared to render it impregnable," he noted in his journal. The house was tolerable but Wolfe was "so ill above stairs as not to be able to come down to dinner."

There were no commands for Knox so he was free to venture to the edge of the falls to take a closer look and view the enemy's camp. The "natural curiosity," as he called it, was not as high as it looked, at least on the French side – no more than fifty feet; though others thought differently. He pondered the impressive rush of water: "It is amazing to see so stupendous a cataract from such an insignificant brook."

Standing on a high point, scribbling notes on a piece of paper, he was almost shot for his trouble. "I was hastily called by one of our sentinels," he wrote, "when, throwing my eyes about, I saw a Frenchman creeping under the extremity of their breastwork to fire at me. This obliged me to retire as fast as I could out of his reach." When Knox thanked the guard for alerting him to danger, the soldier said the fellow had snapped his piece twice; the second time, Knox had turned away just in time.

The following day Murray returned from his expedition on the upper river and reported that General Amherst had taken both Ticonderoga and Crown Point, forcing Bourlamaque to retire to Île-aux-Noix with three thousand men, who he claimed were determined to defend it to the last extremity. Closer to home, General Wolfe was recovering and preparing to withdraw from the Montmorency camp.

"We are likewise assured," Knox wrote, "that the whole number of men in arms throughout this province do not exceed twenty-five thousand, including Regulars, Indians and Canadians from the age of sixteen to seventy: that the latter are very discontented and would cheerfully surrender their capital if they had people of resolution among them to excite and encourage a revolt."

15

Wolfe's Letter to Pitt

"When the artillery and troops are landed, a corps will be left to service the landing while the rest march on and endeavour to bring the Canadians and French to a battle."

— JAMES WOLFE, 1759

For the people of Quebec a more desperate summer can scarcely be imagined. On the night of July 12 mortars lobbed from Point Lévis racked up three hundred direct hits. Before the British set up a battery on Point Lévis, French engineers had assured residents that only Lower Town was in danger. But they were wrong. Along with many other buildings in the heart of Upper Town, the Ursuline convent was severely damaged and the nuns fled to the General Hospital. Two weeks later an observer said, "[A]ll the centre of Upper Town was gutted, including the cathedral." By August 8, 152 houses near the wharves had been reduced to ashes and the church, Nôtre Dame des Victoires, was destroyed. The French, dangerously low on gunpowder, responded with a feeble show of cannon fire.

As summer melted into fall, the quality of life in the colony worsened. Captain Joseph Goreham and his Rangers raided farms downriver, seized any animals they could find and burned dozens of fine old houses. Redcoats gathered cartloads of vegetables to meet Wolfe's demands, leaving farmers to scrabble in the dirt for the leftovers. Private citizens hunted game and dined on salt cod, a dish they had once despised as fit only for sailors. Wolfe's men confiscated most of the cattle, and the colonists consumed all the pigs, sheep and goats. Reluctantly, they added horsemeat to their diet. By all accounts Canadians had far more horses than they needed and, at first, the consumption of horsemeat helped ease the shortage of food. But even this source dried up and the spectre of hunger once again haunted ordinary people. Just as worrying as all these problems was the governor's order to scoop up thousands of young men for the militia – it meant women, children and old men had to bring in the harvest.

The life of officials remained much the same as before. Their tables were laden with rich food and they drank good wine, but the scene had shifted from town house to country estate. Faces at the table changed when members of the elite joined the army or sailed for France. The glittering charades in the intendant's palace were scaled down in L'hermitage, Bigot's hideaway near Charlesbourg, but gambling was still a favourite pastime. The thinly disguised hatred between Montcalm and Vaudreuil was now glaringly obvious when they met on official business. Their two orbits seldom intersected at social events.

Montcalm still had a band of loyal officers around him, but he missed airing his complaints to Bourlamaque (stuck on Île-aux-Noix) and venting his frustrations over a glass of wine with Bougainville (pounding up and down the river road, wearing out the horses). In happier days, Montcalm had found Lévis a genial fellow but, since he remained on good terms with the governor, Montcalm feared he might tell tales. Montcalm found it difficult to curb his tongue, and once the governor heard a bit of gossip it was only a ship away from the Court of Versailles.

Rumours reached Quebec that Amherst was heading for Montreal and Lévis was dispatched to cope with the crisis. It was all talk, of course – Montreal wasn't even in Amherst's dreams let alone his game plan. But no one in power seemed to realize it – not Vaudreuil, not Montcalm, not even Wolfe, who still had vague hopes that Amherst would join him soon to assault Quebec. But with Lévis in Montreal, the general's worries about loose talk became a moot point. These were lonely days for the Marquis de Montcalm.

Meanwhile, Bigot was in L'hermitage risking all his money, dropping as much as two hundred thousand livres a night at the gambling table. He still clutched at the idea that he could recoup his losses from the king's revenues. After all, people still paid taxes; it was just harder to collect them. Bigot was agitated by the growing number of poisonous letters from the minister of marine, Nicolas-René Berryer, especially one that questioned his non-distribution of gifts to the Indians. (Actually, Bigot had sold the cargo and kept the money.) There was a tidal wave of overdue bills on his desk that the minister in Paris refused to pay from the royal treasury and Bigot wondered if his patroness, Madame de Pompadour, had abandoned him. In the back of his mind, he envisioned the situation if the French lost their colonies in North America. Bigot and all his colleagues would be hauled back to France, perhaps to face an inquiry. Was it possible that he, the great Bigot, would see the inside of the Bastille?

Fortunately, things were brighter in his love life. Major Péan, the cuckolded husband of Angélique, had returned to France with a considerable fortune, leaving his wife to preside over the intendant's orgies. In Bigot's case, crime did pay, because at a time when many of the king's men were feeling deprived of sensual pleasures, the intendant found wine, women and gambling more available than ever before.

The thick stone walls of Bigot's country hideaway had been built in the previous century to resist attacks from warring Iroquois, and the ruins of a defence tower were still visible in the garden. The place was peaceful now. The gabled façade overlooked a rippling brook, giving it a fairy-tale air, and a single leafy lane leading into the estate made it easy for Bigot's hirelings to guard his privacy. Yet even here, servants talked. Stories leaked out about wild parties, duels, seductions, kidnapping and even murder. The people of Quebec, suffering from too much bombing and too little bread, repeated the tales, adding touches of their own. It was said, for example, that the intendant's palace in town was "plain" compared with his country house, where the gilt chandeliers and huge oil paintings cost more money than the whole population of Canada earned in a lifetime.

In the eighteenth century the poor were accustomed to, if not exactly delighted by, the huge gap between themselves and the rich. It had always been that way and, if they hadn't been hungry in the summer of 1759, they might not have been so quick to condemn. But many people *were* hungry, and they came to hate Bigot and his cronies. So far, they had respected Governor Vaudreuil; after all, he was Canadian and avoided the excesses of Intendant Bigot and his sidekick, Joseph Cadet. But times were changing and colonists now realized their governor's simple-minded strategies had endangered them. The rich saw things differently. Their privileges were taken for granted and there was no change unless the death of a friend or relative sent a chill down some aristocratic spine. People with power and money were often immune to the inconveniences of war.

Until that final summer, the governor had presided over the council and shared many grand events with the intendant and the general, but it was believed that he had never stolen from the king. Vaudreuil's supporters took the line that he merely looked the other way while others profited. Whether Vaudreuil shared the wealth or not, he and his wife lived in considerable style; he was the king's representative and, as governor, he had at his disposal the Château Louis in Quebec, a lavish house in Montreal and a country place, La Canardière, near Beauport.

Vaudreuil was given the nod for doing a good job as governor of Louisiana. Yet not everyone viewed him in a kindly light. Lord Loudon, commander of the British Army in America in 1757, blamed Vaudreuil for cruelties practised by Canadian troops. "[T]he knowledge I have of Mr. Vaudreuil's behaviour when in Louisiana, from his own letters, and the murders committed at Oswego and now at Fort William Henry, will oblige me to make those gentlemen sick of such inhumane villany [sic] whenever it is in my power," Lord Loudon wrote.

Discrimination against the regulars by colonials was a chief bone of contention in Canada. Colonel Bougainville, himself a regular, complained, "We are treated as the Spartans treated the Helots," adding, "Vaudreuil is a timid man, who can neither make a resolution nor keep one. When V. produces an idea he falls in love with it as Pygmalion did with his statue."

In August 1759, Montcalm could no longer ignore the fact that the French position in North America was crumbling. The loss of Fort Niagara, Ticonderoga and Crown Point was a severe blow, as was the British reoccupation of Oswego (a fort he himself had once seized). Both sides believed that only Brigadier Bourlamaque and his small force on Île-aux-Noix stood between Amherst's army and the swift capture of Montreal. Despite his promotion to lieutenant-governor and his friends, Montcalm was a lonely gladiator.

When Prime Minister William Pitt read Wolfe's report on the failure at Montmorency Falls, it almost unhinged him. He was fifty-two years old and at the peak of his political power. The king, the cabinet, in fact the whole country, depended on him to win the war against France. Mentally he was a giant, but physically he was frail. In his public school days gout had prevented him from playing athletic games and severe fits of depression had frequently confined him to his bed. When he was forty, he told his sister, Ann, that he had a "disorder of the bowel." Doctors believed that most of Pitt's problems were inherited: gout was common among his relatives, several of his ancestors were said to have been violent and the family history was riddled with rash marriages, bitter feuds and outright madness. King George II hated William Pitt, but in the late 1750s His Majesty was forced to conclude that the government would collapse without him.

Despite his flaws, Pitt was such a magnet that when he made a speech in Parliament there wasn't an empty seat in the house. Members listened to him as they would to Handel's *Messiah:* hushed and hypnotized. According to Lord Chesterfield, "Mr. Pitt carried with him an unpremeditated strength of thunder and the splendour of lightning." Others admired his melodious voice, his piercing eye and his overwrought acting. Most of his political peers admitted he had the finest mind in England, although a few believed him to be a dangerous lunatic.

However outlandish Pitt's plans might have been for England, he was the only man in power who had any plans at all. In the fall of 1759 he was consumed with the idea of creating an ever-expanding Empire, and one of the pillars on which his scheme rested was a smashing victory at Quebec. He had handpicked Wolfe for the job, placing his faith in a young firebrand who promised miracles. And so, when he read Wolfe's devastating description of the failed assault on July 31, his vision blurred. Yet he could not ignore Wolfe's lucid letter: "The obstacles we have met in the campaign are much greater than we had reason to expect … I could not flatter myself that I should be able to reduce Quebec." It was a warning – failure at Quebec was likely. Wolfe then went on to admit his part in the debacle at Montmorency Falls and later, in the same document, added, "I found myself so ill, and am still so weak, that I begged the general officers to consult together for the general utility." Here, he referred to his request for advice from the brigadiers. Near the end of the letter Wolfe remarked, "By the list of disabled officers, many of whom are of rank, you may perceive that the army is much weakened. In this situation there is such a choice of difficulties that I own myself at a loss how to determine."

Pitt's delicately balanced mind must have tilted when he read such a confession. Yet he did not doubt its accuracy; rather, he caught

Wolfe's despair, something the author hadn't foreseen when he reported in such agonizing detail. Pitt being Pitt, he instantly passed the news along to his cabinet and from there it reached the public.

On September 3 Wolfe wrote a second letter, this one to the secretary of state, the Earl of Holdernesse, conveying much the same message. "The Marquis of Montcalm has a numerous body of armed men (I cannot call it an army) and the strongest country in the world," Wolfe wrote. "I am so far recovered as to do business; but my constitution is ruined without the consolation of doing any considerable service to the state and without any prospect of it." After reading this letter, Pitt and a large portion of the population virtually went into mourning.

At the Court of Versailles, the picture was just as bleak but for different reasons. Madame de Pompadour and the king now worked in a room where the red lacquered walls were covered with maps instead of Boucher paintings. A story made the rounds that Pompadour used artificial "beauty spots" to mark the position of her army on the continent. Although it wasn't publicly acknowledged, the country was low on funds, the French navy a mere shadow and the army commanded by incompetent generals. Neither king nor marquise held out any hope that Canada would get enough support to defeat the English. The leaders there needed to do what they could with what they had.

Wolfe's problems were equally devastating. His army was riddled with disease, his brigadiers considered him a figure of fun and his commander, Major-General Amherst (far from posing a threat to Montreal), had gone into the business of building roads and forts. Wolfe was on his own.

Part Three

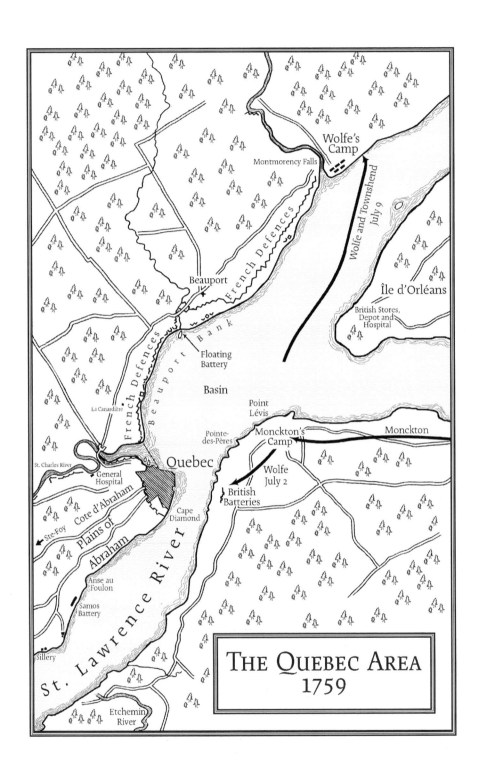

Wolfe's
Camp

Montmorency Falls

Wolfe and Townshend July 9

Île d'Orléans

British Stores,
Depot and
Hospital

French Defences

Beauport

Floating
Battery

Beauport Bank

French Defences

Basin

Point
Lévis

Pointe-
des-Pères

Monckton's
Camp

Monckton

La Canardière

Quebec

St. Charles River

General
Hospital

Wolfe
July 2

British
Batteries

Côte d'Abraham

Ste-Foy

Plains of

Cape
Diamond

Abraham

Anse au
Foulon

Samos
Battery

St. Lawrence River

Sillery

Etchemin
River

THE QUEBEC AREA
1759

16

A Hazardous Scheme

*"I would cheerfully sacrifice a leg or an arm
to be in possession of Quebec."*

— JAMES WOLFE, August 1759

Laudanum, a painkiller consisting of opium suspended in alcohol, is usually associated with dreams. Thomas De Quincey's *Confessions of an English Opium Eater,* describing his architectural fantasies, provides an excellent example of how the drug normally works. But laudanum had a very different effect on General Wolfe. After a dose on September 5, he arose from his sickbed to supervise the exodus of three thousand redcoats from Montmorency Falls to Île d'Orléans, where they had first landed. Perhaps it looked like a backward step to the French. To Wolfe, it was part of a grander plan.

Montcalm assumed his opponent was gathering his troops to sail for home, which was what *he* would have done in similar circumstances, when in fact the Englishman was conspiring to bring about the Frenchman's downfall. Watching Wolfe's latest idiocy from the west bank of the falls, Montcalm made a half-hearted attempt to cut off the British before they embarked and, when that didn't do the job, let loose a brief fusillade at the loaded boats in midstream. The British didn't flinch. In fact, they hung around for four hours pretending to threaten Beauport and then rowed calmly to the western tip of Orléans. In the evening, with all regiments safely ashore, the general pitched his marquee between the 43rd and 78th, much to the delight of diarist Knox, who wrote, "His Excellency dined in our camp and was heard to say that he had just received a letter from General Amherst." A message from the commander-in-chief was such a rare event that Wolfe turned it into dinner conversation. Amherst claimed it took all his heavy artillery to blow Bourlamaque out of Fort Ticonderoga and then Crown Point, implying the French had put up a stiff fight. At first, Wolfe took this to mean Amherst would soon be rushing to his aid with thousands of men, a vision so intoxicating he lost his head and beamed for the duration of the meal.

Alone in his tent, Wolfe had second thoughts. Hadn't French deserters told Brigadier Murray a different story back in August? According to them, Bourlamaque had "abandoned both forts and fled to Île-aux-Noix, allowing the British to walk in unmolested." Given that scenario, Amherst's victories seemed less impressive. Wolfe reread the letter carefully and realized he had jumped the gun – his commander-in-chief hadn't promised to join him at Quebec, at least, not *this* year. Once again Wolfe's mood sank into despair.

Wolfe would have been more depressed if he'd known what was going on at Crown Point. Amherst was mesmerized by the number of armed vessels Bourlamaque had assembled to protect his little island and, when he heard another had been added, felt compelled to build an armed sloop as insurance. Besides, it was late in the season, and his ardour cooled with the weather. Soon lakes and rivers would freeze, wiping out any chance of a successful attack from the water. God knows, he had plenty of projects to keep him busy: begging Albany for winter provisions for his two pet forts, making hay while the sun shone to feed the workhorses he had collected throughout the summer, and demanding back wages for his troops.

Construction at Crown Point was going full tilt (in the end, the renovation would cost the British government three million pounds sterling), and new roads on either side of Lake George were a credit to him. As for Amherst's own winter plans, he talked of the fancy balls, rich dinners and fine wines he would share with his friends in New York society. He had no intention of toughing it out on the frosty shores of Lake Champlain.

Where Major-General Jeffrey Amherst spent the winter of 1760 and his curious method of getting there will be described later.

After dark on September 5, the 43rd, Captain Knox's regiment, forded the Etchemin River on the south shore of the St. Lawrence. They found the current swift, the stones slippery and the water thigh high, but managed to make it to the other side. The following day, the Light Infantry, 28th, 35th, 47th, 58th, Louisbourg Grenadiers and Monckton's regiment joined them, with the Grenadiers on the right, Bragg's on the left and senior regiments in the centre. Colonel Howe's Light Infantry formed the vanguard and Major Dalling's brought up the rear. Two files from each platoon were assigned to cover the flanks with the following orders: "When the woods are out of musket-shot, they [the platoons on the flanks] are to keep near to the battalion, and when within musket-shot, to march within the skirts of the woods." The British had learned the dangers of moving through the forest without special vigilance.

As the troops were about to set out, word arrived that General Wolfe had suffered a relapse and might be dying, whereupon a cloud of doubt gathered over the camp. Even so, the march went forward under heavy fire from the French across the St. Lawrence. The ever-optimistic Knox found a silver lining – his regiment boarded the frigate *Seahorse,* where Captain Smith and his officers entertained them in "a most princely manner." This treatment applied only to officers, of course; life for enlisted men continued in the same old way.

By evening, with the bulk of the army mustered at the Etchemin, a second bulletin swept through the ranks – Wolfe was out of danger and already aboard the *Sutherland,* running the show. The troops breathed a sigh of relief; but not the three brigadiers, who were still smarting over past rebuffs and what they believed to be their leader's incompetence and tactical errors.

In response to Wolfe's request a week earlier for advice about where he ought to land the army, the brigadiers offered several droll suggestions. Wolfe might "land twenty-five hundred men with more to follow in the night without great loss." And the place? Somewhere on the upper river between Jacques-Cartier and Cap-Rouge. Indeed, the landing itself might have worked well in that area, but the army would have had between twelve and fifteen miles to march through enemy territory before reaching Quebec. The brigadiers also mentioned that army transports might carry enough supplies for *two months.*

Because they had brought up the question of landing as high as Jacques-Cartier, the brigadiers later claimed they had first proposed such a scheme and Wolfe did not deserve so much credit for the victory. Doubt still haunts this part of Wolfe's story. In fact, Townshend and Murray claimed Wolfe had hijacked their plan. Wolfe's own letters prove otherwise. To his Uncle Walter, Wolfe wrote in May 1759,

> The town of Quebec is poorly fortified but the ground around about it is rocky ... If I find that the enemy is strong, audacious and well commanded, I shall proceed with the utmost caution and circumspection, giving Mr. Amherst time to use his superiority. If they are timid, weak and ignorant we shall push them with more vivacity, that we may be able before the summer is gone to assist the Commander-in-Chief. I reckon we shall have a smart action at the passage of the river St. Charles unless we can steal a detachment up the river St. Lawrence and land them three, four, five miles or more above the town and get time to entrench so strongly that they won't care to attack.

By August 28, when Wolfe dictated his request to the brigadiers, he had toyed several times with plans to land upriver. The suggestion offered by the brigadiers concerning provisions – that two months' worth was needed – is so absurd it is scarcely remembered. A two-month supply of food implies that Wolfe had that much time in which to execute the assault – which is false. Saunders had warned Wolfe he intended to pack up his ships and go home within a week. And what if the British lost the battle? No official plan existed to keep large numbers of British troops on Canadian soil that winter unless they occupied Quebec as a victorious army. Were the brigadiers' pathetic suggestions the best Wolfe's senior officers could come up with? The beleaguered general must have wondered if he and his brigadiers were on the same planet.

Wolfe's last letter to his mother, dated September 1, began, as usual, "Dear Madam" – a common form of address at the time. In it, James employed his ironic style without revealing how desperate the situation was. "My writing to you will convince you that no personal evils, worse than defeats and disappointments, have fallen upon me. The enemy puts nothing to risk, and I can't in all conscience, put the whole army to risk."

The expression "no personal evils have fallen upon me" was meant as a joke. A personal evil had indeed befallen him – he was so sick he tried to make light of it, knowing his mother would understand. Those close to him felt it was only a matter of time before he collapsed again, and Wolfe had told both Prime Minister Pitt and Lord Holdernesse that his "constitution was ruined." On September 6, when James Wolfe joined Admiral Holmes near Cap-Rouge, he was propped up with drugs, was disenchanted with Amherst and hadn't the faintest idea how long he could function as commander. Only four days after dashing off that cavalier remark to his mother, he was again flat on his back. A miracle would raise him one last time. Or was it his own spirit combined with that old black magic called laudanum?

When he boarded the *Sutherland* to take charge of the Quebec operation, General James Wolfe had seven days to live.

On September 7 Wolfe cruised upriver on the sloop *Hunter,* escorted by a squadron of twenty-two vessels. At Cap-Rouge he scanned the French floating batteries and fortifications around the inlet. On a whim, or so it seemed, he ordered his troops to pile into flatboats and his warships to bombard the shore. Colonel Bougainville, thinking it was a full-scale raid, brought his cavalry pounding down the beach to return fire. Just as things were really hotting up, the rains came and Wolfe withdrew. Perhaps he was only teasing the French or trying to confuse them.

On the morning of the 8th, it was still pouring and at least half Wolfe's army was drenched. Concerned as always about the comfort of his soldiers, he sent them ashore at the village of Saint-Nicolas on the south shore of the St. Lawrence. Bougainville, watching the scene through his spyglass, was puzzled. Were the redcoats crazy? What did this mean? Apparently it didn't occur to him that the British were soaked to the skin and simply drying out their uniforms and stretching their legs. But Bougainville wasn't the only French officer who misread Wolfe's scenic tours up and down the St. Lawrence. Vaudreuil received reports of Wolfe's antics with growing disdain. "The movements of these vessels, the removal of heavy artillery from Point Lévis and the lateness of the season all combined to announce the speedy departure of the fleet," he wrote to Bourlamaque, who was still stuck on Île-aux-Noix. "Everything proves that the grand design of the English has failed."

Montcalm's note to Bourlamaque, scrawled at about the same time, took a somewhat doleful view: "The night is dark; it rains; I am in my boots. My horses are saddled. I wish you were here for I cannot be everywhere and have not taken off my clothes since the 23rd of June." This may have been an exaggeration, since Montcalm was given to dramatic flourishes when he was agitated. On September 11, less than forty-eight hours before the battle, Montcalm dispatched a final note to Bourlamaque (perhaps his last written communication to anyone): "I am overwhelmed with work. I give the enemy another month to stay here."

Even at this late date, Montcalm wasn't worried about defending the heights near the town – he believed a large body of troops couldn't scale them. As he remarked to Vaudreuil during one of their rare meetings, "I swear to you that a hundred men posted there would stop their whole army."

Four days before Wolfe and his army materialized on the Plains of Abraham, he was chafing at the foul weather, his wretched health and his fading hope of glory. The ninth of September brought high winds and still more rain. He huddled in his ship's cabin with Admiral Holmes, sifting through dribs and drabs of information they had squeezed out of French deserters. One such crumb claimed the French intended to send shiploads of badly needed food and ammunition to the capital on the night of September 12. Wolfe, looking for a way to turn a bit of information to his own use, wondered if the enemy ships might serve as a cover for his flatboats; a wild card, certainly, but he filed it away.

Amherst's journal in early September gave the impression that he and Wolfe were fighting two different wars. True, Wolfe had a separate command, but Amherst was still his commander-in-chief and theoretically, they had the same goal – to conquer Canada before the snow fell. Yet Amherst made only a few casual references to military action on the St. Lawrence.

On September 1 Amherst believed that Bourlamaque's position on Île-aux-Noix was "very strong." The next day, French deserters dragged back to Crown Point for questioning admitted that Bourlamaque had a new sloop with sixteen guns. Amherst immediately ordered a party to attack and "try & burn it … The Enemy is trying to have a superior force by water." Amherst complained, as if this were a novel idea, "I sent to Captain Loring to come to me that I may build a sloop as soon as the brig is finished."

On September 3, Amherst noted that the guns ordered from Fort Edward had arrived at Crown Point, and the next day he sent a party of thirteen under Sergeant Hopkins to set fire to the new French sloop moored off Île-aux-Noix. Fear of Bourlamaque's naval strength ruined Amherst's hope of proceeding on to assault Montreal. In fact, his obsession with the "invincible" little island could be construed as an excuse to postpone an attack until spring. On September 5, he mentioned cutting a road to Fort Oswego; the day after that he sent out a party of ninety men to search for the enemy along the shores of Lake George, but they saw nothing and returned to base. On the seventh he directed the making of hand grenades, "which may be of service if I should have an opportunity at trying to surprise Montreal." This was vague language for a man supposedly hurrying north to the St. Lawrence River.

On September 8, Governor Pownall sent word from Albany that he had been told by a ship's master just arrived from Wolfe's camp that the British were "talking of fortifying" Île-aux-Coudres and Gaspé for the coming winter. People were saying that Wolfe probably wouldn't assault Quebec this season. Amherst responded, "I flatter myself, notwithstanding the Master's news, Mr. Wolfe will take Quebec." It was a rare show of support for Wolfe's abilities, but included no promise to assist him in the coming battle.

Amherst's entry on September 9 was devoted to the problem of supplying spruce beer for the army's good health, particularly the colonials "who, if left to themselves, would eat fried pork and lay in their tents all day long."

Wolfe spent the first week of September weighing the risks of a major attack on Quebec, but between bad weather and his own ill health his will to assault the fortress again wavered – would he or wouldn't he set a definite date for the siege? His senior officers were anxious to hear what he had to say. Wolfe's indecision ended abruptly when Admiral Saunders, drumming his fingers in the Quebec Basin, announced it was time to take his big ships home. He gave Wolfe a few days to either fight or pack it in. On Monday, September 10, as Amherst was making up his mind to procure a large supply of spruce beer, Wolfe set out to find the magic gateway to the heights. His party included Monckton, Townshend, Holmes and Carleton, observing the village of Sillery from a spot on the south shore.

It was one of those crisp autumn days when the air is like crystal, and Wolfe noticed a small cove and a trail zigzagging up the steep cliff. The sight made his heart flip. He'd been aware of l'Anse au Foulon for some time, but he'd never been able to make out so much detail. Yes! This was the place! His mind skipped forward – given a moonless night and a bit of luck, landing on this slender curve of sand just *might* be possible. A cluster of small tents at the top of the path indicated a sentry post, but there was no sign of life. Obviously, the French saw this area as completely secure. Wolfe saw it as a window of opportunity.

Wolfe had studied the winds and tides along the river even after the disaster at Montmorency Falls. Saunders had managed to sail his big ships upriver as far as Cap-Rouge by taking advantage of strong easterly winds. Now the winds had turned westerly, perhaps for only a few days, but it suited Wolfe's latest plan – if only the rain would hold off. Well, some chances had to be taken in any worthwhile enterprise and, when he considered the benefits, Wolfe was sure he was right to make his move. L'Anse au Foulon was the place, and September 13 was the day.

Although two of Wolfe's brigadiers were with him on that fateful Monday, he didn't disclose his final plan to them. Deserters passed back and forth between French and English camps almost every day. And if even one man learned the secret, he might tell Montcalm – who would then post a regiment at the top of the path. If that happened, the French could blow Wolfe's advance party right out of the water. Wolfe did, however, confide in his close friend Colonel Ralph Burton the same night, but said nothing to his brigadiers – which showed how little he trusted them.

When Wolfe got back to the *Sutherland* that afternoon, a surprise awaited him: Saunders had sent Captain James Chads of the *Vesuvius* to organize the landing boats. Wolfe was always willing to accept a gift from the gods, and he made Chads the subject of an extraordinary general order the next day:

> *To the Army before Quebec September 11, 1759.*
> Captain Chads, of the Navy, has received the General's direction in respect to the order in which the troops move and are to land: and no officer must attempt the least alteration, or interfere with Captain Chads' particular province, lest as the boats move in the night there may be disorder and confusion among them.

Conferring so much power on a captain was unheard of and created an instant buzz in the officers' quarters. The question on everyone's lips was "Who is this Captain Chads?" Not much was known about the man then, nor is much known today. Chads was approximately the same age as General Wolfe and had been on the Rochefort expedition in 1757. It's possible Chads commanded the ship that carried Wolfe to Île d'Aix after the British captured the island. In any event, Saunders felt that when it came to moving troops over water, he was the man for the job. At the eleventh hour Chads joined Rear-Admiral Holmes and General Wolfe in secret consultations. Chads, and Chads alone, knew every detail concerning the landing at l'Anse au Foulon. The three brigadiers were left out in the cold.

At Crown Point the same day, Amherst received a visitor. Major Robert Stobo, a self-promoting officer, once a prisoner in Quebec and now looking for employment, came directly from the British camp with the latest news. Most of Wolfe's army and a chunk of the navy, he told Amherst, were fifteen miles upriver from Quebec and ready to sweep down upon the capital. Amherst was so unimpressed by Stobo that he barely noted the man's arrival. More importantly, he showed little curiosity about Wolfe's present situation. Perhaps he was preoccupied with a little intrigue of his own making.

As far back as August, Amherst had unsuccessfully tried to achieve a détente with some of the eastern tribes. In September, he had sent Captain Kennedy and Lieutenant Hamilton to territories south of the St. Lawrence River with letters of introduction to the chiefs, saying the officers were to be treated as his ambassadors. Escorting them were a native Ranger called Captain Jacobs and four Stockbridge Indians. As well as the introductions, they carried papers for General Wolfe outlining Amherst's future plans. Amherst must have known that if these plans fell into the wrong hands the situation could be extremely dangerous, but he believed that the Indians would treat Kennedy and Hamilton as honoured guests. Like most British officers, Amherst had little grasp of the intricacies of Indian politics.

Kennedy's mission was benign enough: he was merely to ask the various chiefs to assist the British army or, if they couldn't promise that, to remain neutral in the current struggle. Amherst's orders to Kennedy read in part, "Go through the settlements of the Eastern Indians with a proposal from me and take their answer to Mr. [sic] Wolfe whom I have directed to treat them accordingly."

The Kennedy party accidentally wandered into a group of Abenaki hunters from the village of St. Francis, who captured them and seized their papers. The two Englishmen were then given, or sold, to French officers in Montreal. Amherst was, of course, furious when he learned about the incident from Captain Disserat, a messenger from Île-aux-Noix who had come to negotiate an exchange of prisoners. (It was merely a coincidence that Stobo showed up at Crown Point on the same day.) Disserat was astonished at Amherst's angry reaction when he told him about the fate of Kennedy and Hamilton.

The French officer figured Amherst would be happy to make the trade and retrieve his officers but, instead, the commander did a slow burn over what he called "the gall of the St. Francis tribe who had insulted not only me, but the King of England!" Amherst was well aware that American border settlers hated the St. Francis Indians because for years they had committed unspeakable cruelties against American settlers. They belonged to the Abenaki tribe, but had converted to Catholicism and received regular visits from a priest. The village boasted a church with a steeple and a bell.

Amherst was right about one thing: every segment of society on the eastern seaboard feared the Indians from St. Francis. If he wiped them out, Amherst thought, it would be a credit to him and to the British. And yet, it could be argued that when the British stooped to the same acts of depravity, they became no better than their victims. It seems this idea didn't occur to General Amherst.

As the negotiations with Captain Disserat continued, Amherst couldn't get the St. Francis incident out of his mind – and within twenty-four hours, a plan was set in motion. On September 12, he noted in his journal, "I ordered a detachment of 220 chosen men under the command of Major Rogers to go and destroy the St. Francis Indian Settlements on the south side of the St. Lawrence, not letting anyone but Major Rogers know what it was about or where he was going."

Rogers and his Rangers left Crown Point on September 13 (the day Wolfe and Montcalm clashed on the Plains of Abraham) guided by a handful of Mohawks provided by General Amherst. Some of the Mohawks (who often switched sides from English to French and back again without explanation) got wind of the proposed raid on St. Francis and betrayed Rogers to Canadian bushrangers lurking in the neighbourhood. The defecting Mohawks pretended to be incensed on behalf of their former allies, the St. Francis Indians. But it was well-known they detested the Rangers, and their personal feelings were at least partly to blame for the betrayal.

The Canadians and the Mohawk deserters set out in pursuit of the Rangers and, after only three days, stole a stash of boats and provisions Major Rogers had left behind. When Rogers discovered the loss it came as a serious blow, forcing his party to travel the rest of the way on foot – a distance of some two hundred miles – without rations. A less egotistical leader might have returned with his followers to Crown Point to pick up new supplies, but Rogers plunged ahead, saying he feared his French pursuers more than he feared Mother Nature.

Rogers was the only man who knew the way forward without a map, so most of the men stayed with him. Noticing they were demoralized and hoping to buck them up, the major gave a stirring rendition of Amherst's orders, a portion of which ran:

> Remember the barbarities that have been committed by the enemy's Indian scoundrels on every occasion where they had an opportunity of showing their infamous cruelties … [T]ake your revenge but don't forget [that] though those villains have dastardly and promiscuously murdered women and children of all ages, it is my orders that *no* women or children are to be killed or hurt.

Although the men rallied, it was a bad start to a venture already fraught with danger. In the next three weeks, the Rangers made an incredible journey; Rogers, a charismatic wonder-man, led them through icy bogs and trackless thickets on a diet of shrivelled berries and uncooked squirrel. One of their own scouts warned Rogers that the Mohawks and Canadians were close behind, a piece of information that spurred the men on more than any speech by their leader.

A few deserters did manage to get back to Crown Point. They reported that the Rangers were in trouble, but Amherst didn't order a rescue team. Shortly afterward, Rogers dispatched a request for provisions to be left at a well-known depot where he could pick them up. Amherst honoured that request, but there seemed to be a curse on the whole affair. When Rogers and his starving men reached the supply drop, someone had been there first and made off with the boats and every scrap of food.

Meanwhile, the Rangers staggered on, many without shoes or moccasins, their clothes in tatters. There was no game in the area – even Rogers was mystified by the aura of death that hung over the land – and finally the men were reduced to eating the roots of water plants. Day after day they pushed on, cold and wet and hungry, often leaving their dying comrades behind. At times they took shelter among clumps of fallen logs that cut the wind. Lighting a fire was taboo in this bleak landscape, since smoke was the great betrayer. By October 4, when the detachment reached the St. Francis River, it numbered only one hundred and forty – they had lost eighty men. The river was shallow, and Rogers showed his followers how to make a human chain so they could safely cross to the eastern bank. They were still fifteen miles from their target.

One frosty day, just before dawn, the Rangers hid in the bushes at the edge of St. Francis. When the mist cleared they could see at least two dozen shacks, not in neat rows but all higgledy-piggledy, as if they'd been tossed down by a giant hand. A huge stump shaped like a drum stood in a central clearing, surrounded by tall poles draped with hairy scalps waving in the wind. The place was silent. Rogers figured a celebration the night before had left the whole village in a stupor. He ordered his men to fan out, keep silent and let no warrior escape.

The Rangers loaded their rifles. Major Rogers gave the sign, and the men rushed toward the shacks – shrieking, smashing in doors and set-ting fire to the buildings. Although the Rangers were all exhausted and some were half-dead, they managed to murder two hundred warriors in the next half-hour and even recapture the few who got away. An uncounted number of Indian women and children burned to death inside the blazing shacks. Others fled into the woods.

Before long, the screaming and shooting stopped. A reek of burning cloth and roasted flesh fouled the air. Rogers rushed down to the river to make sure not a single warrior escaped by canoe. It was essential to prevent news of the slaughter from reaching other settlements.

When the Rangers first arrived at St. Francis, Rogers had posted a guard near the central drum where prisoners were to be deposited. There he found eight settlers – three women and five children – for whom he was now responsible. Afraid that his French pursuers would arrive at any moment, Rogers bellowed, "The French are coming! Let's get out of here!" But starving men must eat, and his raiders stopped long enough to chew a little dry corn and fill their pockets before scurrying off.

Rogers checked out the bleak landscape with his sharp blue eyes, spotted the laggards and rounded them up. Their French and Indian pursuers were nowhere to be seen and, taking the women and children with them, the Rangers vanished into the trees, leaving the doomed village to burn itself out. The slaughter had lasted exactly one hour.

In the British camp across the river from Cap-Rouge, Wolfe posted general orders on Tuesday, September 11. Once the troops knew an attack on Quebec was imminent they cheered. Quartermaster-Sergeant John Johnson of the 58th, yet another diarist with the expedition, thought he understood their reaction. "The men were ready," he wrote, "how could it be otherwise, being at the heels of gentlemen whose whole thrust, equal with their General, was for glory?"

As usual, the three brigadiers saw things differently. They were outraged, not because the battle was scheduled but because the precise landing place wasn't named in the orders. Wolfe hadn't informed them privately, either. Obviously they no longer enjoyed his confidence – hardly surprising after months of bitterness and mistrust. It was doubly maddening to the brigadiers to discover that Admiral Saunders (still aboard the *Neptune* preparing a feint against the Beauport lines) knew all the details, as did Admiral Holmes. Even the upstart Captain Chads was in on the secret. By the time the brigadiers met with Wolfe on the morning of September 12, they had worked up such a head of steam that words were raw and sharp. Although Wolfe must have known why they were so angry, he later confessed to a close friend that meeting them that day was like stumbling into a bear pit.

Wolfe's last day was a mixture of risk and rage. Like a crazed gambler, he was betting everything on a single throw of the dice, and the stakes were high: his reputation, the blood of his men, the glory of England. He was so wound up he had little need of medication. His scheme was hazardous for several reasons. There was a chance his army might be squashed between Bougainville's patrol from the west and Montcalm's army from the east. And to add to his concerns Wolfe was well aware that if forced to retreat, he had no escape route. And if he won, he had no specific plan for ruling Quebec.

A member of Wolfe's staff, present at meetings that day, described how the three brigadiers stormed out of Admiral Holmes' cabin late in the afternoon and retired to their own quarters to hash over the way Wolfe had handled matters. After they'd left, Wolfe burst into an explosive rage, saying they had "brought him up the river and now flinched: two of them were cowards and one was a villain." Even Captain Chads, encouraged by the acid tongues of his superiors, expressed doubts about certain aspects of Wolfe's scheme. The general retorted that Chads ought to have spoken up sooner and that he, General James Wolfe, would take full responsibility for any changes he made to the earlier plan.

For Wolfe, a dithering Chads must have been the last straw, and yet by evening the general's natural tenacity and ambition had restored his buoyancy. At about 8:30, just as he was trying to clear his mind for the task ahead, a letter arrived from the three brigadiers: "Sir," it concluded, "as we do not think ourselves sufficiently informed … we must beg leave to request from you distinct orders … as to the place we are to attack."

Wolfe's reply was brief: "It is not a usual thing to point out in the publick orders the direct spot of an attack, nor for any inferior officer not charged with a particular duty to ask instructions upon that point." But he went on to answer the question anyway: "At the Foulon, distant two miles or two and a half miles from Quebec."

Even Admiral Holmes, who had been supportive of Wolfe throughout the summer, was dubious about the night's adventure. Long after it was over, he gave his opinion of the affair: "It was the most hazardous and difficult task I was ever engaged in."

Major-General James Wolfe retired to his cabin for a rest, rose from his bed at about one in the morning, ate breakfast and, with the help of his valet, François, prepared for the most important day of his life. On the whole, Wolfe dressed conservatively: white breeches, white linen shirt and an embroidered waistcoat. His scarlet frock coat, with its gilt buttons and gold braid denoting his rank, was brand new. The coat was lined with blue silk. Some accounts have him wearing soft leather gaiters, but one report states unequivocally that he wore tall black boots which François had polished to a high shine. Wolfe had ordered a great many pairs of boots before he left England. The British had brought no horses, so it's highly unlikely the star of the show would wear gaiters when he was compelled to lead his army on foot. As usual, his hat was big, black and jaunty. He was always meticulous about his clothing.

17

Enemy Forces Seem Considerable

"I will fight them with an ardour and even a fury which exceeds the range of their ambitious designs."

– GOVERNOR VAUDREUIL, 1759

Early on Wednesday, September 12, General Montcalm, Chevalier de Johnstone (a Scot serving as his aide) and Major Monteillard (commander of artillery) tramped along the Beauport lines inspecting the latest gun emplacements. The sky was sooty with the threat of rain. Monteillard noticed the general was all nerves. Over and over, in his distinctive staccato delivery, he insisted Wolfe was about to strike – he could feel it in his bones. Monteillard tended to agree with him. From the trenches, he had already observed a lineup of British warships in the basin and there was a great deal of unusual activity.

Together, the three French officers watched boatload after boatload of armed redcoats weave in and out among their own frigates. In smaller craft, sailors were taking soundings. Judging by the distant flash of cannon, the guns of Point Lévis were still bombarding Quebec. Surely this unholy stir was the prelude to some major action! The marquis reminded himself it was far better to receive the attack at Beauport than anywhere else, for here he was supported by two thousand regulars and several thousand militiamen. Even so, the thought wasn't particularly comforting.

Montcalm, still dedicated to the king's cause despite his quarrels with his fellow officials, tormented himself with doubts about his preparations. What more could he have done to protect the colony? He had begged for more guns at Quebec, but Vaudreuil wouldn't listen. Inside the town walls, the garrison was on constant alert although no one really thought Wolfe was mad enough to launch himself at Lower Town. To the west, near Cap-Rouge, Colonel Bougainville's cavalry, now fifteen hundred strong, was keeping watch on Admiral Holmes' potty armada as it sailed mindlessly up and down the St. Lawrence. The worst thing for Montcalm, however, was the way Vaudreuil countermanded at least half his orders and made decisions without consulting him.

For the last few days, Vaudreuil had been peppering Bougainville with orders like "I need not say to you, Sir, that the safety of the colony is in your hands" – so vague, so meaningless. On top of that, cavalrymen were mixed with Vaudreuil's colony troops and militia and Montcalm had no idea how such amateurs would meet a real crisis. The members of the cavalry guarding the western area, like all the troops, were constantly hungry and exhausted (Bougainville had told Montcalm this in his letters). Only six days earlier, Montcalm had tried to raise Bougainville's morale with a friendly note: "The most important point, my dear Bougainville, is to follow every move-ment of the corps which you have on the water in front of you. You will thus always be on the spot to deal with their embarkation."

Weary and dispirited one minute, keyed up the next, Montcalm wondered if what he'd written on that occasion was really true. What exactly could Bougainville do but race up and down the coast on horseback hoping to prevent a landing? For the past several days, the British hadn't shown any inclination to go ashore; perhaps they never would. Montcalm found it frightening to recall that he and Vaudreuil *did* see eye to eye on one important issue – Beauport would be Wolfe's target. To agree with the governor caused Montcalm to doubt his own instincts. It was unlike Wolfe to do the obvious just as it was unlike Vaudreuil to be right about anything even vaguely connected with the military.

In the dusk, Montcalm spotted redcoats marching back and forth along the south shore. What could they be up to now? Nothing, his companions replied. They were just trying to keep warm. The distant boom of cannon still drifted down from the capital, a constant reminder of how destructive the British guns could be. On the spur of the moment, Montcalm made a decision. Every last soldier at Beauport must spend the night in the trenches.

Chevalier de Johnstone knew his chief was wrestling with an equally difficult problem, the safety of supply barges he expected that night from Cap-Rouge. "I'm afraid the English will seize them," Montcalm confided to Johnstone. "We have only a few days' provisions left." At the moment, the defenders of Quebec were reduced to two ounces of stale bread each day, although Montcalm had noticed that rationing did not apply to Cadet, Bigot or their hangers-on. The intrepid officials were still stuffing themselves with plump chickens the peasants had earlier stuffed with precious seed grain.

By one in the morning an attack from British ships in the basin had failed to materialize. Reluctantly, Montcalm dragged himself back to the Salaberry house with its imposing steep roof (the Canadian answer to heavy snowfalls) and elegantly shuttered windows (designed to keep out cold winds). He lay down in his clothes, but he could not sleep. His mind was still buzzing with annoyances inflicted upon him earlier by the interfering governor.

Only two days earlier, Montcalm had assigned the Guienne Regiment to guard the Plains of Abraham – and Vaudreuil had promptly recalled them to Beauport just to flaunt his own authority. The governor was weak and silly, clinging like a leech to powers inherent in his position, especially anything involving the army. War or no war, Vaudreuil meant to rule even if it cost King Louis the colony.

There were so many examples of Vaudreuil's inept orders that Montcalm couldn't begin to count them. Only yesterday, the general had installed Captain St. Martin as commander of the post above l'Anse au Foulon and Vaudreuil had replaced him with Captain Duchambon de Vergor, one of his lackeys. Of course, the Foulon was perfectly safe. Montcalm himself had sworn to Vaudreuil that the English couldn't land there unless "they'd grown wings." This fellow Vergor couldn't do serious harm, but reversing Montcalm's order showed a lack of respect and tonight, on this dismal, soul-destroying watch, it seemed anything was possible – even flying British soldiers.

A hard look at Vergor's history would have revealed flaws enough to upset any commander. The man had been a captain in the colonial marines, stationed in Louisbourg in the early 1750s when Bigot was intendant there. Fate put Vergor in a position to do the intendant a huge favour: he rescued Bigot from fighting a duel over a woman, a scandal that would have ruined the intendant if it had become public. Bigot, always on the lookout for fresh bandits to help him cheat the king, enlisted Vergor and taught him the fine points of fraud. "Profit by your place, my dear Vergor," he wrote. "Clip and cut – you are free to do as you please – so that you can come soon to France and buy an estate near me."

In 1755 Captain Vergor was in command of Fort Beauséjour, where he followed Bigot's advice, selling off supplies meant to feed hungry labourers and keeping the money for himself. That was the year the English decided to seize the fort. Vergor, afraid for his life, surrendered before the English had time to mount an attack. Captain Vergor was court-martialled for cowardice but was acquitted on the strength of Bigot's warm-hearted testimony. Stripped of his rank, Vergor made his way to Quebec and might have vanished from the pages of history but for his connections in high places. His father once had been governor of Louisbourg and so, with a little help from

Vaudreuil and his friends, the captain was reinstated and allowed to continue his military career.

At l'Anse au Foulon, Vergor was about to play a small but significant role in Wolfe's victory and Montcalm's defeat.

On the eve of battle, Wolfe's troops ate their supper on the frigates moored opposite Cap-Rouge. By nine o'clock, in the darkness, they dropped quietly into flatboats sheltering on the far side of the *Sutherland* and unseen by the French to the south. For the next five hours they sat in full uniform on hard wooden boards, back to back, four men across, packs at their feet. Sailors trained to row heavily loaded boats, and some carefully picked officers, were crammed fore and aft in each vessel.

During the night, the west wind cooled and uniforms grew damp under fitful showers. Sandwiched in tightly, the men were ordered not to talk or move. At 2 a.m. the *Sutherland* hoisted a single lantern, cueing a ten-mile journey in total darkness. Because absolute silence was essential they took no horses; guns and carriages would be man-handled up the steep cliff and, during the battle, Wolfe would have no choice but to stride back and forth on foot while Montcalm surveyed the scene from his glossy charger.

Captain Chads, Colonel Howe and General Wolfe sat in the first boat while the other craft formed a line behind, each one close enough to see the vessel ahead. Helmsmen with muffled oars and closed mouths guided them to the middle of the St. Lawrence, where a combination of current and wind carried them downstream. Captain William DeLaune and his twenty-four Light Infantrymen (volunteers for the first climb up the cliff), Major Barré (one of Wolfe's aides) and two Highland officers (Captain Simon Fraser and Captain Donald Macdonald) were in the first boat, as well. The Scots were there to answer any challenges that might come from French sentries along the riverbank. As Jacobites (supporters of Catholic King James II of England) they had seen service in France and spoke the language.

There are several points of view on the "Elegy question." Some people believe that during the journey Wolfe quoted from Thomas Gray's *Elegy Written in a Country Churchyard*, adding, "I'd rather have written those lines than take Quebec"; others deny it ever happened. There are people who claim he might have quoted from the poem *on some occasion* but not that night, when so much depended on silence. One author says Wolfe pulled a copy of the book out of his pocket and read it aloud, which would have been a small miracle given the often-described blackness of the night. We know that Wolfe brought the poem with him to Quebec – it was a gift from his fiancée, Katherine Lowther – and there is no doubt he read it because marginal notes are in his handwriting. But his general orders on September 11 called for strict silence in the boats, and it's hard to believe a man as focused as James Wolfe would spout poetry when hundreds of lives, perhaps thousands, depended on reaching the goal without detection.

When he prepared his final strike, Wolfe left little to chance. A lighted lantern on the *Sutherland*, still moored at Cap-Rouge, became a guide for Captain Chads, who had to stay in the middle of the river to avoid rocks and shoals. Once Chads could no longer see even a twinkle from the flagship, he needed to find a new point of reference, particularly when he headed for the north shore. Historian Duncan Grinnell-Milnes, in his book *Mad, Is He?*, gives the clearest explanation of this vital stage. By prearrangement, the *Hunter* was moored above the Etchemin River, half a mile from the south shore; that made it practical for Chads to use it as a marker. Captain Smith hung a lantern on the *Hunter's* bow at the time the boats were due to appear; Chads saw the signal and turned the convoy sharply in the direction of the cliffs. Even if the French sentinels at Sillery had noticed the light, it conveyed nothing. The *Hunter* had no intention of moving for some time.

Despite all these precautions, disaster nearly struck when the leading boat, carrying Chads and Wolfe, came up on the *Hunter* suddenly and Captain Smith, thinking it was the enemy, prepared to fire. Wolfe avoided trouble by quickly identifying himself. Crossing the river was rough on the oarsmen – they lost power from both tide and wind and had to pull harder than at any other time during the voyage. Once the fleet came under the shadow of the heights and headed downriver again, the tide tugged it forward. Next Chads had to find Wolfe's cove, l'Anse au Foulon, in total darkness. The first challenge from the enemy came as they passed under the guns at Sillery.

"*Qui vive?*"

And Captain Simon Fraser replied, "*France, vive le roi!*"

"*A quel régiment?*"

"*De la reine.*"

"*Pourquois ne parlez-vouz plus haut?*"

The quick-thinking Fraser said he was speaking softly because he didn't want to draw the attention of English boats on the river. A second voice then urged the first one to let the convoy pass because the ships must be transports sent by Colonel Bougainville. Since the post had received no word of a cancellation, the questioners let it go at that. The exchange was helpful to Chads because it told him he had reached Sillery. But he still had to land at exactly the right moment or be swept downstream.

In the distance British cannon thundered from Pointe-des-Pères and Point Lévis, a comforting sound to the British. Captain Chads now had to find the exact spot Wolfe had chosen. He remained cool at this crucial moment. When he thought it right, Chads turned toward the cliffs and the other twenty-seven boats followed. Soon they were scraping the stony beach. Two boats that overshot the mark ended up five hundred yards downriver. It was now 4 a.m.

Colonel Louis-Antoine de Bougainville, still patrolling the north shore road from Cap-Rouge to Sillery, had a low regard for celibacy, a condition that may have played a part in the night's drama. As darkness fell on the night of September 12, Bougainville stared at the cluster of

British ships anchored in the St. Lawrence and could see nothing stirring. Glancing at the cloudy sky, at the sameness of the scene, Bougainville longed for excitement. After riding along the river road all day he was exhausted, but he was also profoundly bored. Eager for action, he expected none. That the world would tilt and bring the war directly to this spot in the wilderness seemed highly unlikely. All he knew for sure was that soon the British army would sail for home; that Saunders, Holmes and Wolfe would vanish over the horizon; and Bougainville himself would return to a devastated Quebec.

As a dashing young gallant, his thoughts naturally turned to love. It so happened that his cousin's wife, Madame de Vienne, had arrived recently at Cap-Rouge seeking refuge and was, at this very moment, a guest on a farm twenty miles from where he languished. Hadn't his cousin begged Bougainville to look after the lady? Convinced nothing important was in the cards that night, he decided to pay her a visit.

Later that evening, when several British frigates moved down-stream, Bougainville was occupied elsewhere. Nor was he present when a string of small boats slipped away under cover of darkness. His men were grateful for his absence since it guaranteed them a good night's sleep. The colonel missed breakfast, too, but nothing appeared to have happened while he was gone, so what did it matter? It had slipped the attention of the watch that several of Holmes' ships were missing.

At 8 a.m. an official letter arrived for the colonel from Vaudreuil, but it's not known how early Bougainville actually read it. "It seems quite certain that the enemy has made a landing at l'Anse au Foulon," Vaudreuil had written. "We hear a few small volleys. Monsieur le Marquis de Montcalm has just left with a hundred men as reinforcement. As soon as I know for certain what is going on I shall inform you."

Vaudreuil had added a postscript even more vague: "The enemy forces seem considerable. I do not doubt that you will be attentive to his movements and follow them. I rely on you for this."

18

The Plains of Abraham

"When I went to war, I did the best I could."
— LOUIS-JOSEPH, Marquis de Montcalm, 1759

Minutes after he hit the beach, Wolfe realized he was at least a hundred yards east of the path he had chosen to get his army up the cliff. As he peered up at the inky sky, he hesitated. Could DeLaune's men, weighed down with sixty pounds of gear, scale an almost perpendicular wall? Even in the half-light the general saw that rough stones and scraggy bushes were the only help they were likely to get. Boats were piling up behind him, creaking and grating over gravel, and curses grew louder as seventeen hundred restless men waited to step ashore.

Wolfe, surprised that French sentries hadn't already sounded the alarm, made a snap decision: "I don't think you'll make it, lads, but you can try." And he waved Captain DeLaune forward. It was all the encouragement they needed. DeLaune and his band scrambled up the face, showering loose stones and soggy dirt on the ground below. To James Wolfe, waiting with the others, every noise was a punch in the gut. The sentinels up there on the bank must be deaf not to hear such a racket! Yet nobody tried to stop his climbers. DeLaune had just reached the top and pushed ahead into the trees when one of his men accidentally bumped into a sentry. This time, it was Captain Macdonald who saved the day, ad-libbing in rapid French that he had come to relieve the post. His quick thinking bought them a few more seconds – time enough to surround the French camp before the slow-witted guard started shouting.

Despite this clumsy start, the British managed to pull off the ambush. They owed something to luck, of course. Vergor, the officer in charge of the post, thinking there was no danger, put on his night-shirt, rolled into his blanket and fell asleep. His men followed suit, and so, when the first few redcoats came over the top, the whole camp was snoozing. Rousted into the cold morning air, the French began firing at random, hitting each other as often as they hit the enemy. Vergor headed in the direction of Quebec, took a bullet in the heel and was captured. Later, rumours began to surface that he was in league with the British, but it seems unlikely; he wasn't clever enough to be a spy. Vergor's sloppy behaviour that night was typical of the way he had lived his life. An alert sentry might have stopped Wolfe's men at the edge of the cliff. The famous battle might never have been fought, and the history of North America would have been very different.

Only twenty minutes had elapsed from the time the first boat was dragged up on the beach to the coup on the heights. The wide, zigzag path Wolfe had spotted two days earlier was found to be clogged with fallen trees. Colonel William Howe's infantry joined DeLaune's men in clearing it and, within an hour, the British were on the heights in such numbers they succeeded in knocking out Samos and Sillery, the two nearest batteries. Wolfe was now free to assemble his troops. From the beach, the fleet of flatboats began ferrying soldiers from Point Lévis while the *Hunter* and several frigates brought troops from a point farther up the river. Light showers made life uncomfortable for a time, but failed to stop the operation.

After making sure his troops were crossing safely, Wolfe set out along the nearest road to size up the field. To the east he could see a peaceful landscape: not a soul was stirring. Apparently sentinels on the fortified wall still didn't know he had landed, and he figured he'd have time to bring up a good portion of his army before they discovered the truth. To Wolfe, all signs read *Go!* His volatile spirits shot up and his aches and pains fell away. Nothing could stop him now. Quebec had been on his mind for a year. He had pored over maps, grilled deserters and dreamed of the heights so often the area was curiously familiar.

The prize lay just ahead. He could make out the lowering Laurentians to the north, wrapped in dark evergreens and dripping yellow birch trees. Along the river's edge, patches of scrub brush and alders stood ready to hide enemy snipers and the bumpy grassland rolled gently toward the Buttes-à-Neveu, a ridge screening Quebec from his view.

Wolfe soon glimpsed open ground with space enough to deploy his troops in conventional form and allow him to observe Montcalm's battalions when they came spilling over the ridge. He pictured the marquis' frustration when he discovered James Wolfe had chosen the place and the time – and had even set the rules. In a sudden flash of understanding, Wolfe realized all his hopes were bound up in this common patch of earth. Today's battle was to be the sum of everything he had worked for since he first heard his father's military stories, read a history book for himself and studied maps of ancient wars. Somehow, the elements had combined to bring him here. An aide once remarked that in battle Wolfe wore a certain look, "radiant and joyful beyond description." Surely, on the morning of September 13, tall and slim in his scarlet coat, rushing toward his awful destiny, Wolfe wore his glory face.

At Montcalm's headquarters the situation was very different. Major Montbeillard, commander of artillery and keeper of Montcalm's journal, recorded the first alarm: "A little before daybreak, around six o'clock, some musket shots were heard above Quebec. We had no doubt that a convoy of provisions we were expecting had been discovered and perhaps captured."

Montcalm had received no cancellation involving the supply boats from Cap-Rouge and still hoped they would arrive that morning. An hour after the first shots were heard, one of Vergor's men staggered into the hornwork by the bridge, shouting that the British were on the heights above the Foulon. No one believed him. They thought he was mad with fright.

The general himself had spent a sleepless night and was disturbed at dawn by the guns at Samos and Sillery. Without investigating, Montcalm assumed they were firing on English ships passing down the river. In fact, the two batteries were trying to repel Wolfe. For some reason, Montcalm expected the governor would keep him informed, although Vaudreuil had never done so in the past. After waiting an hour and hearing nothing, Montcalm and his aide Chevalier James Johnstone set out for the governor's headquarters.

At 7 a.m. Montcalm met Vaudreuil on the road in front of his house. The governor told him that one hundred regulars from the regiment of Guienne were already on their way to the ridge west of the town. After a brief discussion, Montcalm grew agitated because Vaudreuil insisted that Wolfe intended to attack the Beauport lines and the bulk of the army must remain in the trenches. Scowling, General Montcalm rode toward the pontoon bridge, and as he crossed the St. Charles River, caught sight of the "scarlet thread." "This is a serious business, my friends," Montcalm remarked to his escort. "They are where they are not supposed to be!" Riding on, Montcalm reached the Buttes-à-Neveu, on the western side of Quebec's fortified wall. Although only half Wolfe's force was on the Plains, Montcalm was stunned to see them in formation. An officer standing near him described the general's reaction: "He had expected a battalion. He found an army."

The sight of two thousand redcoats galvanized Montcalm. He sent Johnstone galloping back to Beauport with a dispatch demanding all regiments report to the heights at once. But Johnstone found Vaudreuil had already given orders that not a single soldier was to leave the area. A frustrated Johnstone argued and pleaded, but Vaudreuil stubbornly refused. Although the battle had not begun, the three-year feud between Montcalm and Vaudreuil endangered the French cause.

More warnings that Wolfe had landed came to light. As early as 3 a.m., a French patrol in a canoe saw English boats at the edge of the St. Charles and an officer took it upon himself to move a field gun and a detachment of militia to stop any possible invaders. At 4 a.m., Chevalier de Bernetz, temporarily commandant in Quebec because commandant Jean-Baptiste de Ramezay was in the General Hospital with a fever, hoisted a red flag over the citadel. It was a prearranged signal that the British had landed.

Unfortunately, no one in the governor's camp paid the slightest attention. At 5 a.m., yet another fugitive from Vergor's detachment arrived at Beauport with news that the English had landed at the Foulon. Again, nobody believed him because, according to Major Montbeillard, "We knew so well the difficulties of penetrating at this point. The sound of gunfire wasn't taken seriously because it soon stopped." At 5:45 a.m., Vaudreuil received a report from Chevalier de Bernetz that there had been a landing at the Foulon; but, as no more musket fire was heard, everyone assumed the English had gone away. Later still, a patient in the General Hospital looked out his window, saw the red jackets of British soldiers and summoned others to be his witness. All the patients were dismissed as hallucinatory, and the confusion worked in favour of the British.

Montcalm, with the troops he had managed to muster, viewed the English army through his spyglass and estimated that Wolfe had assembled about two thousand men. The general confided to one of his aides that he couldn't believe this was Wolfe's entire army, and he was right; the number of redcoats on the heights would soon double. Montcalm also observed that the British hadn't brought up any of their big guns, and a frisson of hope gave him a lift. If he could concentrate all his forces before the enemy had time to set up more cannon, he might still drive them off! But time was short, so Montcalm again sent Johnstone to beg Vaudreuil for more regulars. Again, the governor was adamant: "No troops will move from Beauport!" Johnstone argued, but Vaudreuil refused to budge and, as a result, the Scotsman rode back to the general empty-handed. A desperate Montcalm jumped on his most powerful horse and pounded to Vaudreuil's headquarters where, according to witnesses, "the two men argued bitterly."

The governor insisted he was in command of the defence of Canada and that his orders superseded those of General Montcalm. Wolfe, he shouted, intended to launch his full force at Beauport. The English presence on the heights was merely a ruse, and the bulk of the French army must remain at Beauport to repel Wolfe when he appeared. A furious governor explained to an apoplectic general that Quebec could be held with guns and troops from the town garrison along with the Guienne Regiment already on the Buttes-à-Neveu. As a consolation prize, Vaudreuil threw in a few sharpshooters from a company of bushrangers plus two hundred Indians.

To the governor, the situation was simple. Montcalm must hold out until Bougainville arrived from the west with his magic militia and down-home dragoons – perhaps fifteen hundred in all. Whether they were "elite" troops as some writers later reported, or mostly militia, colony troops and a single regiment of regulars as others believed, is arguable. More dangerous to the French army than its size was the vague note Vaudreuil had dispatched to Bougainville earlier that morning, promising he would send more information as soon as he had it. At that point Bougainville was to head for Quebec and join the battle.

Just how Montcalm managed to extract Vaudreuil's promise to send the four remaining battalions of regulars, along with most of the militia and colony troops, is difficult to establish. But no matter how it came about, they were an hour away from the scene. Luckily for Montcalm, affairs moved slowly on the English side and his reliable French regulars arrived in time for the battle. Their departure left about fifteen hundred men to defend the Beauport lines.

What changed the governor's mind? Did Montcalm finally admit that in the spring, the Court of Versailles had given him authority to make all military decisions if Wolfe should assault Quebec? Vaudreuil had received a letter telling him exactly the same thing, at exactly the same time, but he kept it secret. Perhaps, when it was time to conduct the defence of the capital, the governor faced the truth: he had neither the experience nor the temperament for such a task.

The field known as the Plains of Abraham was, according to some sources, named after Abraham Martin, a river pilot who had lived in the small village of Stadacona beside the St. Charles River a century ago. Martin had ventured west across the great rock where the fortress of Quebec would some day stand and claimed the field as his own, though it's unlikely he ever farmed it. On the day of the battle, the field belonged to the nuns of the Ursuline convent in Upper Town and, while some have said it was "abandoned," Captain John Knox described it as a mixture of corn fields and rough grass.

The "Plains" made up one section of a plateau two hundred feet above the St. Lawrence River, about a mile wide and one and a half miles long. The field is sometimes described as "a square mile." Fringed by bushes and clumps of trees, it could be seen clearly from the buttes near Quebec's fortified wall and from the edge of the woods on the western end.

The British forces numbered forty-five hundred, about half the number Pitt had promised when Wolfe signed up, but were trained to stand firm and fight in the open, the ultimate test of a good soldier in those days. Louis-Joseph, Marquis de Montcalm, had roughly sixteen thousand men at his disposal, although only a quarter of them fought in the battle on the Plains. Of those, only five battalions were regulars from France and able to match Wolfe's troops; the rest were poorly trained colonials and raw recruits. Wolfe, in his last letter to his mother, summed it up best: "The Marquis de Montcalm is at the head of a great number of bad soldiers, and I am at the head of a small number of good ones."

When the battle began, Montcalm was trapped in the scenario he had feared so long. All summer he had kept his troops behind barricades despite Wolfe's ploys to lure him out. Keenly aware of the town's shaky walls, he dared not risk a long siege. A shortage of gunpowder and the uneven quality of his fighting force multiplied his worries. And now, Wolfe had somehow contrived to draw him into a conventional battle on an open field.

As the seconds ticked by, Montcalm spotted two British field guns ready to blow up his first line. Not realizing one of the guns was useless, he assumed he needed to start the battle before the enemy had time to haul up still more cannon. In his haste, Montcalm had arrived from Beauport that morning without his artillery, but had managed to borrow three field guns from the Quebec garrison. "We cannot avoid action," he admitted to his aide Montbeillard, the artillery officer who kept Montcalm's journal. It was his last and most melancholy remark.

In the eighteenth century, battles were often a spectator sport. The siege of Quebec was ideal mass entertainment. A large portion of the population had fled the capital because of the bombardment, but there were hundreds still in town who had nowhere to go, as well as merchants, importers and rogues ready to steal from abandoned houses. As the regiments of France and the colony troops tramped through the town, their friends and relatives hung out of windows urging them on, cheering General Montcalm – now their favourite official. Crowds spilled out of the western gates, probably driven by the eternal fascination with death and destruction.

At nine o'clock that morning, the armies were a quarter of a mile apart, too far for musket fire to be accurate but close enough to see each other. Indian and Canadian sharpshooters, hiding in the scraggy bushes and clumps of stunted evergreens, were able to pick off redcoats often enough to alarm their companions. Sounds of fife and drum mixed with sharp commands. At the west end of the open field, Wolfe's six regiments were deployed from right to left with the Louisbourg Grenadiers closest to the river, then the 28th, 43rd, 47th, 78th (which included Fraser's Highlanders) and, finally, the 58th on the far left near the Sillery Road. The line stretched out, long and fragile, two men deep. Wolfe had trained them to fight in this formation but had never tested it in battle. This was the birth of the "thin red line."

The French formed in columns across the east end of the field from right to left: the Quebec and Montreal colony troops in light grey coats with red or blue facings; French regulars (La Sarre, Languedoc, Béarn, Guienne and Royal-Roussillon) in white; and, finally the Trois-Rivières and Montreal colony troops closest to the St. Lawrence, in greyish white coats with black edging. Montcalm wore a dark blue frock coat with gold trim, the wide sleeves falling back to reveal snow-white shirtsleeves each time he waved his sword.

Song and story had long portrayed soldiers standing shoulder to shoulder (and up to this point, it was true), but under Wolfe the men stood eighteen inches apart. The wider space between soldiers was intended to shore up the strength of the new formation. Once positioned on the field, the first line took an oblique step sideways, creating a gap through which the second line could safely fire. This doubled the firepower of a single volley. The real test would come when troops were ordered to stand perfectly still waiting for the

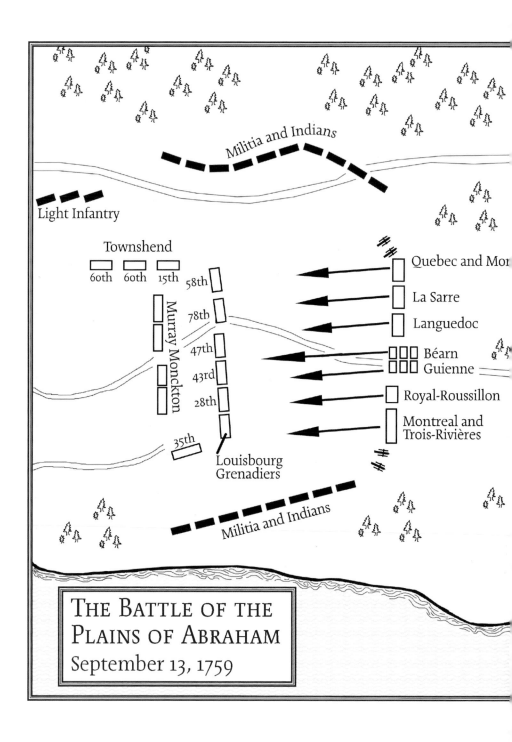

Militia and Indians

Light Infantry

Townshend

60th 60th 15th

58th

Murray Monckton

78th

47th

43rd

28th

35th

Louisbourg
Grenadiers

Militia and Indians

Quebec and Mo[r]

La Sarre

Languedoc

Béarn
Guienne

Royal-Roussillon

Montreal and
Trois-Rivières

THE BATTLE OF THE
PLAINS OF ABRAHAM
September 13, 1759

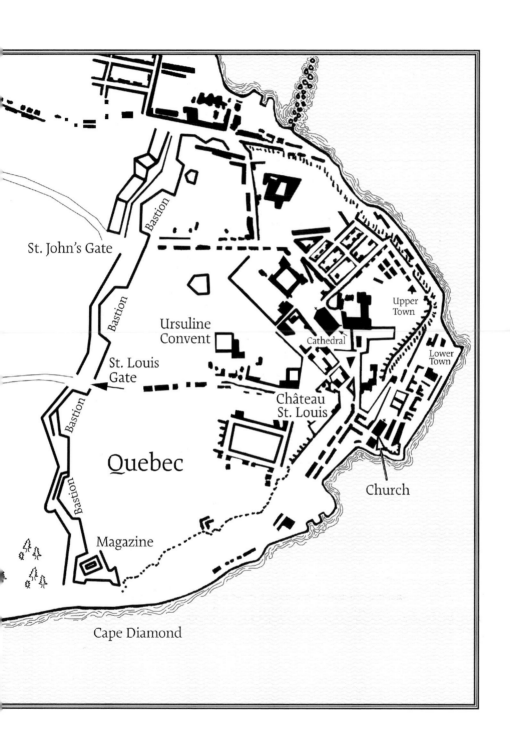

St. John's Gate

Bastion

Bastion

Bastion

Ursuline
Convent

St. Louis
Gate

Bastion

Cathedral

Upper
Town

Lower
Town

Château
St. Louis

Quebec

Church

Bastion

Magazine

Cape Diamond

enemy to come within forty feet. Such control required rigorous training and nerves of steel, and Wolfe was risking everything on the innovation. Not all his officers approved, many still preferring the old-fashioned way: columns seven or eight men deep. They looked stronger and seemed to offer hope that sheer bulk could resist any thin line, whatever the colour of their coats.

While Wolfe waited for Montcalm to make the first move, he ordered his troops to lie down in the grass to lessen their chances of being hit by snipers as well as to conserve energy. He had removed his black cape before reaching the field, and his bright red frock coat was a beacon as he strode up and down the front lines reminding his men not to fire too soon, to reload quickly and to take their second shot before the French recovered their wits.

As senior brigadier, Robert Monckton commanded the right, James Murray was on the left and George Townshend's men were at right angles to Murray, lining the Sillery Road and occupying scattered farmhouses. A rise on the left, where the 15th and 58th met, offered Wolfe an excellent view of the field and he saw the Royal-Roussillon, the last French regiment to arrive, puffing up the steep road from the St. Charles River.

In those golden moments just before the battle, with birds singing in the trees, the sweet smell of autumn in the air and the bedazzlement of soldiers in their *opéra bouffe* outfits, war was brilliant theatre. There was an exquisite pause for effect. A brief silence before the spell was broken. At ten o'clock, Montcalm gave the order to march. Trumpets sounded, drums rolled, flags fluttered and the white-coated regulars from France, the grey-clad colonials and volunteers, wearing a variety of outfits and brandishing their own rifles, stepped out smartly, anxious to prove they could beat the British.

British battalions, watching the white tide rolling toward them, stood like stone statues, cool and resolute. Even a hardened Continental army might have trembled at the sight of their iron will.

The moment had come for Wolfe, the recent invalid, to draw on his inner strength. The general, so frail only days before, now moved briskly and barked his orders with the hint of a smile. Those who saw him up close were surprised by the hot flush on his cheek, his air of excited anticipation.

Despite Montcalm's fears, the British did not outgun the French. British seamen and soldiers dragging two brass six-pounders up the cliff had damaged one in transit and, though the gun couldn't be fired, they set it up anyway, just for effect. Captain York, in command of the only gun that worked, placed it in the centre of the front line, pointed directly at the Béarn Regiment's dense white column, eager to blow them away. Montcalm, without heavy artillery or fresh support from Bougainville and his thousand horsemen, prepared to cut through the red ribbon strung out across the Plains.

As the enemy moved inevitably toward him, Wolfe ordered the regimental colours removed to a safe place. Watching Montcalm in action for the first time, Wolfe saw not a phantom, but a man of flesh and blood, bent on the destruction of the British army. The plump little general plunged up and down the lines on his powerful horse, waving his sword to inspire his troops. Wolfe, thinking and dreaming about Montcalm for so long, felt as if he knew the man intimately. The sight of him alive, courageous, animated as he was himself, sparked Wolfe's own battle-fever.

For a brief time, the French received only spasmodic fire, but it was enough to tear holes in their lines. The ground was uneven and the militia was mixed with the regulars, causing stumbles and hesitations. Some colony troops slipped toward the trees, looking for cover and weakening the centre. Montcalm tried to keep his columns together, hoping to smash through the British lines by sheer bulk. On the surface, it seemed plausible. How could a line two-deep resist the weight of a line eight-deep? Despite the alarming drift on both

French flanks, officers urged their men forward. In the centre, the drums beat like a great noisy heart.

Preparing to meet the first barrage, Wolfe sent Captain York and his overworked cannon behind the lines. For the time being, his job was done. Skirmishers on both wings of the British force, trying to push back enemy sharpshooters, returned to their units. As Wolfe scanned the action, everything seemed in order. Yet it was the British who made the first error: their left flank, positioned near the Sillery Road, fell back in a disorganized withdrawal – and French rangers were only too eager to take advantage. The 15th tried to uproot these lone riflemen with brisk fire of their own, causing a minor tempest that drew Wolfe's attention. He hustled over to investigate, and seconds later a ball hit him in the wrist, severing a tendon. The wrist bled heavily and Wolfe found someone to tie a handkerchief around it. Stuffing his dripping right hand inside his coat and waving his cane with the left, he tramped toward the centre. French troops were firing at random and a ball struck Wolfe in the groin. He staggered, almost went down, but quickly recovered his balance. Fortunately, his thick coat cushioned the blow.

Wolfe reached a knoll on the far right between the 28th and the Louisbourg Grenadiers, once again discovering a spot that gave him an overview of the field. Still the French came on, although it could not be said they were marching "in good order." Suddenly, the sun came out, highlighting the bloody action about to begin. On command, the British army drew to attention, muskets in place, drummers and commanders standing slightly in advance of the centre. Wolfe held his cane aloft.

When the French were exactly forty paces distant, Wolfe's cane swished down. Carleton gave the order to fire and the Louisbourg Grenadiers blew the faces off the Guienne's front line. Platoon by platoon, British fire swept on down the line, so perfectly timed and executed it sounded like a single shot. Following the Grenadiers, the 28th blasted the Béarn, directly in front of them. The French lines reeled back, wrapped in blood and smoke. In all, the British fired four volleys a few seconds apart and the fourth was incomplete only because Wolfe took a musket ball in the breast and collapsed.

Writing in his journal a short time later, Knox described the first volley this way: "The 43rd and 47th gave them [the French] as remarkable a close and heavy discharge as I ever saw performed at a private field exercise ... the French say they never opposed a shock [such] as they received from the centre of our line ... our troops in general and particularly the central corps, having levelled and fired ... *comme un coup de canon.*" And after the third volley, "they gave way and fled with precipitation so that, by the time the smoke vanished, our men were again loaded."

As the fourth volley began, and Wolfe sank slowly to the ground, the Highlanders roared, threw down their muskets and waved their broadswords in the air. Bagpipes keened and one hundred huge men in bright-coloured tartans took off after the fleeing French.

Near the edge of the field, Wolfe was dying. Three or four officers clustered round him, but he refused to let them call a surgeon. "It's all over with me," he said, closing his eyes. One of his attendants, glancing up from the dying man to check the action on the battlefield, called out excitedly, "See how they run! See how they run!" It was enough to bring Wolfe to life for another few seconds. "Who run?" "The enemy, sir, they give way everywhere."

Wolfe craved victory to the end. From deep inside, he found strength enough to give one last command, one he considered essential to winning the day: "Go one of you, to Colonel Burton. Tell him to march Webb's Regiment down to the Charles to cut off their retreat from the bridge."

Although Captain John Knox didn't witness Wolfe's death, he questioned everyone present to get an accurate account and, to the best of his knowledge, Wolfe's last words were "Now, God be praised, I will die in peace."

Montcalm, still on horseback and caught in the rush toward the gates of Quebec, took a random shot in the stomach and slumped forward. Two soldiers running alongside managed to keep him in the saddle as they slipped through one of the western gates seconds before it slammed shut. A woman on the street recognized Montcalm, saw the blood pouring from the wound, and shrieked, "O my God! My God! The marquis is dead!" Montcalm, ever the gentleman, was reassuring: "It's nothing," he responded. "Don't be troubled for me, my good friends." The soldiers took him as far as Dr. Arnoux's house, where he was carried inside.

The British had won! Yet, at the end of the day, the French were still inside the fortress and the English, now commanded by Brigadier George Townshend, were camped on the Plains. It would be five days before the French formally surrendered. But there were still scenes to be played out. Melodrama was never far from centre stage.

Wolfe Killed, Montcalm Fatally Wounded

"If I had been sole master, Quebec would still belong to the King."
— GOVERNOR VAUDREUIL, September 13, 1759.

Between ten-thirty and noon on September 13, the bulk of Montcalm's troops rushed through the gates of St. Louis and St. John into the arms of a shaken population. The remainder scurried across the front of the ramparts and down the slope to the suburb of St. Roch with dozens of screaming Highlanders chasing after them, waving their bloody swords.

Shades of Dettingen: a British victory best remembered for the escape of the entire French army while George II and his son the Duke of Cumberland lingered on the battlefield accepting compliments on their victory. Now, sixteen years later, Townshend unwittingly created an echo of that old disaster when he failed to pursue the French and instead remustered his troops on the Plains of Abraham. As a result of Townshend's decision, the losers occupied the fortress for five more days.

Vaudreuil arrived on the Buttes-à-Neveu well after the smoke had cleared, like some decrepit old actor who had missed his cue. His critics said he was merely covering his assets: if he found a French victory he would claim a share of the glory, and if he stumbled on defeat he could always blame Montcalm. Vaudreuil himself was vague about the reasons for his late entrance but, as usual, brutally frank about the French regulars' poor performance. They were, he said, "so panicky even *I* couldn't stop them!" His solution to the Sturm und Drang swirling all around him was to head for the temporary safety of his headquarters on the St. Charles River.

Chevalier Johnstone, Montcalm's aide, was more circumspect. He left the fleeing army and took up a position north of the town where he expected to watch the disaster in relative safety. Instead, he was caught in a hail of bullets from British infantry, his horse severely wounded and his uniform torn. Johnstone managed to reach a meadow down by the St. Charles, dismount and seek refuge in the fortifications at the bridge. He found the high command in utter chaos.

"It is impossible to imagine the disorder and confusion in the Horn Work," the Scotsman later wrote. "M. de Vaudreuil listened to everybody and agreed with the one who spoke last. On the appearance of English troops near the St. Charles River, two old captains of the Béarn Regiment cried out that the place would be taken by assault, sword in hand, that we all should be cut to pieces and nothing could save us but immediate capitulation."

A disgusted Johnstone noticed axe men already chopping down the pontoon bridge and warned them that by doing so, they would cut off any French troops left behind on the Quebec side of the St. Charles. The destruction stopped. In the governor's office, he found Vaudreuil, Bigot and a number of other officials drafting the articles of surrender. Vaudreuil rudely told Johnstone he had no business there because he was Montcalm's friend. Johnstone retired immediately, furious to see them "giving up so scandalously."

While Johnstone mourned the loss of life and lack of pride among the colony's leaders, his friend Montcalm was dying. Brigadier Sénezèrgues, once second-in-command, was mortally wounded and Brigadier St. Ours already dead. The demoralized French appeared to be without a leader. Yet how could this be, Johnstone wondered. The fearless Vaudreuil had boasted for years that *he* was the supreme commander and would save Canada or die. Now that he was in sole charge, Vaudreuil hadn't the faintest idea what to do. Those who saw him in the first few hours after the retreat said he ran about hysterically, asking everyone's opinion and accomplishing nothing.

Late that afternoon, with a breathtaking lack of sensitivity, Vaudreuil wrote to his old enemy Montcalm, asking for advice. Montcalm, in great pain and attempting to arrange his personal affairs before he died, dictated a cold reply to the addled governor. In it, he outlined three choices. He could fight again; could retreat to the village of Jacques-Cartier, some thirty miles upriver, to reorganize the army; or could give up the colony immediately. A week later, Vaudreuil, once more in the business of portraying himself in a shining light, wrote a letter to the minister of war, M. Berryer, claiming both he and Bigot had wished to resist but all their senior officers decided to capitulate. In the face of such opposition, Vaudreuil swore, they retreated to Montreal. "Monsieur the Marquis de Montcalm," he threw in with gratuitous scorn, "unfortunately made the attack before I joined him."

The behaviour of the victorious British was only marginally saner than the pathetic goings-on among the French. Shortly after Wolfe was carried off the field, Brigadier Robert Monckton suffered a serious wound. Command of the British expedition then devolved upon Brigadier George Townshend, the man who had tormented Wolfe for the past three months. All summer Townshend had trivialized his leader by drawing coarse cartoons and spouting diatribes directed at any young officers foolish enough to listen. By chance, Townshend had become general of the army, but a week before the battle he had very different expectations. Writing to his wife on September 6, he wrote, "General Wolfe's health is bad. His generalship is not a bit better. I never served so disagreeable a campaign as this. One month more will put an end to our troubles, our campaign is over."

Whether or not Townshend heard Wolfe's dying order, to pursue the French, doesn't matter. He put a stop to *all* pursuit, in any direction. Next, he scanned the tumultuous scene and decided to stay put, eat lunch and take a rest. In his own good time, he sent his army to entrench on the plains. Many believed the appearance of Bougainville and his cavalry emerging from the woods at Townshend's back intimidated the new general – although he claimed his troops were too exhausted to fight a second battle, especially with a fresh body of troops.

An examination of conditions shows this is absurd. Colonel Bougainville's men could hardly be called fresh. They had marched fifteen miles over rough roads that morning and for weeks had been riding up and down the river road. There is disagreement on the size of Bourgainville's detachment, but Montcalm himself believed he had one thousand men scattered over a fifteen-mile strip. It's highly unlikely the colonel had time to gather his entire force before setting out for Quebec.

Were these troops "elite", as some historians claim? Or were they untrained militia mixed with a hundred or so French regulars and a handful of Indians? Whoever they were, they couldn't have been in much better shape than the British. Bougainville declared that when he saw the strength of the British opposed to him, he retreated because he had no hope of outfighting them. Townshend, like Wolfe, was at Dettingen and knew what happened when the victor failed to pursue his beaten enemy. He had commented on that very situation at the time: "The French, to the surprise of every one, were suffered to escape unmolested. The king halted and the Enemy was suffered to quietly repass their bridge over the Main." How different his view was when *he* was in command, and the enemy was allowed to "repass their bridge" over the St. Charles!

Up to the moment when the fatal ball struck Wolfe in the chest, he had conducted the battle brilliantly. Had he lived, Wolfe would have dealt with Bougainville's arrival in the same way. Bougainville was astute, but he was still green, scarcely a match for a leader like Wolfe. The French colonel was twenty-seven years old and had dabbled in law, had been a member of the French parliament, and was a creative mathematician, none of which had prepared him for the military. The British troops had proven their mettle on the field; their blood was up and they were eager to chase that enemy all the way to Montmorency Falls if necessary. Bougainville showed his grasp of the situation when he decamped from the place so quickly.

On September 13, after the brief battle was over, the British lugged more cannon up from the beach and took possession of the commodious General Hospital. The number of British dead, wounded and missing totalled 664, leaving approximately four thousand men still fit to fight. Although Vaudreuil claimed the French losses were only 640, when the British picked up wounded and buried the dead they estimated French losses at fifteen hundred. The truth lay somewhere in between.

At midnight, the French garrison still occupied Quebec and the British had settled down for the night on the battlefield. Yet none of the British sentries or scouts appeared to notice that thousands of men, horses and baggage carts were struggling west along the Ste-Foy Road. Vaudreuil and his ad hoc committee ordered the evacuation of the main Beauport camp to begin between nine and ten that evening, and one of his own officers later described it as "a flight not an orderly retreat." How did they find their way in the darkness unless they carried torches? Surely *somebody* must have seen that long line of bright lights, and yet General Townshend made no attempt to stop it. For the second time in one day, the French army was allowed to get away.

Hysteria infected the French camp. Troops abandoned artillery, ammunition and valuable provisions, and Vaudreuil, who must have

known Quebec's cupboard was bare, forgot to inform the commandant, Ramezay, who was once again in charge of the garrison at
Quebec. However, Vaudreuil *did* remember to send Ramezay a draft
of the articles of capitulation, along with a note telling him not to hold
out until the fortress was taken by assault but to give up as soon as the
food supply ran out. Ramezay himself was none too sharp (he may still
have been feverish) but, eventually, it did occur to him to send a party
to bring in supplies left at Beauport. By the time his soldiers got there,
the camp had been picked clean by hungry farmers and roving Indians.

The loss of the Beauport provisions was a serious blow to both
garrison and townspeople. Before climbing into his calèche for the
overland journey to Montreal, Vaudreuil sent a messenger ahead to
Lévis at Jacques-Cartier, begging him to take command of the entire
army. Thus did Lévis become a general of France. On September 14, a
ragtag crowd could still be seen moving along the Ste-Foy Road following the troops. It doesn't seem to have occurred to Vaudreuil that
he had left the capital of Canada in the lurch. The word "morale" was
not in his vocabulary.

Inside a ruined Quebec, ten thousand souls, military and civilian,
expected protection. Because of the bombardment, shelter was
scarce. Why did Wolfe continue shelling Quebec long after he'd
proven he could raze the capital whenever he chose? By battering the
place all summer (they were still firing sporadically the night before
Wolfe landed at the Foulon), Wolfe was destroying the barracks and
solid houses his troops would need in the coming winter. Was it pure
revenge? Was it frustration over Montcalm's stubborn refusal to meet
him on the field? The question is just as fascinating as the often-
asked "Why did Wolfe take the field without establishing a secure
supply line and escape route for his troops?"

On the evening of September 14, Ramezay held a council of war to
decide whether the French should give up. A record of this meeting
still exists. It records that the town might have held out longer if there

had been adequate food, but they had rations for only a few days. Of the fourteen officers who gave their written opinion, thirteen voted for capitulation. With this almost unanimous vote, Commandant de Ramezay, obeying Vaudreuil's written instructions, moved slowly toward surrender.

That same evening, as Montcalm lay dying, Commandant de Ramezay paid the general a visit. After politely asking about his condition, Ramezay came to the point – should he hoist the white flag? He confessed he was at a loss. Montcalm's mind was perfectly clear. For him, the days of placating military and civil authorities were over. Ramezay and his officers had failed to support Montcalm in the spring, when he offered ways of improving Quebec's defences. They had thrown their weight behind the governor's puerile opinions and were therefore as much to blame for the defeat as he was himself. Montcalm noticed that Ramezay was more concerned about his own problems than he was about Montcalm's approaching death.

"I will neither give orders nor interfere any further," the marquis told his visitor. "I have much business that must be attended to, of greater moment than your ruined garrison and this wretched country. My time is short, therefore pray leave me." Later, he dictated a note to Ramezay containing the same answer he had given Vaudreuil.

Montcalm cared about the soldiers who had served under him and sent a touching note to General Townshend on their behalf: "Monsieur, the humanity of the English sets my mind at peace concerning the fate of French prisoners and Canadians. Do not let them perceive that they have changed masters. Be their protector as I have been their father." But he was appealing to the wrong man. Townshend intended to leave Canada in less than two weeks, but even if he'd stayed to govern, he had no interest in men at the bottom of the social ladder. In his eyes, soldiers were like cattle.

There were Frenchmen in high places, however, who still respected duty: Bishop Pontbriand, dying of cancer, found the strength to administer the last rites to Montcalm. No coffin was available for the fallen general, and an old man who did odd jobs for the nuns put together a rough box. Late in the evening of September 14, the courageous and unhappy marquis was laid to rest without due honours; no tolling bell, no gun salute, no special guard.

General Montcalm was buried in a bomb crater near the front of the chapel in the Ursuline convent, a hole enlarged to accommodate the makeshift coffin. Francis Parkman described the service as one conducted by "three priests from the Cathedral and attended by several nuns, Ramezay with some of his officers and a crowd of civilians." They lowered the body into the ground by torchlight and some wept for the only member of the ruling set untouched by scandal. Even at the time, the ceremony was thought by many to foreshadow the demise of the colony itself.

Meanwhile, French officials were trying to rally. On September 17, General Lévis met Vaudreuil in the village of Jacques-Cartier and agreed to march the army back to Quebec to engage the British a second time. Put like that, it sounds quite civilized. But Gordon Donaldson, in *Battle for a Continent, Quebec 1759,* tells a different story: "De Lévis stormed into Jacques Cartier and took command of the beaten army. He was now a General of France and he damned Vaudreuil for giving up so easily and only just fell short of calling the Governor a coward."

Lévis' forces were shrinking fast. Militiamen drifted home to harvest what was left of their crops, and his Indian allies were vanishing at an alarming rate. General Lévis knew he had to act quickly. Vaudreuil, still indulging himself in a fanciful view of recent events, dispatched a rosier picture to the Court of Versailles. "I was much charmed to find M. de Lévis disposed to march with the army towards Quebec," he wrote. Vaudreuil didn't say Lévis would actually *lead* the troops, rather that Lévis would move "towards" Quebec. To the troops hearing the order to march back over the route they'd just covered, it must have sounded like lunacy. But crazy or not, by night-fall on September 18 the French army had reached St. Augustin, only a few miles from the stricken fortress.

Brigadier-General Townshend (temporarily in command because Wolfe was dead and the senior brigadier, Monckton, lay wounded) was busily setting up batteries aimed at Quebec's western side. The troops brought up sixty guns and fifty-eight howitzers, Knox wrote. And even if they had acquired horses, much of the hard labour still would have fallen to the privates. That was the way of war before the machine age.

Although Townshend had assumed command on the field because Monckton was wounded, he was in no hurry to relinquish his authority after Monckton recovered. Officers under Townshend felt he was determined to have his own name on the documents of sur-render. From September 13 to September 18, Brigadier Townshend went through the motions of command (keeping Monckton out for political reasons) and his thoughts were already on the voyage home.

French officials realized the British terms were generous and they were anxious to end the game before the British had a change of heart. Garrison troops would make their exit with proper ceremony, and the regulars and some officials would be returned to France on the earliest possible ship. Citizens were to retain their property, their Roman Catholic religion and their language, provided they signed a paper swearing allegiance to the British crown. The bishop, the clergy, churches and convents would be protected from violence and theft. French leaders knew a brass ring when they saw one and grabbed it; in that century, treaties were usually much less forgiving.

Commandant de Ramezay raised the white flag on September 17 and Townshend arranged for all necessary ceremonies to take place. Even so, turning over Quebec to the British wasn't accomplished without a touch of drama. Only a few hours after the white flag went up, Bougainville pounded into town on horseback carrying bags of biscuits and a promise from Lévis to fight again. But even if Bougainville had arrived before the verbal agreement, Commandant de Ramezay had no faith in the enterprise. He had witnessed the army's headlong retreat on September 13 and refused to trust the regulars a second time. The capitulation would become a reality the following day.

On the morning of September 18, with British naval guns trained on the town, Brigadier Townshend and Admiral Saunders signed the surrender. That evening fifty artillerymen came through the St. Louis Gate pulling a gun carriage bearing the British colours. Townshend was escorted to the Château Louis (the French governor's official residence), the whitecoats marched away and the redcoats took their places.

In the Quebec Basin, General James Wolfe, suitably embalmed, lay in a stateroom on the *Royal William,* the ship that would carry him home.

Down south, around Lake George, the British weren't quite so successful. Amherst had whiled away the summer mending forts and making roads. In early September he turned to building ships, a good idea if he'd started a month earlier – before the weather had turned chilly. Yet Amherst was still bothered by the idea that he ought to make an attempt to take Montreal. Where had the summer gone? Île-aux-Noix, bristling with guns, still squatted like a plump porcupine in the middle of the Richelieu River, and he regarded it as a major barrier between himself and his target. Even if his transports managed to slip past the island's gunfire, they still would face several armed vessels on Lake Champlain. Amherst seemed unwilling to admit it was too late to assault Montreal and, announcing that he needed one more brig and one more sloop, he implied he would still head north.

Once again, Amherst's lumbering pace and poor priorities set the stage for failure. On September 1 his scouts reported that all the French soldiers who had abandoned Ticonderoga and Crown Point were presently shoring up gun positions on that irritating little bastion of an island Île-aux-Noix, adding that Bourlamaque now had one hundred cannon.

"That can't be," Amherst wrote in his journal, as if by doing so he could make them disappear. "[B]ut they certainly got together all [the cannons] they could and I suppose some come from ships that escaped Mr. Durrell [*sic*]. If those ships had not got up [the St. Lawrence River] Canada would probably be ours." The reference was to Admiral Durell's feeble attempt to blockade French transports back in May.

Deserters told the British that the French had just launched a brand-new sloop, bringing their total to five. In response, Amherst ordered Major Ord to prepare "fire darts to screw in and I'll try to burn it." A fire dart was an early James Bond–like device that required a skilled swimmer who could sneak up on an enemy ship and attach it to the hull. In those days there were no rubber suits or fitted goggles to help keep out the cold, and underwater work was very unpleasant.

Captain Loring's crew was scheduled to begin building a sloop on September 3, but heavy rain delayed the start. Undaunted, the major-general dispatched his four best swimmers to place fire darts under Bourlamaque's latest sloop. But before they could accomplish anything, the men were captured. At the same time, Amherst received a letter from Albany saying British officers in Canada were thinking of fortifying Île-aux-Coudres (downriver from Quebec) and leaving a fleet to winter on the Gaspé coast. His colleagues in Albany also said Wolfe had little hope of capturing Quebec this season. But Amherst said he still had faith in Wolfe, a rare occasion when he showed an interest in Wolfe's fate.

Exactly one month later, Amherst began gathering his forces for the expedition to Montreal, although he was still waiting for the new brig – the *Duke of Cumberland* – and the sloop *Boscawen*. His scheme was deceptively simple: "Captain Loring will try to cut the enemy [ships] off from Île-aux-Noix which is the only sure way of taking them."

It was October 11 before Amherst was ready to sail north on Lake Champlain and, as usual, the gods were waiting to blend comedy and tragedy. The first night out some Highlanders in a bateau mistook French sloops for their own and came under fire. A few were taken prisoner, the boat was set adrift and the vessel and the remainder of the crew were rescued. The next night the weather turned nasty and Amherst's men quickly became exhausted rowing in such high winds. As a result, he ordered all boats to take cover in a sheltered bay. Most of the troops were safely put ashore to "boil their pots," although there is no record that they actually ate hot food. Next morning, Amherst added, "In the night a man in a dream cried out 'Murder!' and another, in his sleep, fired his piece and burnt a sergeant of the Grenadiers very much."

Stormy weather prevented the British from moving on Lake Champlain. Captain Loring, moored several miles north on the *Duke of Cumberland,* sent word he had chased an enemy schooner and trapped it between two islands. But unfortunately he had run aground himself just as he came within firing range. Eventually, Loring's ship floated free and he again gave chase, this time cornering the French in a small bay by anchoring the *Cumberland* across the mouth to prevent the enemy's escape. The end of the story was left to the imagination.

The sailors who had brought the letter from Loring to Amherst found they couldn't return because "the water run [*sic*] as high as some seas in a gale of wind." They had no choice but to remain with Amherst. In the middle of October it was still raining heavily, the lake was "much agitated" and Amherst had given up hope of setting sail for Île-aux-Noix. At night the temperature sank to zero; during the day gales threatened to destroy the ship. Amherst, a man devoted to the obvious, noted, "This would be nothing if it was a month earlier but every day is a great loss of time when I can't stir from here."

Winter was almost upon him yet he acted as if the weather had somehow ambushed him. Captain Loring, he figured, would be expecting support by now – so he dispatched two loaded whaleboats to the *Duke of Cumberland*. It soon became obvious that the men had to turn back, and the expedition was called off. On October 18 two letters arrived by an overland route, one from Brigadier Gage at Oswego, who told Amherst that Quebec had fallen on September 13, and the other from the lieutenant-governor of New York, confirming the victory and adding that Wolfe was dead.

The news produced very little reaction from Amherst. "This will, of course, bring Mons. de Vaudreuil and the whole army to Montreal so I shall decline my intended operations and get back to Crown Point where I hear the works go on but slowly," was his comment. Not a word of regret about Wolfe's death; not a single huzzah for the British victory at Quebec. Amherst's chief concerns were the postponement of his voyage to Montreal (one can almost hear his sigh of relief) and the lack of progress being made on his expensive renovation of Crown Point. Amherst's journal entry on October 19 sounded more like a justification for his own conduct than a simple observation: "The wind being northerly and an appearance of winter having set in, it would take me ten days more to get to the Île-aux-Noix and, as my intention of sending a detachment to destroy Caughnawaga and surprise Montreal can no longer be executed, I ordered the troops back to Crown Point."

Amherst and his fleet arrived at the ever-evolving fort of his dreams on the twenty-first of October. It was a month before his troops were ready to make the journey south to Albany and New York, where they would move into winter quarters. Yet even knowing he must transport thousands of men by boat on lakes and rivers that never went a winter without freezing, he felt no urgency. Plodding paperwork and written orders for garrisons under Amherst's command kept him busy. One morning, at the end of November, he looked out the window and noticed it was "snowing fast." It was time to go south.

20

Holding the Fort

"They despaired, they triumphed and they wept:
for Wolfe had fallen in the hour of victory."
— HORACE WALPOLE, London, 1759

Quebec lay in ashes. Wolfe's long bombardment had turned the capital into a ghost town. Down by the docks, three hundred houses
were piles of rubble and the imposing bishop's palace on Mountain
Street looked haunted. In Upper Town every major building was
damaged in one way or another. The cathedral was a burned-out
shell and, inside the church of the Récollets, exploding bombs had
tossed up skulls and bones long buried underneath the floor. People
with relatives or friends living in the country fled there for shelter;
others struggled to survive inside the fortress.

British soldiers roamed the streets, stood guard duty on every
corner and overflowed the barracks. Hundreds of privates still slept
in tents although everyone knew something had to be done about
that before the snow came: winter was written on the sullen sky.
Justice was swift and harsh: theft and rape were punishable by flog-
ging and sometimes by hanging. But hungry men no longer feared

death and, despite the severity of the punishments, the crimes continued. On September 18, when Brigadier Murray became military and civil governor, ten thousand people huddled inside the walls. The town larder contained barely enough half-rations to feed six thousand people for a few days.

From the beginning, hundreds were sick and dying and the numbers grew at a frightening rate because no one, including doctors, understood the threat posed by tainted water or the importance of quarantining infectious patients. Thirty-seven years would pass before Edward Jenner discovered a vaccine against smallpox, and a century would go by before Louis Pasteur developed the germ theory. Doctors had only recently grasped that fresh citrus fruit and spruce beer helped prevent scurvy. Most medical men still used leeches to extract quarts of blood from patients who could ill afford to lose a dram. Doctors were scarce and nurses, usually untrained males willing to do the dirty work, could be more of a threat than the original complaint. Exceptions were the compassionate Ursuline nuns who ran the General Hospital and the smaller Hôtel-Dieu. The sisters took in sick and wounded from both armies.

This, then, was the chaotic capital General Murray inherited. Unlikable as he was, the grim little Scotsman was probably the best man to handle the horrors of peace. Rumour had it that he liked the French Canadians *too* well, might even be a secret sympathizer, a Jacobite! Whether this was true or false, keeping the townspeople alive was not Murray's only challenge. The fear of raids lurked in the background. Canada was far from beaten. General Lévis was out there in the forest with his patchwork army, cooking up God only knew what Machiavellian schemes to claw back the capital.

Army rank and file worked so hard they had little energy left for griping. In the days immediately following the occupation, British detachments buried the dead, hauled away stinking rubbish, gathered firewood and levelled trenches they'd recently dug on the Plains.

Others hurried to unload provisions from British ships still moored in the harbour: flour, sugar, tea, salt pork and rum, clothing and blankets to keep the army from freezing to death in the coming winter. Finding fresh meat, vegetables and fruits to offset the steady salty diet was a top priority and yet scurvy continued to spread through the population. The supply of spruce beer, favoured by Wolfe, had run out. And the wretched town could expect no help from their allies in New England and Nova Scotia, for soon Quebec would be an island in a sea of snow and ice. Every earthly plague checked in – smallpox, typhoid, venereal disease and dozens of fevers still unnamed. Medicine of any sort had always been in short supply, but now Canadians and British soldiers alike depended on whatever the naval surgeons agreed to leave behind. The best of times was past. The worst lay just ahead.

The great ships sailed on October 16 with Rear-Admiral Charles Saunders and Brigadier-General George Townshend aboard the *Stirling Castle*. Brigadier-General Robert Monckton took ship for New York to come under the command of Major-General Amherst and recover from his wound. Colonel Guy Carleton and Major Isaac Barré, who had lost an eye, sailed for England. James Murray remained in Quebec, the first governor-general under British rule. Murray had longed for power, had envied Wolfe, and here he was, a little king in a frozen landscape. Murray had won the prize, but it had lost much of its glitter. Life in Quebec was, for a time, a miserable affair.

Ten battalions, all the British artillery and a company of Royal Americans, remained in Canada with Murray – their shared task, literally, to hold the fort. Among the officers was Captain John Knox, a man eminently qualified to survive the coming ordeal and, at the same time, keep a record of it. Hadn't he endured five months in Fort Hell, otherwise known as Beauséjour? Hadn't he shared the thrill and the pain of the Battle of the Plains of Abraham? Details of his first winter in Quebec, so carefully noted in his diary, combine the captain's own experiences with observations about common soldiers. As a captain, Knox lived a cut above the privates and non-commissioned officers, but he was one of those rare men who sympathized with those below him while being grateful his lodgings were better than theirs. "On 5 October," he wrote, "I removed to the tenement assigned me for my quarters, a cart-house and stable called by the inhabitants *un hangar;* a spacious but unfinished apartment with a closet [toilet]: a loft for hay and a manger at one end for horses from which I was separated by a stone partition. With the assistance of a good stove and some carpentry work my habitation was rendered tolerably comfortable."

Within a week of establishing his curious lodging, Knox was sent to guard the General Hospital, where his duties included the prevention of plunder and rape by soldiers and transients. Because the British were uneasy about their own safety (trapped in snow and surrounded by the enemy), every person leaving the hospital – including medical men, officers and domestics – needed a passport to go to town. It was also Knox's job to seize all firearms and ammunition left behind by the French.

Knox considered himself lucky to get such an assignment. For one thing, he ate, as he put it, "at the French king's table" in the company of captured enemy officers and their wives. At first, his new companions spoke in Latin to conceal what they were saying, never dreaming a mere English captain would understand. Knox changed that by quoting Virgil to them and, surprised by his expertise, the French contingent stopped using their secret code. Little is known of Knox or his background, but this incident shows he was an educated man, which meant he likely came from a moneyed family.

During the time Knox guarded the hospital, he ate "dinner" between 11 a.m. and noon and, though the food was indifferent, the coffee was laced with brandy. Supper, which the French called the *grand repas,* was served between six and seven o'clock in the evening, and food was always plentiful. Knox was supplied with a spoon, a four-pronged fork, a napkin and a plate, but was informed he must bring his own knife and a supply of wine. At table, his personal valet served him with help from domestic staff hired by the nuns. Knox, who appears to have been a generous soul, shared his wine with fellow diners and observed they "by no means disliked it." Most wine came from France and Knox would have bought his supply from the transports.

Captain Knox had been on duty for three days when the Mother-Abbess (the sister of former Commandant de Ramezay) invited him to take an English breakfast in her spacious apartment. He found a group of nuns sitting around doing needlework. Two large silver pots, one for coffee and one for tea, were placed on a table in the middle of the room. The menu was Spartan: a plate of sliced buttered bread, and a loaf of uncut bread with butter (and a knife). Unfortunately, the tea was so strong Knox couldn't drink it and he settled for milk. Nevertheless, he viewed his stint at the hospital as an oasis in the hard life of the garrison and was reluctant to return to his residence in *"un hangar."*

Life among the privates was grittier. At first, they had kept warm by burning old fences and scraps of wood from smashed houses. Early in December, the custom was forbidden and soldiers were forced to cut trees in the surrounding forest and drag them long distances over deep snow, a chore that reminded Knox of his terrible winter in Fort Beauséjour. Troops cut up blankets from supplies abandoned by the French to make socks and gloves. All posts at Point Lévis and on Île d'Orléans were shut down for the winter and the troops moved into Quebec. Women camp followers went along, their allowance cut by a third. To qualify, they were expected to meet certain requirements: mainly being "useful to the soldiers," cleaning or doing laundry for both men and officers. Though sex was never mentioned, women were ordered to "reside in the men's quarters," which strongly suggests it was expected. Female sutlers were not permitted to benefit from such arrangements because they were thought to be making a living and were, by implication, self-supporting. No provision was made by the army to send women back to England or any other destination, should they take sick or be abandoned by husbands or lovers. The life of a camp follower was precarious, at best.

On the bright side, soldiers half-frozen in their inadequate uniforms were given bits of clothing from supplies the French had left behind – uniform jackets, waistcoats, hats, powder horns, moccasins, scraps of flannel and damaged linens (meaning underwear). Men detailed to cut firewood wore creepers – clogs with metal cleats on the soles – at a cost of five pence a pair. While the freebies helped keep soldiers warm, they created a comic appearance. In their mix-and-match uniforms, privates looked less exotic than their fur-draped officers and were never quite as warm.

Knox wrote, "Our guards on the grand parade make a grotesque appearance in their different dresses: and our inventions to guard against the extreme cold are various beyond imagination. The uniformity of the clean, methodical soldier is buried in the rough fur garb of the frozen Laplander. We resemble a masquerade rather than a body of regular troops."

Knox often failed to recognize his old friends with fur hats pulled down to their eyebrows and mufflers wrapped around their faces. But even with that much protection, frostbite remained a constant hazard.

In another part of the forest, down by Lake Champlain, Jeffrey Amherst was about to take the longest hike of his life. He had finally given up the idea of attacking Île-aux-Noix this season and made no more mention of Quebec's fall or Wolfe's death. It was as if he had no connection with Canada's fate. Perhaps he expected officials in Albany to keep in touch with General Murray and pass the word on to him.

November blew in with a hard frost; it was so cold and windy, all work on the fortress at Crown Point came to a halt. While doing his paperwork in relatively comfortable quarters, Amherst received a letter from Vaudreuil, now snugly ensconced in his Montreal mansion, about a routine prisoner exchange. Amherst was agreeable to the request. After all, such a piece of business cost him nothing and would look good in his reports to London.

In the course of being questioned by Amherst, a prisoner pointed out that in Montreal, people were gossiping about Major Rogers and his "gang" burning St. Francis and slaughtering the natives. Amherst's response, as recorded in his journal, was defensive: "I fancy he is mistaken about women and children and that some Indians and Canadians attacked Major Rogers in his retreat at night." Amherst knew perfectly well that he himself had ordered the raid, although it was also true he had specified no women or children were to be harmed. Perhaps he made the entry in an attempt to distance himself from the St. Francis raid.

Late in November, Amherst was still dawdling at Crown Point, deep in plans to move his troops to winter quarters. On November 26, standing on the shore of Lake Champlain, he spied chunks of ice and popped out of his coma just in time to set out on the long road to New York. The first lap of the journey, a boat trip to Fort George, was accomplished before nightfall. Amherst's little fleet was the last to sail on Lake George that season.

After warming up on the overnight stop, Amherst marched his troops over fourteen miles of military road that connected Fort George with Fort Edward on the Hudson River. When he described the walk as "fine marching but there was no riding," he spoke for himself. Perhaps it *was* fine for a general wearing handmade boots and heavy socks, woollen underwear, a fur overcoat and a muffler around his face. Amherst was forty-two years old and obviously robust, or he wouldn't have started out on such a venture. His rank as commander-in-chief of the British Army in America ensured an adequate escort and sufficient baggage handlers.

Thousands of privates moving through the same icy landscape wore moccasins rather than leather shoes because they kept the feet warm. It's unlikely any soldier owned a winter overcoat – the garment is never mentioned. When the weather was bitter, the men wrapped blankets around their shoulders like capes. The lucky ones wore heavy "leggins," mufflers and hats with earflaps.

To give Amherst credit, though, he never whined about feeling cold or tired, even after walking twenty-five miles over rutted, snow-covered roads. Luckily, the wind was usually at his back. If he relied on the occasional jolt of brandy to keep going, he never admitted it. His attitude, as reflected in his diary, was so enthusiastic about frosty weather that he went out of his way to accompany troops to Saratoga, a little side-trip that added miles to his journey.

Perhaps his blood really *was* different from that of other men. He declared, "It is better to lay [sic] in a good warm wood by a blazing fire than to pitch a tent in the open." On December 2, an attempt was made to move the army from Fort Edward down the Hudson by boat but the river was frozen and the plan was abandoned. From that point on, everybody was forced to walk. A large number of troops were destined for New York and, on December 5, General Amherst made a seven-day plan for the first leg of the march. The Royal Americans faced a one hundred–mile walk to Elizabethtown and were assigned the west bank of the Hudson. Prideaux's, about to trudge 170 miles to a camp near New York, took the road along the east bank.

"I set out on foot, crossed the river and walked 22 miles to Kinderhook," Amherst noted on December 6. "The road is such a distance there is no view of the river and not above half-a-dozen poor cottages on the whole road. Kinderhook is a pretty open spot; about one hundred families are settled in the place."

From that point on, Amherst's diary was a guided tour complete with helpful hints for anyone who cared to follow in his footsteps. In Claverack he was taken in by Mr. Hauteboon and given refreshments. After a rest, the general covered another fourteen miles before fetching up on the doorstep of Justice Tinbrooks. "The country is well settled with farm houses and has woods of oak and pine," he wrote. Next day, his first lap covered 22 miles to the DeWitts, whose property stretched right down to the Hudson and where, in the general's opinion, the peasants lived well. His descriptions continued on the same light note until at last, on December 11, he caught sight of the mouth of the Hudson River. That night he dined with the lieutenant-governor of New York and his journey was over.

It's unfortunate that Amherst didn't give an account of his feelings when he again tasted civilized life. What did he eat for supper that first night? Was the governor's food rich? Was his wine up to snuff? Did Amherst bask in front of a blazing fire with a glass of good port, knowing his trials were over for the winter? Regrettably, the general didn't pass on any details. He merely closed his journal.

21

A Public Scandal

"However glorious this victory was, and however important in its consequences, it was very dearly bought ... the loss of a genius in war is a loss that we know not how to repair."

– EDMUND BURKE, *Annual Register,* 1759

Wolfe, wrapped in his long black cloak, was carried down the steep road at l'Anse au Foulon and rowed out to the frigate *Seahorse.* Captain Thomas Bell, one of his aides-de-camp and a family friend, prepared the body. Whether Wolfe was embalmed as we understand the term or "immersed in brine," as one report suggests, depends on the source. The body was sealed in a stone shell taken from the cistern of the convent of the Ursulines, the sort of coffin that would permit the use of liquid preservative. On September 23, Bell escorted the body aboard the man-of-war the *Royal William,* and they set out on the long voyage home.

As the British officers prepared to leave Quebec, General Monckton, still the ranking officer, expressed the hope that George Townshend would remain as long as possible. "There are many things to do which I am convinced you will be good enough to assist me in," Monckton wrote. But there was little chance of that! Townshend was on a mission:

to reach London at the earliest possible moment, defend his reputation and stir up the muddy waters swirling around Wolfe's name.
Monckton had never been as anti-Wolfe as Murray and would be of
little use in the present difficulties. By contrast, James Murray was an
angry, envious man. And although he was slated to carry on as civil
and military governor in Canada, he might still be useful. Townshend
let Murray know Wolfe's friends were already whispering malicious
tales about the three brigadier-generals and offered to act for Murray
as well as himself when he got back to London. Murray swallowed
the bait. "Since so black a lie was propagated," he wrote, "I think
myself very happy that you will be on the spot to contradict whatever
ignorance or faction may suggest." The "black lie" was that the
brigadiers had wished to land thirty miles farther upriver and had
never approved of Wolfe's choice of the Foulon. It was partly true
but, since Wolfe's victory proved him right, such a tasty bit of gossip
could not be allowed to drift about the posh clubs or appear in letters
to the editor.

Saunders sailed for England on October 16 aboard the *Namur*,
taking Townshend with him. That same night, Townshend's first dispatch announcing the taking of Quebec landed on Pitt's desk in St.
James' Square, London. It couldn't have come at a better time. Only
three days before, Pitt had received Wolfe's despairing letter of
September 2 in which he confessed to the disaster at Montmorency
Falls. Now, with a miracle to report, Pitt spent the night scribbling
notes to king and cabinet trumpeting that England was blessed and
his own foreign policy flourishing.

At a levee the next day, the king remarked to Pitt, "All your plans
have succeeded." And Lady Hervey, a political junkie and royal hanger-
on, gave her opinion in writing: "Quebec is certainly a great acquisition
but 'tis gold bought too dear. Woolfe [*sic*] is an irreparable loss, such an
head, such an heart, such a temper and such an arm are not easily to be
found again." Major Barré arrived the next day to confirm the news,

and word radiated from London throughout the countryside and to other cities. Bonfires sprang up everywhere, champagne flowed at the tables of the rich and a tidal wave of cheap gin swept over the poor. Wolfe's death was a tragedy, but England bowed to his greatness.

Not everyone toasted Wolfe, of course. Tobias Smollett, a popular novelist, sniffed, "All was rapture and riot and Wolfe was exalted to a ridiculous degree of hyperbole."

Unlike poor Montcalm, whose funeral service was simple to the point of sadness, Wolfe was given an elaborate farewell. The body arrived at Spithead on November 16 (after almost two months at sea) and the burial took place four days later. The *London Chronicle*, November 17–20, 1759, described the coffin's journey from Spithead to Portsmouth:

> On Saturday, November 17, at seven o'clock in the morning the body was lowered out of the ship into a twelve-oared barge, towed by two twelve-oared barges and attended by twelve twelve-oared barges. Minute guns were fired from ships at Spithead, from the time of the body's leaving the *Royal William* to its being landed at the point at Portsmouth, which was one hour. At nine, the body was put into a travelling hearse, attended by a mourning coach and proceeded through the garrison.

The entire garrison and a crowd of silent civilians gathered to watch the cortege as it wound through the town. Cannon boomed and muffled bells tolled until it moved out on the road to Blackheath, east of London, where the body lay in state for three days in the front hall of the family mansion. A funeral attended by relatives and friends took place in St. Alphege Church nearby, and Wolfe was buried in the family crypt beside his father.

Only a few months earlier, Henrietta had buried her husband and, when news came of her son's death, she sank into a deep depression. Within two weeks, Thomas Bell and William DeLaune delivered Wolfe's personal belongings and the miniature portrait of Katherine Lowther. Mrs. Wolfe forced herself to read James' will and was shocked to discover that his bequests amounted to £7,000, considerably more than the value of Wolfe's estate. It seemed to jolt her into action. Friends and even Henrietta herself suggested Wolfe didn't understand his father's will – which seems ludicrous given his reputation as a scholar and a realist. It was simple enough: the old general had left everything to his widow. In the last letter James wrote to his mother, he assured her that he approved of the terms of his father's will; so why would he expect any large sum of money from the estate? It's possible, of course, that Wolfe Sr. changed his will after James sailed for Quebec. It seems more likely that Wolfe was depending on his army back pay to cover everything. Henrietta, supporting her son to the last, said she would see that all his commitments were honoured and began her crusade to collect from the army by asking William Pitt for his advice.

Wolfe made his will on June 8, 1759, while he was aboard the *Neptune* en route to Quebec and, as usual, expressed himself clearly. Katherine Lowther's portrait was to be set in jewels to the amount of five hundred guineas and returned to her. He left £1,000 each to Colonel James Oughton, Colonel Guy Carleton, Colonel William Howe and Colonel George Warde. (He added a codicil on July 2, just before the attack at Montmorency Falls, leaving £1,000 each to his uncle, Walter Wolfe, and his cousin Edward Goldsmith.) The fact that he had failed to include his old friend William Rickson was remarked upon, but no explanation ever surfaced. The additional £2,000 suggests that Wolfe firmly believed there would be enough money to fulfill his wishes – he would never have knowingly burdened his mother with debt.

As for his possessions, he left his silver plate to Admiral Charles Saunders, a man he had come to admire, and his camp equipment, table linen and wine to the officer who succeeded him. His books and papers went to Colonel Carleton and a hundred guineas each to six officers he had befriended during the campaign. Wolfe bequeathed fifty guineas to his valet François, and twenty to Ambrose. His clothes were to be divided among the two personal servants and three footmen. All members of his household staff were to be paid a year's wages and their board until they reached England or found a new job. The balance, if there was anything, was to go to his mother.

Henrietta received a well-worded brush-off from Pitt. It wasn't his department, the Prime Minister wrote, passing her along to the Duke of Newcastle, a man who not only disliked Wolfe for his own reasons but also was George Townshend's uncle. Newcastle informed Mrs. Wolfe that back pay at the level of major-general was out of the question because Wolfe had held the rank temporarily. When she asked for back pay owed at a colonel's level, the duke refused it outright.

Nevertheless, for some people, there was money to be made out of the latest popular hero. Parliament voted £3,000 for a memorial sculpture of Wolfe for Westminster Abbey; art patrons commissioned busts; and several artists painted pictures of Wolfe's death that were copied and sold in various forms, although they bore little resemblance to the Plains of Abraham, Wolfe or the battle scene. While the government could find money for the sculpture, it denied Mrs. Wolfe's request for money due the conqueror. With the help of her nephew Edward Goldsmith and the schoolmaster, Mr. Swindon, Henrietta continued to badger the self-described "grateful government."

Brigadier-General George Townshend and Admiral Charles Saunders appeared before Parliament in January 1760 to receive thanks for their part in winning Canada for England. By this time, a bitter feud between the supporters of General Wolfe (officers who had fought at Quebec, such as Carleton, Barré and Saunders) and General Townshend (influential figures such as the Duke of Newcastle, Horace Walpole and Adjutant-General Richard Lyttleton) had become a public scandal. People gossiped about Townshend's chilly references to Wolfe in his dispatches and his less-than-subtle attempt to take credit for capturing Quebec. A nasty pamphlet appeared anonymously, criticizing Townshend; and he, believing it was the work of the Duke of Cumberland, challenged Lord Albemarle, one of Cumberland's close friends. The king heard about the upcoming duel and stopped it before a shot was fired. All this lent a distinctly unpleasant tone to the Wolfe cult, but ordinary people persisted in seeing Wolfe as a hero, right up there with Marlborough and, later, Wellington.

Between December 1759 and April 1760, the inmates of Quebec were painfully aware of the unseen enemy all around them. *Coureurs de bois,* Indians and deserters arrived at the gates even in the coldest months with horrendous tales about French preparations for the next siege of Quebec. General Lévis was supposedly planning to eat his Christmas dinner in the Château St. Louis. He led fifteen thousand men, many of them rehearsing with scaling ladders against handmade snowbanks. During a random raid on the British outpost at Lorette, the French rustled a herd of cattle belonging to the British. A party went out from the fortress and, after a vicious skirmish, retrieved their property, but the incident gave the British a fright. On another occasion, a French detachment brazenly occupied Point Lévis across the river and the British, finding this intolerable, dragged cannon across the frozen St. Lawrence to blow them away. The ensuing scrap cost them twelve dead and twenty wounded and the French took twelve English prisoners. French losses were not made public, but Knox believed they were heavy because he saw "great quantities of blood on the snow everywhere in their rear."

None of these sallies had much effect upon the fortress itself – they were mere bee stings on an elephant's leg. And yet, no matter what indignities were thrust upon them, the French residents of the capital prayed that Lévis would wait until transports from France arrived in the basin. They were sure to be loaded not only with food, but with the ammunition he'd need to win back the capital.

Vaudreuil, wintering in Montreal, tried to restore his tattered reputation by boasting to his friends and scratching out wordy letters to be sent on the first ship leaving for France. General Lévis, a jovial fellow, was willing to get along with anyone, even a windbag like the governor, if it meant regaining Quebec. To give him his due, Vaudreuil had improved his spy system since the September defeat and now had agents inside Murray's army feeding him accurate tidbits about British problems. He knew the death toll from scurvy and other diseases was close to catastrophic. The previous October Murray had seven thousand men in fighting trim. By April 1760 the figure was forty-eight hundred; some were dead, and the rest were either ill or had deserted. Hospitals were filled with patients and two or three soldiers died every day.

Vaudreuil had already composed a report to Minister Berryer claiming he had "arrived just in time to take the most judicious measures and prevent General Amherst from penetrating into the colony." However, Amherst's journal revealed that his plans to attack Île-aux-Noix were delayed so long the whole scheme fizzled out; Vaudreuil had had nothing to do with saving Montreal that last winter, but that was the kind of personal propaganda the governor so readily spewed out.

In April, eleven thousand soldiers in the main French camp at Jacques-Cartier were judged enough to make a fresh assault on Quebec. A story circulated that Lévis intended to divide his troops into three sections of five thousand men each and attack three important outposts near the capital. "They flatter themselves," Knox wrote, "that from the weakness of our garrison [due to] sickness and mortality, we shall surrender to their superior army." Still seeking a cure for scurvy, British officers were handing out rations of ginger, but with little effect.

A final clash between the British and the French was inevitable, and both sides stepped up their preparations as the weather warmed. Serious gamblers put their money on the French to win.

22

A Final Clash

"We drove them back as long as we had ammunition,
until our cannon were bogged in deep pits of snow."
– SERGEANT JOHN JOHNSON, 58th Regiment, April 28, 1760

The final battle for Quebec in the spring of 1760 was divided into three parts: the French raid on Ste-Foy; a two-hour struggle the next day on the familiar Plains of Abraham; and a two-week siege of the fortress, brought to an end by the arrival of the British fleet. Governor-General James Murray's fast response to the arrival of Lévis' army on the Plains was impressive, but when it came to gamesmanship on the field, he earned a goose egg. Apparently, he'd learned nothing from Montcalm's mistakes the September before and, although the circumstances were different, the result was much the same.

General Lévis, a courageous and clever warrior, landed his army at Cap-Rouge, fifteen miles above Quebec, and hoped that by marching through the woods to the Plains of Abraham, he would take General Murray by surprise. He succeeded until 3 a.m. on the morning of April 27, when a fluke changed the odds. Before dawn that day, a sailor on a British frigate that happened to be wintering at the docks near Lower Town heard faint cries for help coming from the river. The captain of the *Racehorse* put out a rescue boat and the crew scooped up a French soldier clinging to a huge chunk of ice. The man was half-dead, but plied with rum and warmed by a fire, he stopped shaking long enough to tell his captors he was an artillery sergeant with Lévis' army. In the hope that he had useful information, the sailors wrapped him in a blanket and hauled him up the hill to General Murray's headquarters in the Château Louis. A good grilling, they thought, might yield results.

Under questioning, the sergeant claimed he and six other men were on their way to join Lévis' army when a ferocious storm capsized the boat, dumping them in the river. The captive was more robust than his companions, since he had managed to hang on to an ice floe until the current carried him to Lower Town. It was then that he began to shout for help. The prisoner warned his captors that the French squadron, presently at Cap-Rouge, consisted of several frigates, sloops and smaller craft – all loaded with enough guns and provisions to service twelve thousand men. (Later, the figure turned out to be seven thousand.) The sergeant added that everyone in the Lévis camp was convinced that if the French fleet reached Quebec first, carrying enough men and provisions, a French victory was certain.

Murray had reason to agree. During the stressful winter, he had found time to examine the fortified walls and had reached the same conclusion as Montcalm, three years before: they were so badly constructed that a battering from heavy artillery would reduce them to dust. Knowing these things, General Murray decided to challenge Lévis on the Plains before he had time to set up his cannon.

The French mustered every man available to take back Quebec: regulars from France, colony troops, militia and Indian allies. To support this army, they stripped the countryside of food, ammunition, horses and ships. General Lévis, Governor Vaudreuil, citizens and ordinary fighting men all realized the coming battle would be their last chance to escape British domination.

After establishing his camp at Cap-Rouge, Lévis decided to attack the British outpost at Old Lorette. "It was a frightful night," the recently promoted general wrote, "so dark that but for the flashes of lightning we should have been forced to stop." The small band of red-coats defending Old Lorette fell back on the village of Ste-Foy. By morning, heavy rain had turned to drizzle and Lévis, peering out from thick evergreens that edged the plains, could see the church and houses occupied by the British. Having no idea how numerous the British were, Lévis thought it wise to wait until nightfall and slip past the place without a fight. Why not head straight for Quebec?

Murray didn't wait for Lévis' strategy to unfold. Warned by the floating informer that the enemy was at Cap-Rouge, the general rose early on the morning of the 27th and led a small force toward Ste-Foy. His intention was to rescue soldiers marooned in outposts close by. As the British plodded along the snowy Ste-Foy Road they came under French fire and Murray suspected a trap. The wily French hoped to lure him into the woods, but he was too smart to fall for that old trick. Although he could catch only glimpses of his enemy through the trees, he fired his field guns, which, Knox reported, "galled the French immensely." The upshot was that the British refused to be drawn into the forest and the French hunkered down, determined not to be drawn out.

It soon became apparent that neither combatant was prepared to engage in an all-out fight. Instead, Murray blew up the church, which he'd earlier turned into an ammunition dump, and marched back to Quebec. The score was a handful of dead and wounded on each side and two drenched armies. While the British made an orderly retreat, the French made a half-hearted attempt to pursue. But British field pieces held the enemy off. Captain Knox described the French as "firing and shouting at a great distance." It wasn't the first time Knox had tut-tutted his disapproval of Gallic hollering. If things went wrong, he much preferred the grim silence of the British.

Murray called the whole thing off and returned to Quebec, so the first encounter between the two armies petered out. But his men weren't ready to quit. They hadn't had a real "go" at the French, nothing to show for the day's effort except hundreds of wet red jackets. With the British safely back in the fortress, officers tried to console their disgruntled men with an extra ration of rum and permission to dry out beside blazing fires fuelled by scraps of wrecked houses from the suburb of St. Roch.

The following day, April 28, Murray marched out the St. Louis Gate for the second time, to confront an even bleaker landscape. The leafless trees wept moisture from a recent storm, the distant hills looked threatening. Mushy snow concealed deep holes in the road, making it difficult for troops who were dragging the gun carriages. The British formed on the Buttes-à-Neveu while General Murray and his party sauntered up the road to reconnoitre.

French troops were well dug-in when Murray and his army came into view on the ridge. As the second wave reached Sillery Wood, it flowed over the adjoining Plains. (This was almost the same ground Wolfe had occupied the autumn before.) Lévis, on horseback, was caught between the two opposing forces and, suddenly realizing the danger, he took cover in the trees, drawing some of the troops along with him. Murray saw movement, mistook it for a genuine retreat and felt compelled to pursue. At least, that's the reason he later gave for ordering his army to shift to marshy ground. In minutes, his foot soldiers stood knee-deep in icy water and his artillery was swallowed up in slush.

A short distance away, near Ste-Foy, a fierce scrimmage erupted between French Grenadiers and British Light Infantry over possession of Dumont's windmill – a well-known landmark – and its outbuildings.

The British infantry dashed toward the enemy, not realizing their artillery was stuck in the snow behind them. In minutes they were stopped cold by a feisty captain from the Béarn Regiment who managed to whip his men into a frenzied attack. Murray's infantry (reduced in strength and weakened by sickness) reeled back into the arms of their own troops, a blunder that prevented anyone from firing. It took several minutes to disentangle the infantry. When the men were free again, they discovered all their officers were dead or dying and had no choice but to retire.

After an awkward lull, the scrap over possession of the mill and buildings started up again, passing back and forth from French to British until nobody held the prize. It was then that Murray realized his big guns were half-buried in holes filled with slushy snow. Since they couldn't be moved and couldn't fire, he was forced to abandon them. That's when the impossible happened. *British troops were ordered to fall back!* It was unbelievable, it was infuriating, but the men obeyed and, in the process, left many wounded behind. Later, it was said that Indians and French bushrangers scalped those who couldn't escape.

Knox wrapped the extraordinary order in his usual patriotic verbiage: "It was a command they were hitherto unacquainted with and some men cried out, 'Damn it, what is falling back but retreating?'" Despite loud criticism from the lower ranks, the British army retired in good form and Knox later speculated their calmness was one reason the French didn't pursue. French accounts paint a very different picture – *they* say the British retreat was a "disorderly flight." After it was over, Knox accused French officers of handling their men roughly; he summed it up: "Judging from their losses, that fell on the flower of their troops, they were heartily sick of the struggle."

The British had lost eleven hundred from all ranks, much higher than the figure given for Wolfe's victory in 1759. According to the French, their own losses were between six hundred and eight hundred, but the statistics seem to have vanished. Knox suggested that if a thousand fresh troops had suddenly appeared to support the British, they might have driven off the enemy or, short of that, the enemy never would have dared encamp so close to the walls of Quebec when it was over.

Next morning, General Murray announced he had only 3,140 men well enough to fight. Sergeant John Johnson disagreed with the figure and used strong language to make his case. Johnson was usually respectful when referring to the officer class, but on this occasion he questioned the official numbers because, he said, many soldiers were "half-starved, scorbutic skeletons" and shouldn't be included. Johnson also dared to criticize Murray's tactics, describing the general's "mad, enthusiastic zeal" that nearly lost the fruits of Wolfe's victory. Historian Francis Parkman put it less harshly when he wrote that "the fate of Quebec trembled in the balance."

After the second battle for Quebec ended so disastrously for the British, Murray defended his strategy in a letter to Prime Minister Pitt: "We had a very fine train of artillery – [therefore] shutting ourselves within the walls was putting everything on the chance of holding out from a wretched fortification."

Military men on every level had something to say about the way affairs were handled in Canada after Wolfe died. With the British army once more inside the fortress, Sergeant Johnson explained the retreat this way: "We were too few and too weak to stand an assault." Morale was indeed low among the rank and file. Drunkenness and the plundering of private houses spread through the town. Defeat spawned violent behaviour, a reaction easier to understand after reading an official pamphlet from the Museum Restoration Service, which says, "For the most part, the common soldier had been born poor – had never known any life but hunger, sickness, pain and filth. The existence of a soldier in the British army of the eighteenth century was at best, one step above a penal colony." Only victory could bring a sense of relief, and that was temporary.

Following the undignified flight of the British army that April day, the lower ranks turned into packs of demented demons, roaring through town chasing women and destroying property. Somebody had to restore order, and General Murray was just the man for the job. He stopped the drunken orgies by smashing all the sutlers' rum barrels and ended the looting by hanging the leader. Within three days, Quebec was relatively calm again. Every man worked; convalescents filled sandbags and those who were strong enough reinforced the walls and dragged the captured French guns up the hill to the ramparts. Everyone believed the French would soon besiege Quebec.

Among the officers, an attempt was made to behave like gentlemen. General Lévis presented General Murray with spruce beer for his table because he'd heard Murray liked it. Under a flag of truce he also sent spruce boughs so the British could make beer for their men. Murray, not to be outdone, gave Lévis a whole Cheshire cheese. Lévis returned the compliment with a brace of freshly shot partridges. The opposing generals might have been the best of friends.

At the same time, Murray rushed to increase his firepower on the ramparts and Lévis and his followers were far from idle. In fact, they were digging trenches close to the western wall, along the back of the Buttes-à-Neveu. Partridges or no partridges, Murray set up 150 cannon that would soon pour down burning shot on his hard-working enemy. On the French side, progress wasn't quite so impressive. By the end of May (when the siege was over) they had managed to plant only one heavy gun.

Such activity cost a lot of effort and countless lives, but both sides knew the issue would be decided by which fleet first appeared in the Quebec Basin, French or English. Lévis could not continue to besiege Quebec without substantial help, and he needed it soon. As for Murray, on May 1 he sent the *Racehorse* to Louisbourg and Halifax with letters begging officials in both places to rush ships to his aid: either they did what he asked or the game was lost.

Lévis' siege of Quebec lasted two weeks. For people inside the fortress, it seemed more like two months, marked as it was by a painful food shortage, fear of French cannon and an outbreak of life-threatening fires. On May 4, when gunners attacked a French sloop that happened to be passing downriver to the gulf, sparks fell on an open chest of ammunition. The chest blew up, wounding three British soldiers and scorching several others. Only luck prevented the flames from reaching a second open chest of explosives and endangering a section of the ramparts. The intendant's palace nearby, one of the most impressive buildings in town, was spared. But outbuildings, boats and naval stores along the St. Charles River were badly damaged. Thinking the French would take advantage of the chaos, gunners on the west wall kept up a steady barrage all night. Apparently they didn't know the enemy hadn't enough ammunition to do them real harm. Once the fires were under control, troops on both sides went back to work as if nothing had happened.

The French camp was running out of food. For the five thousand men in the trenches, rations were a quarter-pound of fresh meat and a half-pound of bread doled out each night. Each soldier received a quarter of a cup of brandy. Things were worse for the British army. No wine was to be had, although Murray ordered brandy to be distributed among the men. Only servings of fresh food would have been more tempting to British officers than a steady supply of decent wine. Knox, who seldom complained about anything, declared the salt pork inedible.

On the night of May 8, British artillerymen fired all night along the west wall, and at times every gun and mortar in the fortress was in action. The same French sloop they had spotted going downriver on May 4 was now seen working her way back up to the Foulon. British soldiers on the ramparts hailed her in a sporting way without firing, but she snubbed them. As the small ship sailed haughtily by, a British officer shouted across the water, "Why don't you stay downriver to pilot up the French armada?"

When the first sail appeared on May 9, Murray ordered the British flag hoisted over Cape Diamond – more in hope than certainty. The scene on the ramparts was played out once more as nervous civilians and anxious soldiers held their breath, straining to identify the ship's nationality. At last it became clear: blowing on the wind was the bright red cross of St. George. The frigate *Lowestoff* boomed out a 21-gun salute to the fortress. And once again men threw their hats in the air and shouted until they were hoarse.

Lévis knew he couldn't sustain a siege without reinforcements and supplies, couldn't outgun or outmanoeuvre the British fleet that was bound to follow the *Lowestoff*. And so, reluctantly, he swept back to Montreal with his army, to prepare for his last stand against the invaders.

In London, news of Murray's retreat on April 28 was received with annoyance and astonishment. Hadn't they conquered Canada the year before? Didn't they now occupy Quebec? Hadn't Wolfe taken that stronghold and hadn't they celebrated his heroic feat? This year they had a new problem to worry about. France was still a menace to England's shores and her army was only the width of the Channel away! Later in the summer, when Montreal surrendered, the people of England could scarcely grasp what it was all about. They hadn't the slightest idea how close they had come to losing Quebec and all of Canada, how close to forfeiting control of half the continent of North America.

Eventually, the commercial and political significance of Great Britain's conquest would prove staggering, but three years after the battle on the Plains of Abraham, when France and England finally signed a peace treaty, King Louis XV chose to keep the sugar crops of Martinique and hand over the snowy wastes of Canada. King George III was pleased – he thought it might cheer up his American colonists to have a friend instead of an enemy on that long and difficult border.

23

The Honours of War

"I am resolved, for the infamous part the troops of France have acted in exciting the savages to perpetrate the most horrid barbarities, to manifest to all the world my detestation of such practices."
— JEFFREY AMHERST, September 8, 1760

In May 1760 Jeffrey Amherst, commander-in-chief of the British Army in America, was cooling his heels in Albany, waiting for volunteers from the colonies. Told that recruiting on the eastern seaboard was lagging, the unruffled general remarked, "The Provincials [colonials], I fear, will be very late." But when he got word General Murray had almost lost Quebec in a second battle on the Plains and Lévis was, even now, besieging the town, he exploded. It may have been Murray's blunt way of breaking the news that brought on the temper: the governor informed Amherst that the British fleet had better arrive before the French or England could say goodbye to Wolfe's victory. The warning galvanized Amherst. His letter to officers in Louisbourg ordered ships and men to be rushed to Murray's aid – or heads would roll.

Luckily for the defenders, the British *did* arrive first and Lévis took his army back to Montreal. Amherst, shaken by the spectre of losing

Quebec and, incidentally, ruining his career, sat down to make a plan.
How was he to capture Montreal? The answer was not long in coming:
bottle up the French in the town and attack from three different angles.
He envisioned Governor James Murray sailing majestically upstream
from Quebec, Brigadier William Haviland working his way down the
Richelieu River and Amherst himself leading a thousand men in a fleet
of boats by way of the upper St. Lawrence. Montreal was a fur-trading
centre and its walls had been designed a century before to withstand
Iroquois arrows, not heavy artillery. Amherst did not doubt it could be
captured, but timing was everything. The three armies must converge
near Montreal on the same day – or *almost* the same day.

The capture of Montreal was Amherst's last chance to glean a little
glory. Back in 1758, when the British had successfully besieged
Louisbourg, Amherst got the credit and Wolfe the adulation. At
Quebec, Wolfe became a star and, a year later, his aura still burned
bright. Despite Amherst's high rank, people looked upon him as a
supporting player. Montreal was his chance to change all that. While
his three-pronged scheme was daring enough, it was also a trifle mad.

At the start, the three commanders would be separated by long
distances and could keep in touch only by courier. True, an important
military dispatch might begin its journey by ship, but it usually ended
up in some shaggy fellow's pocket, carried through bear-infested
forests and mosquito-riddled swamps to a target on the move. So far,
there had always been some young whippersnapper eager to accept
the mission, not for money, of course, but to stand out from the
crowd. How skilled in survival, how brave, how honest the messenger
might be were factors the sender seldom weighed. Letters were often
late, stolen or sold to the enemy.

Amherst's colleagues in Albany were surprised when he came up
with such an innovative plan: he was known for erring on the side
of inertia, not for making wild gestures. The idea of three armies
converging at the same place came dangerously close to fantasy, since

a journey through uncharted wilderness was as perilous as a battle. More soldiers died of disease, starvation, drowning and dumb accidents than ever got shot by the enemy. Even so, Haviland and Murray took up the challenge. Amherst had ordered them to boot the French out of Canada, and they would damned well accomplish the task.

Murray left Quebec July 13, with twenty-four hundred men, thirty-two transports, nine floating batteries and a string of assorted small craft loaded with ammunition and provisions. It was quite a cavalcade. Before the troops even boarded, "certain irregularities took place." They had just received their back pay and were primed to celebrate, so it was only natural that drunkenness, fistfights and last-minute flings with women, not all of them agreeable, would slow down departure. But at last the ructions were sorted out and, by July 15, the armada had reached a point midway between Quebec and Montreal.

So far the enemy had offered no opposition, but shortly after the fleet anchored at Trois-Rivières a handful of snipers began firing at random on British ships. This action so angered the irascible Murray that he marched a party of Light Infantry several miles upriver, lecturing the locals as he went along. People, he said privately, seemed too dense to understand their predicament. Murray must have been a persuasive speaker because over one hundred citizens took the oath of neutrality that day. "Who can carry on or support the war without ships, artillery, ammunition or provisions?" he thundered at them. "Consider your own interests and provoke us no more."

Turning to a priest who happened to be standing at the front of the crowd, he was frank: "The clergy are the source of all mischiefs that have befallen the poor Canadians, whom they keep in ignorance and excite to wickedness and their own ruin." Yes, he told the priest, he had hanged a captain of militia and transported a handful of Jesuits to Great Britain for this same lack of cooperation. And he would continue the policy until all inhabitants had signed. "Preach the gospel which alone is your province and do not presume directly or indirectly to meddle with military matters," he shouted at the priest. "The quarrel is between two Crowns."

A spy sent by the French to mix with the British and discover their plans was caught and very nearly hanged. The man saved himself by promising to tell Murray everything and gave the general a great deal of information, some of it highly questionable. There were, said the spy, only four hundred French soldiers posted between Quebec and Trois-Rivières. Two battalions of French regulars and a few Canadians were distributed among islands in the St. Lawrence River and posted on that well-known spot the Île-aux-Noix. The bulk of the French force was camped between Trois-Rivières and Montreal.

If Amherst hoped to reach Montreal from the upper St. Lawrence, he must first pass Île-Royale (now called Fort Lévis), where he would find a modest contingent under Captain Pouchot, the officer who had defended Fort Niagara. Before Amherst's fleet set sail, neither Murray, Lévis nor Pouchot could have imagined the intimidating sight of hundreds of boats loaded with thousands of soldiers swooping down on Montreal. Nor could anyone have foreseen the famously late Amherst arriving punctually, as his schedule demanded.

Murray, still a long way from joining the other two commanders, was much encouraged by the blather dished up by the talkative spy, the gist of which claimed the French army was mutinous, Canadians were deserting in great numbers and the daily ration had been reduced to a quarter-pound of meat and a hunk of stale black bread. Even more amazing, the French had run out of brandy and wine.

At Trois-Rivières, the St. Lawrence narrowed dramatically and Murray sent two armed boats ahead to take soundings. He needed to find a channel deep enough to allow the big ships safe passage. A gathering of Canadians watched this activity from the high banks, rifles at the ready. One brash citizen called out in English, "What water have you, Englishmen?"

"Sufficient to bring up our ships and knock you and your houses to pieces," was the reply.

The exchange seemed to amuse the Canadians and, being a good-natured lot, they invited the invaders to come ashore for refreshments. The British, suspecting their sincerity, refused politely, but their cool response failed to stop the locals from paddling out with a "quantity of greens and salading." To Murray and his officers, fresh vegetables must have seemed an irresistible treat. It's doubtful the lower ranks benefited very much since farmers were short of everything except home-grown produce.

After studying reports on the depth of water and whereabouts of hidden rocks, Murray chose an anchorage close to the south shore. Citizens swarmed aboard without waiting for invitations, offering vegetables, poultry and eggs. They were happy to accept salt in return, a rare and expensive commodity in the colony and one the poor needed to preserve eels and other fish for winter. When the fleet prepared to leave, a colourful mixture of folk lined up along the shore to wave goodbye: French regulars in uniform, *les habitants* and militiamen in civvies, and Indians in breechclouts and face paint. Captain Knox observed a detachment of light cavalry cantering along the beach in blue coats with scarlet facings, their officers in white. Both sides enjoyed the fleet's visit, a pleasant distraction in the warm sunshine. Murray's troops must have found it hard to believe they were at war with these friendly strangers.

When the British reached the island of Ignatius, not far from the mouth of the Richelieu River, everyone went ashore while sailors scrubbed the transports and aired them out. In such a peaceful atmosphere, enthusiasm among the farmers to sign the oath of allegiance to the British rose significantly. A party of thirty men and women, some of them long-time captives in nearby Indian villages, begged sanctuary from Murray and he took them aboard.

Heading upstream, General Murray discovered Brigadier Bourlamaque camped just south of Sorel, actively fortifying the village and encouraging the French to resist. Murray paused long enough to burn houses and crops in the surrounding parish, explaining to anyone who would listen that he must prove to Canadians that he intended to punish all those who didn't cooperate.

By August 15 Murray and the fleet had reached a spot twenty-seven miles from Montreal and, upon receiving conflicting reports on the whereabouts of Haviland and Amherst, began to fret. Was he expected to besiege Montreal all by himself? Five thousand French soldiers were said to be jammed inside the town walls. Their Indian allies had abandoned them and Lévis had hanged three militiamen for desertion – a critical situation for the French if it were true. Still, he was cynical enough reserve judgment. Such tales might be a ruse to make him feel overconfident.

Once again, half the summer had slipped away and Amherst was still a long way from Montreal. As usual, he had followed his own star, spending most of June moving troops and supplies from Albany to Oswego, the port from which he intended to launch his expedition on Lake Ontario on his way to the St. Lawrence. Smothered in organizational details, Amherst still managed to send Major Rogers, safely back from his adventure at St. Francis, to destroy a French ammunition dump on the Richelieu in an effort to help Brigadier Haviland. Amherst had almost ignored poor Wolfe, but this year he was determined to keep in touch with his colleagues. Hearing the French had raised the siege on Quebec brought Amherst temporary relief: it meant he could rely on Murray's support against Montreal.

In early June, Amherst began moving men and provisions along the Mohawk to Oswego. A river in full flood helped float the heavy loads, but there still remained a tricky portage at Oswego Falls where watercraft had to be hauled sixty yards overland on wooden rollers. At this stage his fleet suffered considerable damage and Amherst, who preferred solving logistical problems to fighting battles, came up with a solution. In future, he noted, all vessels needed on Lake Ontario would be built at Oswego, thus cutting out this destructive portage.

By the first week in July, Amherst was ready to sail for Oswego. Fort Ontario had been rebuilt and he planned to make the post his headquarters, saving time and expense. As more and more boats and troops gathered, Oswego became the centre of activity on the eastern end of Lake Ontario. Large-scale movements always drew a great many tribesmen, not only locals but from far away: they loved the hustle and bustle of selling furs and firewater, beads and brandy. Young warriors, looking for battle experience, hoped to join Amherst's expedition.

It was no secret that Amherst didn't like Indians. He could never ingratiate himself with them as Governor Vaudreuil or Sir William Johnson had, and yet he needed them. Indians picked up valuable information over long distances in a way the Europeans could never copy. Their talent for moving swiftly through the wilderness was brilliant and only Major Rogers and his Rangers had ever come close to matching their skills. Whether Amherst liked it or not, he set out for Montreal with seven hundred warriors and their women and children and a small body of Mohawks attached to Sir William Johnson.

Amherst's observations about Indians, as recorded in his journal, often carried an air of disapproval. "[D]uring a bout of heavy rum-drinking a warrior was mortally wounded, an Indian boy died, a squaw drowned and one squaw slept with so many soldiers she looked like dying," he wrote about a streak of bad luck they suffered that summer.

Despite an avalanche of obstacles, Amherst's fleet moved out of Oswego August 10, a vast collection of bateaux, whaleboats and smaller craft carrying ten thousand human beings and a month's provisions. After less than a day's sail, high winds forced the ships to take cover at the mouth of the Sable River and, once again, Amherst's carefully orchestrated timetable was held up by forces beyond his control.

A description of Amherst's next three weeks doesn't read like a formula for changing the history of America. Amherst's boats had barely reached the St. Lawrence River when a French brig, the *Ottawa,* emerged from the mist with her cannon loaded. After a brief skirmish, five British gunboats captured her. Not long afterward, two of Amherst's armed vessels recently lost in the maze of the Thousand Islands heard the gunfire and, following the sound, rejoined the fleet. After a week of travel, the heavily loaded transports had advanced as far as Fort Lévis sitting in the middle of the St. Lawrence, where the small island threatened to cut off access to the first set of rapids. Amherst would have to either sail around or capture it.

Intermittent firing began between British gunboats and the cannon protecting Captain Pouchot's tiny log fort. Before long, the redcoats had landed and established posts and batteries on rocky ground surrounding the blockhouse. Although the fort's wooden walls soon began to splinter, the firing continued for three days until Pouchot was forced to call in all his pickets. Thus far, the British claimed three killed and one wounded: General Amherst had suffered a sprained knee.

Amherst was aboard a whaleboat waiting for Pouchot to cave in when he received a letter from Brigadier Haviland announcing his August 11 departure from Crown Point. From this, Amherst estimated that by the time he reached Montreal, Haviland would be waiting. Pouchot surrendered on the twenty-fifth and the British moved in to take over the ruins of the fort along with quantities of powder, ball and provisions. Although deep in the wilderness, one must observe the niceties of life. On the night of August 26, Captain Pouchot dined with General Amherst.

Before Amherst left Fort Lévis he fell into his old habit, ordering repairs to walls he had just blown apart. Trouble with the Indians surfaced in a detailed report he made later about the taking of Fort Lévis: "I did not permit an Indian to go in." At first glance, the entry sounds mysterious, but he cleared it up later by adding that despite his best efforts, a few Indians managed to find the new burial ground, where they dug up the graves and scalped the dead bodies. He had tried to keep them away but they had outwitted him. Leaving a garrison of two hundred men on the island, Amherst sailed on down the St. Lawrence. Word reached him that Murray was camped near Montreal. All Amherst had to do was shoot the rapids and he would find the Quebec contingent established in a camp near the town.

When the fleet reached the Galop and Long Sault rapids, Amherst sent scouts along the shore to make sure there would be no ambush. "The river current is strong but not dangerous," he noted. "The whale-boats took water several times but all boats came on safe." Amherst was the kind of man who faced natural obstacles stoically. It was human failings that stirred him up and, when he heard that Indians had made off with at least twenty British whaleboats, he was angry.

Conquering the first set of rapids cost the British one corporal and three men, all drowned. It was considered a sustainable loss – human lives, especially among the lower ranks, were worth very little in the eyes of their superiors. When the fleet reached the Long Sault Rapids, just before the river widened into Lake Francis, a French colonial officer, St-Luc de La Corne, appeared on the shore with two hundred men seemingly poised to attack the expedition. However, the famous bush fighter backed off when he heard Fort Lévis was now in British hands: he had no hope of support. A rainstorm kept the fleet on Lake Francis long enough for Amherst to receive a message from Haviland; Île-aux-Noix had fallen, and he was on his way down the Richelieu. (The watershed here caused rivers to run north.) With this bit of good news, Amherst's extraordinary plan suddenly became possible. On the stretch of river between Cedar Rapids and the Cascades, Amherst emptied most of his boats and marched his men along the shore. He hoped to save a great many lives by the tactic and perhaps he succeeded, but his losses were still heavy: eighty-four men, plus twenty bateaux and seventeen boatloads of artillery, including a number of big guns.

So far, things were going his way and Amherst felt so optimistic he was able to deal humanely with a group of district farmers. "I saved all the cattle, sheep etc. for the inhabitants who signed a paper for good behaviour," he noted. The following day, September 6, Amherst's ten thousand men landed at Lachine, on the western end of the island of Montreal. Although the British spotted a detachment of enemy cavalry and exchanged a few shots, the French vanished and Amherst marched his army to open ground, close to his target.

Governor Vaudreuil and General Lévis, staring over the low stone walls at the red sea lapping all around them, were hard-pressed to make a decision. Unlike the dramatic two-tiered Quebec, Montreal was flat: a strip of stone and wooden buildings with a heap of earth at one corner capped with a few big guns. Montreal's *raison d'être* was the fur trade, attracting a mixture of trappers, crooks, salesmen and Indians from faraway places. It was also a haven for naughty officials who spent their nights drinking and gambling and sharing four-posters with other men's wives. Only Mount Royal, rising solidly behind the town, offered any relief in an otherwise undistinguished landscape.

Montrealers from every level of society were alarmed when the English heretics swarmed around the walls. The British reported their own strength at seventeen thousand, but French sources claimed they numbered between twenty and forty thousand. No matter; there were enough of them to convince Vaudreuil that further resistance was useless. On September 7, while Amherst was inspecting his troops, Bougainville arrived with a message from the governor asking for a cessation of arms until he could discover whether England and France had made a general peace. Such confirmation could come only from Albany or London, and it would have meant a long delay. Amherst said no.

In response, the French drew up a new list of demands. Amherst accepted most of them, changed a few and refused the rest. Lévis and Vaudreuil insisted on the "honours of war," which would have allowed the French to march out of Montreal with their arms, cannon and all regimental colours. It was a request that stuck in Amherst's craw. Notes flew back and forth but, in the end, Amherst was adamant. He insisted on "showing the world that England did not condone the cruelties and atrocities committed by Indian allies of France before and during the war."

For officials and military officers forced to return to France, the honours of war were crucial. If they were perceived as surrendering too easily it would reflect badly on their future. They needn't have worried. They *had* no future. Even the powerful officials with the best connections were doomed to spend two years in the Bastille before coming to trial, not as punishment for losing Canada, but for stealing from the king's revenues. As for his ice-bound colony, King Louis was relieved to be rid of it. When peace came in 1763, he held on to his Caribbean possessions and handed Canada to England. People would always prefer sugar to fur, he said.

British occupation of Montreal began with a formal signing ceremony on September 8. Lévis was absent – rumour had it he was busy burning regimental colours rather than surrender them to Amherst. The actual takeover the next day was a low-key affair. A troop of red-coats marched into the Place d'Armes and two thousand whitecoats threw down their muskets and marched away without benefit of drums, trumpets or flags.

The Mohawks under Sir William Johnson were still in town. They had shown up at Montreal expecting Armageddon, and what they got was a handful of white men scratching their names on pieces of paper. French citizens, remembering the massacre at Fort William Henry, feared a bloodletting, but British officials were, for once, in control of the situation. After dishing out plenty of wampum, silver trinkets and brandy, they hastily escorted the Indians to their canoes and waved them off.

That night, ex-governor Vaudreuil gave a dinner in honour of Major-General Amherst. There was a show of good manners by British officers who attended, although Amherst wasn't concerned about such niceties. He got more pleasure out of writing a letter to Prime Minister Pitt announcing his capture of Montreal than he did out of the actual event.

Afterword: 1759–1764

"Since we do not know how to make war, we must make peace."
— DUC DE CHOISEUL, Minister of Foreign Affairs, 1761

In the summer of 1759, Madame de Pompadour sent a spy to get the goods on Intendant Bigot's ever-expanding thiefdom. Pompadour herself had appointed him to the post three years earlier because his friends touted him as a good administrator. But when she discovered he was piling up a huge personal fortune at the king's expense, she flew into a rage. A bit of poaching was one thing; draining off millions belonging to His Majesty, quite another. The king and Pompadour were no longer lovers but she still adored him and, in her eyes, "Do not cheat the king" was the eleventh commandment.

It's difficult to understand why a man as clever as Bigot didn't see the danger – perhaps he was besotted by drink or theft, or both. Obviously, to a woman who worked herself almost to death to stay in power, forgiveness was not on the table. The marquise meant to see Bigot punished.

Pompadour's agent, Querdisien Trémais, arrived in Quebec at a time when French officials were distracted by fear of invasion and ordinary citizens by pangs of hunger. In such a climate, it was easy for the newcomer to pass himself off as an admirer of Bigot and gain access to damning ledgers and correspondence. The agent copied some documents and stole others and, like any good spy, shipped some papers to Pompadour and kept a few as insurance. From that time on, Bigot was doomed.

The terms of surrender at Montreal stated that military officers, civil authorities and resident aristocrats must be transported to France on British vessels as soon as possible. It was November before most of them sailed, and violent storms had already caused havoc on the Atlantic. General Lévis, Madame Pénisseault, ex-governor Vaudreuil and his elderly wife were all in the same boat and came frighteningly close to drowning. Another ship, the *Auguste*, was wrecked and 114 passengers lost, but the tough old partisan St-Luc de La Corne swam ashore and made his way to Quebec on snowshoes. Officials who reached French ports were arrested as soon as they landed, whisked off to Paris and into the Bastille.

Distressing as jail time must have been for men used to great luxury, the rich fared reasonably well. Ex-governor Vaudreuil took along his black servant, his books, tobacco and fine wines. Bigot and Cadet, pleading the need for spiritual guidance, were allowed out every Sunday to attend mass. Those who could pay ordered meals from Paris chefs. Altogether, two dozen men were imprisoned in the Bastille from December 1759 until December 1761, when the trials were finally set in motion. An enormous heap of evidence was put before twenty-seven judges, some of it supplied by Pompadour.

The hearings lasted fifteen months. Cadet confessed and Bigot denied everything until documents bearing his own signature proved him guilty. Bigot and Cadet ended up accusing each other, and both Vaudreuil and Bigot denounced Cadet. If the criminals hadn't caused so much misery to so many people and hastened the end of the French regime in Canada, they might have been seen as comic.

As usual, the windy Vaudreuil had much to say, wrapping himself in the flag and defending the regular officers who, he said, had fought and died for France. These were the same soldiers he had mocked in earlier days, driving Montcalm berserk. Perhaps Vaudreuil's patriotic plea muddled the judges, since he ended up as the only accused acquitted. Probably owing to his noble family connections, Vaudreuil was awarded the Cross of St. Louis and pensions totalling twelve thousand livres, which allowed him to retire to his château and live in genteel poverty. Vaudreuil died at eighty, a lonely old man.

When it came time to pass sentence on Bigot, the prosecutor ascended into the realm of Biblical vengeance. Bigot should be forced to kneel at the gates of the Tuileries wearing nothing but his shirt and a placard reading "Thief" hanging from a rope around his neck. Afterward, he ought to be beheaded. The judges opted for a milder sentence: Bigot was banished from France for life and all his property confiscated. His assets were enough to cover the fine, 1.5 million livres, and the formerly resplendent intendant spent his last years alone in Neuchâtel, Switzerland. He died in 1778.

Cadet was fined six million livres, an appropriate sum since he was the biggest swindler of the lot. He was banished from France for nine years, but he bribed officials to allow him to travel back and forth between France and Canada, where he made land deals and sold goods crucial to an expanded settlement. In this way, the butcher's son amassed an even greater fortune and became a rich landowner in France. Both his daughters married aristocrats. For a while, it looked as if Cadet would die laughing at justice. Fortunately, it all turned out badly. Cadet lost everything and died bankrupt in 1781.

Two dozen minor thieves, all minions of top officials, had no money to pay large fines and no powerful connections to spring them, so they remained in jail, their ultimate fate unrecorded.

After France lost the war, Pompadour's influence declined along with her health – she suffered blinding headaches, chronic indigestion and severe congestion of the lungs. For months she sat upright in a chair because she couldn't breathe lying down. Once elegant, perfectly turned out for every occasion, in her last days the marquise wore a dressing gown over a white petticoat, a touch of rouge and a faint smile meant for the king, who was one of her frequent visitors. On the eve of Palm Sunday, 1764, King Louis noticed she was slipping fast and suggested she call for a priest. Pompadour reluctantly agreed, knowing that once she confessed, she could never see the king again. A priest arrived, Louis retired to his apartment on the floor above, and Pompadour made her last confession.

The king spent Palm Sunday in church. Late in the afternoon, a few friends gathered around the marquise. Growing weaker and weaker, eventually she told them this was truly the end. The priest offered to leave the room, but she stopped him, saying, "One moment, M. le Curé, we'll go together," and died. There was a firm rule that no dead body could remain in the Palace of Versailles, so Pompadour was carried out on a stretcher immediately, covered by a blanket, to be deposited in the Hôtel des Réservoirs, a stone's throw away.

Two days later, a bitter wind blew sheets of freezing rain against the palace walls as the cortege made its way along the Avenue de Paris on its way to the city. The king, without hat or coat, stood shivering on a small private balcony to watch the procession disappear, tears streaming down his cheeks. "That is the only tribute I can pay her," he told his servant Champlost.

General Lévis, a courageous, worldly man known to be unstable in his romantic alliances, deserted Madame Pénisseault and married a wealthy Frenchwoman. While Pompadour was still powerful at Court, she welcomed him, thus securing his social life. Lévis' influential connections in London persuaded Pitt to release him from his promise not to fight in the current war, and soon he rejoined the army in Europe, this time against England's ally, Frederick of Prussia. He was made a duke and a marshal of France and, by dying at the age of sixty-seven, conveniently missed the horrors of the Revolution. His widow and their two daughters weren't so lucky: all three were guillotined. But even so, Lévis didn't escape entirely. A revolutionary mob broke into his tomb in Arras and scattered his bones to the wind.

Bourlamaque, the most intellectual of Montcalm's friends, put his opinions about the loss of Canada on paper shortly after he returned to France, criticizing many facets of French colonial policy. On one topic he agreed with his British opponents: the French had handled the natives badly. Indians, said Bourlamaque, were of limited value as scouts, and lavishing gifts on them produced only greed. They were loyal when their side was victorious, but if it lost they vanished. Bourlamaque acknowledged there had been widespread corruption at the trading posts. Soldiers should not engage in trade, and agents at outlying posts should be changed often to cut back on the amount of fraud. As for the Canadians, they were naturally brave, and with proper training, their young men might have made a fine fighting force. An effective governor, he wrote, ought to be both soldier and statesman, a man who was willing to oversee every aspect of government with sharp eyes. He ought to be deeply concerned with the public good.

Bourlamaque remained in the army, served in Malta fighting the Turks and became governor of Guadeloupe. He died in 1764, the same year as Madame de Pompadour.

After returning to France, Colonel Louis-Antoine de Bougainville became a captain in the French navy and invested some of his own money in an expedition to the South Seas. He attempted to colonize the Falkland Islands for France, but the venture failed. On a second voyage, he circled the globe and produced two volumes about plants and animals he had discovered in the South Pacific. His work as a naturalist was well received. In 1781, as commander of the French fleet, Bougainville helped orchestrate the defeat of Cornwallis at

Yorktown. As an aristocrat, he narrowly escaped being beheaded during the Revolution. Bougainville was much admired in France, and in his later years, Napoleon made him a senator. He died on his Normandy estate in 1811, at the age of eighty-two.

William Pitt remained popular with commoners, but most of his peers continued to see him as a menace to their special interests. Even after Pitt's brilliant success in adding Canada and India to the Empire, George II detested him; and yet, he seemed to know instinctively that England needed Pitt. But fate took a hand and on October 25, 1760, His Majesty got out of bed, went to the water closet and fell to the floor, stone-cold dead from a massive stroke.

The old king's grandson, George III, was 23, not too bright and completely under the influence of the ambitious Earl of Bute. The new king immediately made Bute a privy councillor and first gentleman of the bedchamber. A politician who hoped to end the Whig monopoly, Bute, with the king behind him, forced Pitt's resignation in 1761 and himself became prime minister. Two of his top priorities were to make the monarch supreme over Parliament and to end the war with France. The Treaty of Paris, signed in 1763, brought peace; but in the dustup over putting together an agreement, several imperial gains were thrown away. From the sidelines, Pitt despaired for himself and his country. Bute was never popular with the people but, for a time, Pitt's power continued to weaken.

In 1766, George III had a change of heart. Pitt was recalled to office as lord privy seal and created Earl of Chatham. If only he had been robust he might have made a great comeback but, during the next three years, Pitt was prey to painful gout and moods so black he often took to his bed. He managed to appear in public occasionally but lacked the spirit to dominate the scene. His last speech in Parliament, made in 1768, was a rant against current proposals to break up the Empire. After thundering on for some time, Pitt collapsed and was carried home to die.

Lord Rosebery, one of his biographers, defined William Pitt's importance to England this way: "Twenty years after his death, Britain reached the lowest point in her history. But still she is richer for his life."

General Jeffrey Amherst always seemed to be on the verge of a spectacular breakthrough. Following Louisbourg (when Wolfe's impetuous charge at Freshwater Cove saved the day), Amherst had a series of "almosts." In the fall of 1759, Amherst almost reached Île-aux-Noix on his way to assault Montreal, but winter stopped him cold. In 1760, he came close to getting a peerage for his part in taking Montreal and completing the British conquest of Canada, but the French surrendered without a fight and, instead, Amherst got a knighthood and the position of governor-general of North America.

In 1763, Amherst was preparing to quell Chief Pontiac, the charismatic leader of the western Indians, when he was called back to England to be commander-in-chief of the home army. Before leaving America, he considered killing the rebellious Indians by distributing blankets infected with smallpox. Had he put this scheme into practice, it might have made him the father of biological warfare. It is not clear whether this happened.

For some reason, George III changed his feelings for Amherst (earlier he had seen the commander as "Pitt's man") and announced he was going to present the general with vast acres of land owned by the Jesuits in Canada. Amherst's enemies in Parliament worked against the move and, instead of becoming an instant millionaire, Amherst was given the title Baron Amherst – a nice gesture, but hardly the proverbial pot of gold. Amherst managed to hang on to his army command with the rank of field marshal until he was almost eighty, then retired to his estate in Kent and died in 1797.

Brigadier-General Robert Monckton remained in America. Amherst gave him command of the army in Pennsylvania in 1760 – he was only thirty-four years old – and the following year he became governor of New York. Before the year was out, however, Amherst and Admiral George Rodney, accompanied by Monckton, led expeditions against Martinique, Grenada, St. Lucia and St. Vincent, captured all of them and later received the thanks of the House of Commons for their efforts. In 1778 the never-married Monckton became governor of Portsmouth, and died at the age of fifty-six. Lieutenant-General Monckton was buried in Kensington Parish Church, London, in 1782.

The Honourable James Murray got his wish. Envious of his fellow officers – some were tall (he was short), others rich (he was poor) and still others handsome (a word never used to describe him) – Murray coveted power. With the capture of Quebec, he became the first governor of Canada, ruling the ruined town and scattered colony. In the first awful winter, gossips lionized General Lévis – not Governor Murray – as the great liberator. Lévis was still out there strengthening his army and threatening to besiege Quebec in the spring. It didn't improve Murray's image when people accused him of favouring French peasants over British merchants. Still, he was tough and fearless and stayed on at Quebec until the British government recalled him in 1766.

Murray became governor of Minorca in 1779, a definite improvement over his last assignment, but in 1781 the island was blockaded by combined Spanish and French troops under the Duc de Crillon. The duke offered Murray a bribe to surrender the island and, of course, he refused. A year later, his garrison was so reduced by disease he was forced to capitulate. No blame was attached to Murray's surrender of Minorca; in fact he was rewarded with the rank of full general and the governorship of Hull. Murray died in 1794.

After failing to discredit Wolfe, George Townshend took a year's leave of absence from the army. With influential relatives in positions of power and plenty of money, he was free to do as he wished. Townshend could have loafed through life, enjoying his wife and three children, managing his extensive properties and indulging in outdoor sports. But despite the nasty streak in his nature, Townshend wanted more from life than that; like Wolfe and Murray, he longed for glory.

In February 1761 a notice appeared in the *Gentleman's Magazine*, informing the public that Townshend, at the age of thirty-six, was in command of the second brigade under the Marquess of Granby, whose army of thirty-two thousand was leaving for Germany to support Prince Ferdinand of Brunswick against the French in Westphalia. A year later Townshend campaigned in Portugal against France and her ally, Spain, until a general peace was declared – Spain had run out of ammunition. In any case, winter was almost upon them, so all special service officers along with five thousand British troops were returned to England.

It so happened that Townshend's wife, Lady Ferrers, and their three children had been in Lisbon visiting the general just before the war closed down. It was not uncommon for wealthy officers to import their families when they had an urge, but suddenly Townshend was faced with the problem of getting himself and his family safely home as quickly as possible. Being a man of influence, he dropped a note to his former colleague Admiral Saunders, asking for a lift on a man-of-war, an option not available to the average soldier.

The admiral, who was in Gibraltar, offered transportation on the *Favourite* and said he would send the frigate to Lisbon to pick up the whole family. "Nothing," he assured Townshend, "can be safer on the water; I wish with all my heart there was more room in her, and that Lady Ferrers, yourself and family may have a good passage home." It was signed, "My Dear Sir, Your most faithfull hmble [*sic*] Servant, Chas. Saunders."

The *Favourite* turned out to be not as safe as advertised. She was almost wrecked at the mouth of the Tagus River when her captain, having shifted some guns to give the Townshends more space, edged into the Atlantic amid high winds and a sea that was "mountains high." She drifted broadside onto the bar and was saved from disaster by hitching her anchor to a rock. The ship rolled all night just clear of the breakers, and in the morning the captain was forced to cut the cable and run into a small bay to save her. When the Townshends reached Portsmouth, they learned from a newspaper brought over on the Lisbon packet that they had all been drowned.

Townshend's father died in 1767 and George inherited the title 4th Viscount, as well as the family estates. The same year, he was appointed lord lieutenant of Ireland, a prestigious but thankless post. Townshend's biographer, a descendant, wrote that George Townshend had ruled Ireland wisely – and it may be true. By that time, he'd had some narrow escapes and learned he couldn't always get his own way. The contemporary press was vitriolic in its comments about him, but in 1771 Lord Chesterfield, revered statesman and author, defended Townshend in an essay. Lady Ferrers' death in 1770 probably affected Townshend more than all the cruel attacks by the "pamphleteers of Grub Street," the press of his day.

Upset by the loss of his wife and concerned for his children, Townshend asked Lord North to be relieved of his position in Ireland: "I will be extremely obliged to His Majesty if he will be pleased to permit me to return to His Royal Presence whenever he shall think that some other person may be usefully entrusted with that important charge. The truth is that my health, my fortune and my spirits are much impaired."

Townshend was not allowed to leave his post until November 30, 1772, and the next year he returned to active duty and managed to fight a duel in which he almost killed Lord Bellamont. Yet honours still came his way: an honorary colonelcy in the 2nd Dragoon Guards, master-general of the ordnance and two steps up in the peerage to become Marquess Townshend of Raynham. In 1796 he was made a field marshal and given the governorship of Jersey, a sinecure.

Townshend married again in 1773 and his new wife bore him six children. After his death, at least one of the eulogies made an attempt to be fair, with the comment "No one enjoyed life more than the Marquess Townshend. He suffered indeed some heavy inflictions but he bore them with resignation." Perhaps this was true in later life, but General Wolfe and his fellow brigadiers might not have put it so politely.

More than ten years after the government voted £3,000 for a sculpture of the dying Wolfe, the work was unveiled in Westminster Abbey. Reviews were mixed. At least four top sculptors in England along with one Belgian, one French and one "anonymous" had submitted drawings. Joseph Wilton, then the best-known artist in the field, was chosen. The white marble figure of the hero-general, naked except for a drape across his genitals, is supported (gingerly, it seems) by a Grenadier and peered at by a Scottish Highlander.

Any resemblance to Wolfe as he is described in writings or as he appeared in the few portraits that exist is purely coincidental. The Duke of Richmond, a friend of Wolfe's, dispatched Wilton to view the body when it first arrived at Portsmouth, in the hope of making a death mask. However, the face was too decayed to be of any help, and Wilton used a servant who looked like Wolfe as a model for the head. The statue's body is average for a thirty-something man, but the legs are so muscular they could belong to a trained athlete. Everyone, including Wolfe himself, said he was extraordinarily tall and freakishly skinny, so it's difficult to imagine what Wilton was thinking. In the eighteenth century, naked statuary was in vogue – the neoclassical style was *de rigueur* in painting, poetry and sculpture, especially if the subject was a national hero. Horst W. Janson, in his "Observations on Nudity in Neo-classical Art," has this to say: "Wolfe's nudity is threefold: he is nude like a classical hero, nude like a secularized saint and functionally nude as well, for his uniform is piled on the floor at his feet." This is all very well, but it doesn't work. Wolfe is portrayed as an anglicized Greek god, supported in a distinctly awkward position for a dying man, by soldiers wearing contemporary (at the time) uniforms. Where is the logic?

Meanwhile, poor Henrietta Wolfe struggled for five years to extract from a "grateful government" the money due England's latest hero. She died in 1764 without collecting a penny of James Wolfe's back pay. The bequests in his will and its codicil were honoured from Mrs. Wolfe's own estate, providing yet another dismal example of the biblical David's warning, "Put not your trust in princes."

The modest battle of the Plains of Abraham changed the face of North America, helped push French kings off the world stage and eventually prodded Americans to revolt. Despite a good many mistakes, the British won the overall war because France was bankrupt; the greed of Quebec officials contributed to Quebec's lack of a first-class defence; the Indians, while right about defending their rights, were wrong in their methods. Montcalm lost the most important battle because he was too honest to consort with crooks. Wolfe won because the failings of others affected circumstances and because, already certain of his fate, he was characteristically brave and brash.

Bibliography

PRIMARY SOURCES

Amherst, General Jeffery. *The Journal of Jeffrey Amherst, 1758–1763*. Chicago: University of Chicago Press, 1932.

Bougainville, Colonel Louis-Antoine de. *Adventures in the Wilderness Journal, 1756–1760*. Norman, Oklahoma: University of Oklahoma Press, 1964.

Du Hausset, Mme. *Memoirs of Pompadour & Louis XV*. New York: P.F. Collier, 1910.

Knox, Captain John. *Historical Account of the Campaigns in North America*. Toronto: Champlain Society, 1914.

Stobo, Robert. *The Most Extraordinary Adventures of Robert Stobo*. Boston: Houghton Miflin, 1965.

Townshend, George, 1st Marquess of Townshend. *Military Life of Field-Marshal George Townshend*. London: John Murray, 1901.

Wolfe, General James. *Wolfe's Life and Letters* (edited by Beckles Willson). London: William Heinemann, 1909.

Wolfe, Major-General James. *Journal of the Quebec Expedition*. Montreal: McGill University Museum (copy of original document).

SECONDARY SOURCES

Algrant, Christine Pevitt. *Madame de Pompadour*. New York: Grove Press, 2002.

Chartrand, René. *The French Soldier in Colonial America*. Cape Breton, Nova Scotia: Museum Restoration Service, 1984.

Connell, Brian. *The Plains of Abraham*. London: Hodder and Stoughton, 1959.

Darling, Anthony. *Red Coat and Brown Bess*. Cape Breton, Nova Scotia: Museum Restoration Service, 1970.

Donaldson, Gordon. *Battle for a Continent*. New York: Doubleday, 1973.

Doughty, A.C., and G.W. Parmalee. *The Siege of Quebec and the Battle of the Plains of Abraham*. Quebec: Dussault and Proulx, 1901.

Downey, Fairfax. *Key to a Continent.* Toronto: Prentice-Hall, 1965.

—. *The Canadian Frontier, 1534–1760.* New York: Holt, Rinehart and Winston, 1969.

Eccles, W.J. *Essays on New France.* London: Oxford University Press, no date.

—. *France in America.* New York: Harper and Row, 1972.

Grinnell-Milne, Duncan. *Mad, Is He?* Oxford: Bodley Head, 1963.

LaPierre, Laurier. *1759: The Battle for Canada.* Toronto: McClelland & Stewart, 1990.

Lever, Evelyn. *Pompadour.* New York: Farrar, Straus and Giroux, 2003.

Levron, Jacques. *Pompadour.* London: George Allen and Unwin, 1963.

McLennan, J.S. *Louisbourg.* London: Macmillan, 1963.

McNairn, Alan. *Behold the Hero.* Montreal: McGill–Queens University Press, 1997.

Mitford, Nancy. *Madame de Pompadour.* London: Hamish Hamilton, 1954.

—. *The Sun King.* London: Harper and Row, 1966.

Moore, Christopher. *Louisbourg Portraits.* Toronto: Macmillan, 1982.

Parkman, Francis. *Decline and Fall of the French Empire.* Boston: Little, Brown, 1893.

—. *A Half-Century of Conflict.* Boston: Little, Brown, 1892.

—. *Montcalm and Wolfe.* Boston: Little, Brown, 1884.

—. *The Old Regime.* Boston: Little, Brown, 1893.

Redman, Alvin. *The House of Hanover.* Toronto: Longman's Green, 1960.

Rosebery, Archibald, Lord. *Lord Chatham.* London: Harper and Brothers, 1910.

Rutledge, Joseph L. *Century of Conflict.* New York: Doubleday, 1956.

Salmon, Edward. *General Wolfe.* Toronto: Cassell & Company, 1909.

Schama, Simon. *Dead Certainties.* New York: Vintage Books, 1992.

Stacey, C.P. *Quebec 1759.* Toronto: Macmillan, 1959.

Tintayre, Marcelle. *Madame de Pompadour.* New York: G.P. Putnam's and Sons, 1927.

Walpole, Horace. *Memoirs of King George II (1754–1757).* New Haven: Yale University Press, 1985. (First published, London: Henry Colburn, 1846.)

Waugh, W.T. *James Wolfe, Man and Soldier.* Montreal: Louis Carrier and Co., 1928.

Willson, Beckles. *The Life and Letters of James Wolfe.* London: William Heinemann, 1909.

Wolfe-Aylward, A.G. *The Pictorial Life of Wolfe.* London: William Brendon, 1924.

Wright, Robert. *The Life of Major-General James Wolfe.* London: Chapman and Hall, 1864.

Wrong, George M. *The Rise and Fall of New France.* New York: Macmillan, 1928.

Index